PROGRESS IN ECONOMICS RESEARCH

VOLUME 27

PROGRESS IN ECONOMICS RESEARCH

Additional books in this series can be found on Nova's website
under the Series tab.

Additional e-books in this series can be found on Nova's website
under the e-book tab.

PROGRESS IN ECONOMICS RESEARCH

VOLUME 27

ALBERT TAVIDZE
EDITOR

New York

NOTICE TO THE READER

The Publisher has taken reasonable care in the preparation of this book, but makes no expressed or implied warranty of any kind and assumes no responsibility for any errors or omissions. No liability is assumed for incidental or consequential damages in connection with or arising out of information contained in this book. The Publisher shall not be liable for any special, consequential, or exemplary damages resulting, in whole or in part, from the readers' use of, or reliance upon, this material. Any parts of this book based on government reports are so indicated and copyright is claimed for those parts to the extent applicable to compilations of such works.

Independent verification should be sought for any data, advice or recommendations contained in this book. In addition, no responsibility is assumed by the publisher for any injury and/or damage to persons or property arising from any methods, products, instructions, ideas or otherwise contained in this publication.

This publication is designed to provide accurate and authoritative information with regard to the subject matter covered herein. It is sold with the clear understanding that the Publisher is not engaged in rendering legal or any other professional services. If legal or any other expert assistance is required, the services of a competent person should be sought. FROM A DECLARATION OF PARTICIPANTS JOINTLY ADOPTED BY A COMMITTEE OF THE AMERICAN BAR ASSOCIATION AND A COMMITTEE OF PUBLISHERS.

Additional color graphics may be available in the e-book version of this book.

LIBRARY OF CONGRESS CATALOGING-IN-PUBLICATION DATA

ISSN: 1549-1552

ISBN: 978-1-62808-201-2

Published by Nova Science Publishers, Inc. † New York

CONTENTS

PREFACE

This series spans the globe presenting leading research in economics. International applications and examples of economic progress are invaluable in a troubled world with economic booms bursting like so many penny balloons. Topics discussed include a comprehensive framework for analyzing the risk management in the agri-food sector; university spin-off programs and economic commercialization in the U.K. and Spain; social economic implications from an intellectual capital perspective in the Netherlands; a new two-stage model and money flows in the Chinese stock market; modern macroeconomic research on consumption; and the psychology of public spending.

Risks management studies in the agri-food sector predominately focus on the technical methods and the capability to perceive, prevent, mitigate, and recover from diverse risks. In most economic publications the risks are usually studied as other commodity regulated by the market supply and demand, and the farmers "willingness to pay" for an insurance contract modeled. At the same time, the risk management analysis largely ignore a significant "human nature" based (bounded rationality, opportunism) risk, critical factors for the managerial choice such as the institutional environment and the transaction costs, and diversity of alternative (market, private, collective, public, hybrid) modes of risk management.

Chapter 1 incorporates the interdisciplinary New Institutional Economics and presents a comprehensive framework for analyzing the risk management in the agri-food sector. First, it specifies the diverse (natural, technical, behavioral, economic, policy etc.) type of agri-food risks, and the (market, private, public and hybrid) modes of their management. Second, it defines the efficiency of risk management and identifies (personal, institutional, dimensional, technological, natural) factors of governance choice. Third, it presents stages in the analysis of risk management and for the improvement of public intervention in the risk governance. Forth, it identifies the contemporary opportunities and challenges for the risk governance in the agri-food chain. Finally, it identifies, and assesses the efficiency and prospects of major modes for risk governance in the Bulgarian dairy sector.

Chapter 2 addresses two central research objectives: on the one hand, to identify the different models of spin-off support programmes to be found in British and Spanish universities, and to analyse their differentiated characteristics; on the other, to validate the models identified in the literature. The analysis was performed using data collected by way of a survey, targeted at the heads of university spin-off support programmes, to which the authors applied a statistic analysis. Firstly, the authors applied factorial analysis to identify the most significant variables explaining the characteristics of these programmes. Secondly, using the cluster analysis technique based on the variables identified, the authors classified the British universities on the one hand, and the Spanish ones on the other. Using Anova analysis the authors went on to describe the differentiated characteristics of each of the clusters found. This analysis enabled us to identify four significantly different types of spin-off support programmes in British universities and another four in Spanish universities. It also confirmed that programmes existed in the United Kingdom could be differentiated in terms of resources, university commitment, proactivity and selectivity; in the case of the Spanish universities, as well as these four variables, the authors also found differences in terms of experience and the number of spin-offs created. Among the various types of programmes identified, the authors found one in the United Kingdom and two in Spain that appear to be models for success. The study also confirms the importance of a favourable environment to the success of these programmes, however it does not confirm that the universities tend initially to follow a policy of low selectivity, as indicated in the literature.

Despite the wide breadth of literature concentrating on policy implications for social and economic issues, few articles have examined the linkage between tangible economic results and intangible national intellectual capital (NIC). Chapter 3 is an examination of the co-evolution between tangible and intangible factors in the Netherlands in order to understand the underlying influence that intellectual capital has on the economy.

Intellectual capital at a national level consists of human capital, market capital, process capital, renewal capital, and financial capital. The dataset utilized captures a six-year time period from 2005 to 2010. This time frame is of particular interest as it spans the phases before, during, and after the 2008 global financial crisis. Using this dataset, this chapter examines the co-development of the intangible national intellectual capital and tangible GDP per capita (ppp).

In this manner, the authors present a holistic picture of the Dutch national intellectual capital landscape and perform year-on-year trend analysis. Next, the authors place the Netherlands within the context of 48 countries and compare the Dutch national intellectual capital trend against that of others. This allows for comparison and contrast of the Netherlands with other major countries to provide valuable insight for future social economic policies.

Data analysis shows that there is a high correlation between the intangible national intellectual capital and the economic success as well as the speed of recovery following the 2008 global financial crisis. The result leads to the conclusion that countries with high levels of intellectual capital develop better resilience and ability to weather crisis. The Netherlands is one such example. This study is part of a growing number of studies that focuses on intellectual capital and its impact on modern societies and economies.

Macroeconomic information reported in this chapter showed that the Dutch government navigated the country through the crisis relatively well. NIC related graphs and statistics also indicate that the Netherlands was able to not only maintain but even advance its short-term NIC international competitiveness. However, its long-term NIC has room for improvement. Its top ten NIC ranking among 48 countries may have played a role in facilitating its national development and helped withstand the financial turmoil.

The direction and calculation of stock markets' money flows is one of the most difficult problems in financial engineering. Based on existing methods of money flows, Chapter 4 proposes a new two-stage model, by which the authors build an index system, and then empirically analyze the money flows of China's stock market. The results show that, the ratio of net money inflow to outflow in the bull market is above 2.3, and the ratio of net money outflow to inflow in the bear market is above 1.3; the ratio of net inflow to outflow is above 1.78 in the high-growth industries, and the ratio of net outflow to inflow is above 1.54 in the low-growth industries; With respect to individual stock, the ratio of net inflow to outflow over 2 is a high-growth stock. This study also find that the net money flows of past 10 days, 20 days and 30 days have a significant role in the prediction of net money flows for the next 10 days, 20 days and 30 days.

Chapter 5 attempts to provides a rigorous framework that helps resolve this puzzle. This model extends the related literature by examining individuals' inter temporal choices with the consideration of intergenerational interactions. This extension is empirically important because intergenerational transfers account for an important part of aggregate saving. This chapter is based on the same essential idea as Fan, but it develops a different model. The authors' model implies that an individual is more concerned about her offspring's well-being when the offspring's future mean income is lower. In a Markovian game framework, the model shows that the bequests from parents to children decrease with the mean income of future generations. Meanwhile, *ceteris paribus*, an individual's bequests to her children increase with her own wealth. Thus, the model has the following implications. First, at a given point in time, richer people have higher saving rates, because they are concerned that their children are likely to receive lower incomes than theirs. In other words, a household with higher lifetime income saves more in order to leave more bequests to its offspring, who are likely to be worse off. Second, over time, when an economy experiences economic growth and the mean income of the economy rises, individuals will reduce their bequests because their offspring are expected to be equally well off due to the economic growth. Consequently, the saving rate can be approximately constant over time if the impacts of the increase in one's lifetime income and the increase in her offspring's future mean income on her consumption cancel out each other. Thus, this model helps explain the consumption puzzle and reconcile the short-run and long-run consumption functions.

This paper is closely related to Fan, who studied a model that aims to achieve the same purpose as the current paper. However, this paper builds on a model that is very different from Fan. In Fan, it is assumed that parents get utility from their children's future wealth. In contrast, the current paper is in line with Fan, who assumes that parents get utility from the quality of their grandchildren as well as their children. Consequently, the current paper studies a framework in which intergenerational conflicts and intergenerational commonality co-exist. Thus, while it is based on the same essential idea of Fan, this paper examines this important issue from a different angle from Fan.

In what follows, Section 2 summarizes a framework on which the current model is based; Section 3 is the core of the paper, which examines the consumption functions both in the long run and in the short run and provides an explanation for the consumption puzzle; Section 4 further illustrates the intuition of the paper with an example; Section 5 offers the concluding remarks.

The size and role of the government is one of the most fundamental and enduring debates that has attracted the attention of researchers for decades.

Politicians, social scientists, and citizens disagree sharply about the appropriate public spending, as well as the size of government. Many see government as an agent striving to correct the inadequacies and excesses of the unrestrained markets. Others view politicians, public sector employees, and special interest groups as seeking to use the power of the government for their own purposes. The purpose of Chapter 6 is to investigate the reasons that determine the preferred size of government, and the role of government.

In: Progress in Economics Research. Volume 27 ISBN: 978-1-62808-201-2
Editor: A. Tavidze © 2013 Nova Science Publishers, Inc.

Chapter 1

GOVERNING AGRI-FOOD RISKS

*Hrabrin Bachev**

Institute of Agricultural Economics, Sofia, Bulgaria

Abstract

Risks management studies in the agri-food sector predominately focus on the technical methods and the capability to perceive, prevent, mitigate, and recover from diverse risks. In most economic publications the risks are usually studied as other commodity regulated by the market supply and demand, and the farmers "willingness to pay" for an insurance contract modeled. At the same time, the risk management analysis largely ignore a significant "human nature" based (bounded rationality, opportunism) risk, critical factors for the managerial choice such as the institutional environment and the transaction costs, and diversity of alternative (market, private, collective, public, hybrid) modes of risk management.

This paper incorporates the interdisciplinary New Institutional Economics and presents a comprehensive framework for analyzing the risk management in the agri-food sector. First, it specifies the diverse (natural, technical, behavioral, economic, policy etc.) type of agri-food risks, and the (market, private, public and hybrid) modes of their management. Second, it defines the efficiency of risk management and identifies (personal, institutional, dimensional, technological, natural) factors of governance choice. Third, it presents stages in the analysis of risk management and for the improvement of public intervention in the risk governance. Forth, it identifies the contemporary opportunities and challenges for the risk governance in the agri-food chain. Finally, it identifies, and assesses the

---

* E-mail address: hbachev@yahoo.com; Address: Institute of Agricultural Economics, 125 Tzarigradsko Shose Blvd., Blok 1, 1113, Sofia, Bulgaria.

efficiency and prospects of major modes for risk governance in the Bulgarian dairy sector.

Keywords: agri-food chain and risk management; market, private, and public governance; dairy risk management, Bulgaria

1. Introduction

Around the globe the issues of management of diverse (natural, technical, market, financial, criminal, policy etc.) risks in agrarian and food sectors are among the most topical in academic, business and policies debates [Babcock; CIPS; Deep and Dani; EU; OECD; Olsson and Skjöldebrand; Ramaswami; RPDRM; Schaffnit-Chatterjee; Shepherd et al.; Trench et al.; Weaver and Kim]. In the last decades, newly evolving uncertainty, risks and crisis associated with the progression of natural environment, products and technology safety, social demands, policies, economy, and globalization, all they have put additional challenges on existing system of risk management in agri-food sector.

Most risks management studies in agri-food sector predominately focus on technical methods and capability to perceive, prevent, mitigate, and recover from diverse threats and risks [Barker; DTRA and IIBR; Hefnawy; Jaffee et al.; Luning et al.]. In majority of economic publications a Neoclassical approach is applied, the risks is studied as other commodity regulated by market supply and demand, and farmers "willingness to pay" for an insurance contract in relations to agents risk aversion, risk probability and magnitude of damages modeled [Gerasymenko and Zhemoyda; OECD]. Nevertheless, market and private failures are acknowledged, and the needs for public intervention in risk management increasingly recognized. At the same time, risk management analyses largely ignore a significant "human nature" (bounded rationality, opportunism) based risks, the critical factors for the managerial choice such as the institutional environment and the transaction costs, and the diversity of alternative (market, private, collective, public, hybrid) modes of risk management. As a result, the efficiency and complementarities of diverse agri-food risk management modes can not be properly assessed [Bachev, 2012a].

Despite the significant advancement in the risk management technologies and the "menu" of risk reduction, mitigation and copping strategies, a great number of failures and challenges (production, supply chain, food and human safety, environmental etc.) continue to persist in agri-food sector [Dani and Deep; EU; Humphrey and Memedovic; OECD; Luning et al.]. Consequently, a greater attention is directed to the *system of governance* which eventually determines the exploration of technological opportunities and the state of agri-food security [Bachev, 2010a, 2011c].

This chapter incorporates the interdisciplinary *New Institutional Economics* [Coase, 1939, 1960; Furuboth and Richter; North; Williamson, 1981, 1996] and presents a comprehensive framework for analyzing the risk management in agri-food sector.

First, it specifies the type of agri-food risks and the modes of their management.

Second, it defines the efficiency of risk management and identifies factors for the governance choice.

Third, it presents stages in the analysis of risk management and for the improvement of public intervention in the risk governance.

Forth, it specifies the contemporary opportunities and challenges for the risk governance in the agri-food chain.

Finally, it identifies, and assesses the efficiency and prospects of major modes for risk governance in the Bulgarian dairy sector.

The ultimate goal of this paper is to improve the analysis of risk management in agri-food sector, and to assist public policies and risk management strategies and collective actions of individual agents.

2. Framework for Analyzing and Improvement of Risk Management

Agri-Food Risks and Modes of Risk Governance

Risk related to agri-food sector is *any current or future hazard (event) with a significant negative impact(s).* It is either an *idiosyncratic,* accidental, low probability, unpredictable event/threat, or it is *systematic* - a high probability, "predictable" event/threat.

The risk and threat could be of a *natural* origin - e.g. adverse weather, insect attract, catastrophic event etc. They may be of a *technological* origin - "pure" technical failures like tractor's flat tire, engine disorder etc. They are often of *human origin* - individual or collective actions/inactions, "human nature". Frequently, risks are a combination of previous three.

A great portion of risks in agri-food sector are caused or are consequences of a human actions or inactions. The *individual* behavior and actions causing risks may range from:

- *agent's ignorance* – "normal" human errors, lack of sufficient knowledge, information, and training;
- *risk-taking (retention) strategy of individuals* - accepting "higher than normal" risk;
- *mismanagement* - bad planning, prevention, recovery;
- deliberate *opportunistic behavior* - pre-contractual cheating and "adverse selection", post-contractual "moral hazard";
- *criminal acts* such as stealing property or yields, arson, invasion on individual safety;
- *terrorist attacks* – e.g. contamination of inputs and outputs aiming "mass terror" etc.

The *collective actions* which are source of risks are commonly related to:

- *economic dynamics and uncertainty* - changing industry and consumers demands, market price volatility, international competition, market "failures" and disbalances such as "lack" of labor, credit, certain inputs etc.;
- *collective orders* - "free riding" in big organizations, codes of behaviors, industry standards, strikes and trade restrictions, community rules and restrictions;
- *public order* - political instability and uncertainty, evolution in informal and forma social norms and standards, public "failures" such as bad, delayed, under/over intervention, law and contracts enforcements, mismanagement, "inefficiency by design", etc.

The agri-food sector risk could be *faced* by an agri-food sector component - e.g. risk *on* a dairy-farm, *on* a food processor, *on* a trader. The risk could also be *caused* by the agri-food sector - risk *from* farming, from food processing, *from* food-distribution etc.

The risk could be *internal* for the agri-food chain such as hazards cased by one element to another, and staying in or mitigating *within* the sector. It could also be *external* associated with hazard coming from outside factors (such as natural environment, government policy, international trade), and/or affecting external components (consumers, residents, industries, nature).

Finally, the risks could be *private,* when it is taken by individuals, collectives, economic entities (households, firms, cooperatives), industries. The risk is often *public* affecting large groups, communities, consumers, society, future generations.

The risk is big when there is *great likelihood* of a risky event to occur and that is combined with substantial possible *negative consequences*. The later may take a great variety of forms – e.g. damaged human and livestock health and property, inferior yields and income, lost market positions, food and environmental contamination etc.

When risk is considerable it would likely be associated with *significant costs* which sometimes are hardly expressed in monetary terms - e.g. human health hazards, degradared soils, lost biodiversity and eco-system services etc. Thus the "rational" agents maximizing own welfare will be interested to *invest in risk prevention and reduction.*

In a *narrow* ("technical") sense the *risk management* comprises the individual, collective and public *action(s)* for reducing or eliminating risk and its negative consequences. In a *broader* sense the *risk management* is the specific *system of social order (governance)* responsible for a particular *behavior(s) of agents* and determining the way(s) of assignment, protection, exchange, coordination, stimulation and disputing diverse risks, rights, resources, and activities [Bachev, 2011c]. In the particular socio-economic, technological and natural environment, the specific *system of risk governance* "put in place" is intimately responsible for the efficiency of detection, prevention, mitigation, and reduction of diverse threats and risks and their negative consequences [Bachev, 2012a].

The generic *forms* and *mechanisms* of risk governance are (Figure1):

- *private modes* ("private and collective order") - diverse private initiatives, and specially designed contractual and organizational arrangements tailored to particular features of risks and agents – e.g. private or collective codes of behavior, diverse (rational, security, future etc.) private contracts, cooperatives, associations, business ventures etc.
- *market modes* ("invisible hand of market") - various decentralized initiatives governed by the free market price movements and the market competition such as risk trading (selling and buying insurance), future contracts and options, production and trade of special (organic, fair-trade, origins) products etc.
- *public modes* ("public order") - various forms of a third-party public (Government, international) intervention in market and private sectors such as public information, public regulation, public ban, public assistance, public funding, public assurance, public taxation, public contract, pubic provision etc.

Sometimes, the risk management in agri-food sector could be effectively done though *"self-management"* – e.g. production management, adaptation to industry and formal standards, "self-insurance" though keeping stocks, financial reserves etc. For instance, primitive forms of *on farm* risk management through improving *production management* are widespread such as control and security enhancement, application of appropriate (pest, disease, weather resist) varieties, technology and production structure, product diversification, dislocation etc. Similarly, *off-farm* enterprise (and income) diversification is a major strategy for risk management in most of the European farms [Bachev and Tanic].

However, very often, the risk management requires an effective *governance of relations* with other agents – exchange and regulations of rights, alignment of conflicts, coalition of resources, collective or public actions at regional, national and transnational scales etc.

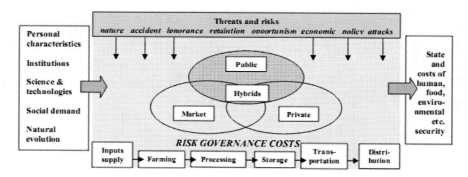

Figure 1. Generic risks, factors, stages and modes of risk governance in agri-food sector.

Accordingly, a risk could be "managed" through a *market mode* (e.g. purchase of insurance, hedging with future price contingency contracts), a *private mode* (contractual or literal integration, cooperation), a *public form* (state regulation, guarantee, compensation), or a *hybrid* combination of other forms.

Efficiency of Risk Management

The individual modes of risk governance are with *unequal* efficiency since they have dissimilar *potential* to reduce the likelihood and the (negative) impact of risk, and command different *costs* [Bachev, 2010a].

Principally, the market or the collective governance has bigger advantages over the internal mode ("own protection") since they allow the exploration of economies of scale and scope in risk prevention and bearing (sharing) negative consequences[1]. However, the risk trading and/or sharing is often associated with significant *transaction costs* - for finding best partners, prices, formulating and disputing terms of exchange, coalition, safeguarding against new risk from opportunistic behavior of counterparts or partners etc. Consequently, *market* and *private sector "fail"* to govern effectively the existing and likely risks in agri-food sector, and there is a need for a *"state intervention"* in risk management - assisting farmers cooperation, public costs-sharing or provision, mandatory insurance regulation etc.

Thus *"governance matters"* and applying a proper structure of risk management is an important part of the overall process of the optimization (effective allocation) of resources.

Following Coase's logic [Coase, 1960] if *property rights* were *well-defined* and *transaction costs* were *zero* then all risks would be managed in the most efficient (socially optimal) way independent of the specific mode of governance[2]. Then individual agents would either sell out their risk to a specialized market agent, or safeguard against the risk through terms of a private contract, or join a risk-sharing organization of interested parties. The risk-taking would be distributed between (exchanged, shared by) agents according to their will while the total costs for risk prevention, assurance, reduction, and recovery minimized. The rational choice for an individual agent would be to get rid of a significant risk altogether – to sell the risk out to a specialized market agent (a risk-taker). Such totally decentralized (market) governance would optimize the risk-taking and minimize the "technological costs" for risk assurance and recovery exploring the entire potential for economies of size and scope at national and/or transnational scales.

However, when property rights are not well-defined or enforced and transaction costs[3] are high then the *type of governance* is essential for the extent and costs of risk protection [Bachev, 2012a]. For instance, an internal (ownership) mode is often preferred because of the comparative protective and costs advantages for "standard" natural or behavioral risk management over the outside (market or contract) modes. What is more, frequently the enormous *transaction costs* could even *block the development of insurance market* or the emergence of

---

[1] Most studies on risk management in agriculture focus on modeling farmers "willingness to pay" for a risk contract in relations to risk's probability and amount of likely damages [e.g. Gerasymenko and Zhemoyda].

[2] In such a world some kind of risks would not even exist or be of no importance - e.g. risks related to adverse human behavior (any opportunistic intention would be discovered at no costs and interests effectively safeguarded).

[3] Transaction costs are the *costs associated with the distribution, protection and the exchange of diverse rights and obligations of individual, groups, and generations* [Bachev, 2010a].

mutually beneficial (collective) risk-sharing organization. It is well known that despite "common" interests and the huge potential for risk minimization the collective organization for risk-sharing are not or hardly developed by stallholders.

Furthermore, the formal and informal *institutional restrictions* could make some modes of risk governance impossible - e.g. risk assuring monopolies and/or cartel arrangements are illegal in many countries while most entrepreneurial risk-taking is endorsed (the "low risk - low profit" principle). Thus, not all modes of risk governance are constantly feasible in any socio-economic settings[4].

What is more, *individual agents differ* significantly in their *capacity to recognize, take, pay for prevention, and manage a risk.* For instance, a risk-taking farmer prefers risky but more productive forms (e.g. bank credit for a new profitable venture); the bigger enterprise can better perceive (hire expertise, collect information) and invest in protection of risks and/or take (absorb negative consequences) of a larger risk, etc. Besides, the individual agents have quite different interests for an effective management of a particular risk(s) since they get unlike benefits and costs from the risk management – e.g. effective environmental management often create costs for farmers while benefit the residents and other industries.

Last but not least important, there is no singe *universal* form for the management of divers type of risks and according to the *specific feature of each risk* (origin, probability, likely damages) there will be different most effective form of governance. For instance, while a low probable "standard" (natural, criminal) risk could be effectively governed by a classical market contract (e.g. purchase of insurance), most behavioral risks require special private modes (branding, long-term or interlink contracts, vertical integration), a high damaging risk from a terrorist attract necessities specialized public forms (intelligence, security enforcement) etc.

Hence, depending on the *kind and severity of risk,* and the *interests and personal characteristics of individuals,* and the *specific natural, economic and institutional environment,* there will be *different (most) efficient* forms of governing a particular kind of risk. Consequently, some *governance mix* will always exist to deal with divers risks associated with the agri-food sector [Bachev and Nanseki].

In many cases, an *effective* risk management leads to a considerable *reduction* or *removal* of a particular type of risk. However, often complete risk elimination is

---

[4] Nevertheless, if costs associated with the illegitimate forms is not high (possibility for disclosure low, enforcement and punishment insignificant) while benefits are considerable, then the more effective governance prevail – large gray or black economies are widespread around the globe.

either very costly ("unaffordable" by individuals, communities, society) or practically impossible (when uncertainty associated with the future events is enormous, the transaction costs are very high etc.). For instance, certain natural risk will always exist despite the available system of risk management. Besides, it is practically impossible to write a "compete" contract (e.g. for insurance supply and trading risk) including all probable future contingencies, and the subsequent rights and obligations of each party. Consequently, some transacting risk will always retain. Therefore, an effective risk management is usually connected with the needs for some *trade-off* between the benefits from reducing a particular risk (saved costs, minimized negative impacts) and the related *costs for the risk governance*[5].

Furthermore, an individual mode of governance could offer an effective protection from different *(multiple)* risks. Besides, an effective management of one type of risk might be associated with exposure to a new type of risk/costs – e.g. the vertical integration eliminates the "market risk" but creates a risk from opportunisms of partners. Moreover, the level of the (overall) risk exposure is typically determined by the *"critical"* (most important) riskand the integral risk is rarely a sum of the individual risks. For instance, if there is a very high risk/threat for stealing the harvest, otherwise important risk for crop pest protection would not be added to the overall risk of the farm[6].

Frequently, there are a number of possible *(alternative)* forms of governance of a particular type of risk – e.g. "risk to the environment" could be managed as voluntary actions of individual farmers, environmental cooperation, private contracts with interested parties, assisted by a third party organization, public eco-contact, public regulation, hybrid forms etc. [Bachev, 2010a].

In certain cases, some forms of the risk management are practically impossible or socially unacceptable – e.g. insurance markets do not develop for many kind of agro-food risks and the *private management* is the only option; the management of many environmental risks and challenges require *collective actions* at local, eco-system, regional or transnational levels etc. In modern societies many type of risks management are *publicly imposed* – e.g. food safety risk is under *public management* and harmonized in the EU, there are strict regulations on GMC, "precaution principle" is mandatory for the environmental related projects and carried out by the state authority, "safety nets" are organized as public projects etc.

---

[5] Thus some "uncovered" risk would normally remain.
[6] That was the case in transitional Bulgarian conditions where due to ineffective low and security enforcement, the entire sub-sectors of agriculture (vineyards, orchards) has been abandoned by smallholders in certain regions of the country because of the extremely high risk/treat of stealing the harvest by organized or individual thieves.

Therefore, a *comparative analysis* is to be employed to select among (technically, economically, socially) *feasible alternatives* the most efficient one – that which would reduce the overall risk to *"acceptable"* level, and which would require minimum *total* (risk assurance *and* risk governance) costs [Bachev, 2012a]. The later must include all current and future costs associated with the risk management – the *current* technological and management costs (for adaptation, compliance, information, certification), risk insurance premium, contracting and coalition costs as well as the (current and future) *long-term* costs for adaptation and recovering damages including associated *transaction costs* (disputes, expertise, low suits etc.) for claiming experienced losses[7].

In any case an *individual, group, community, sectoral, chain, national and international* efficiency of the risk management have to be distinguished. It is often when elimination of a risk for one agent induce a (new) risk for another agent – e.g. the agri-food price fluctuation causes an income risk to the producers but benefits the speculators; the application of chemicals reduces risk for the farmers but produces significant negative effects (e.g. water, soil and air contamination) on the residents, consumers, affected industries etc.

Furthermore, the risk management is only a *part* of the overall governance of divers (production, consumption, and transaction) activities of agents[8]. That is why the total efficiency (benefits, disadvantages, costs saving and risk minimization potential) of the various modes for the individual agents and the public at large are to be taken into account[9].

According to the specific natural and socio-economic environment, the personal characteristics of individuals, and the social preferences, various *structure of risk governance* could evolve in different sub-sectors, industries, supply chains, and societies. In one extreme, the system of risk management would work well and only the "normal" (e.g. entrepreneurial) risk would be left "ungoverned". In some cases, *market* (free-market prices, competition) would fail to provide adequate risk governance but a variety of effective *private modes* would emerge to fill the gap - special contractual and organizational arrangements, vertical integration, cooperation. Often, both market and private governance may fail but an effective *public involvement* (regulation, assistance, support, partnerships) could cure the problem.

---

[7] Most analyses of the agri-food risk management usually ignore the current and likely long-term *transaction costs* associated with the risk management.

[8] E.g. most of the managerial innovations in farming and agri-food chain have been driven by the transaction costs economizing reason [Sporleder].

[9] Frequently minimization of the risk related costs is associated with an increase in production and/or transaction costs, and vice versa. Often the risk elimination costs of one agent brings about a higher security for another agent in agri-food chain etc.

Nevertheless, there are situations when the specific institutional and risk management costs structure would lead to failures of market and private modes as well as of the needed public (Government, local authority etc.) intervention in risk governance[10]. Consequently, a whole range of risks would be left unmanaged which would have an adverse effect on the size and the sustainability of agri-food enterprises, the markets development, the evolution of production and consumption, the state of environment, and the social welfare [Bachev, 2010a].

Depending on the costs and the efficiency of the *specific* system of governance put in a particular (sub)sector, region, country, supply chain etc. there will be *unlike outcome* in terms of *"residual" risks*, and dissimilar *state* and *costs of human, food, environmental etc. security* in different regions and period of time (Figure 1). For instance, when there is inefficient public enforcement of food, labor, environmental etc. safety standards (lack of political willingness or administrative capability) then enormous "gray" agrarian and food sector develops with inferior, hazardous and counterfeit components.

Factors of Governance Choice

The forms of risk management in agri-food sector would depended on the risk type and features, the personal characteristics of agents, the institutional environment, the progress in science and technologies, culture, the social education and preferences, the evolution of natural environment etc. (Figure 1).

The risk features like origin, probability of occurrence, likely damages, scale etc. are important factor for the governance choice. For instance, local technical or behavioral risk could be effectively managed though a private mode while most of market and environmental risks require collective actions at regional, national or transnational level. For a high probability and harmful risks the agents will prefer more secure (and more expensive) mode – e.g. security investment, purchase of insurance, keeping reserves, taking hostages, interlinked organization. Nevertheless due to the lack of economic means many small size farmers can not afford related costs and practice no or primitive forms of risk management – cash and carry deals, product diversification etc. Here there is a need for a third party (Government, international assistance) intervention though insurance, support, safety net etc. schemes to decrease farmers vulnerability.

The personal and behavioral characteristics of agents (such as specific interests, preferences, knowledge, capability, risk-aversion, reputation, trust,

---

[10] Principally, when market and private modes fail there is a strong *need for a public* intervention in agriculture [Bachev, 2011b].

"contractual" power, opportunisms) are important factor for the choice of management form. For instance, some risks are not perceived (unknown) by private and public agents and therefore no risk management is put at all; in some cultures, the cooperative is the preferred mode of agrarian organization; experienced and trained farmer could design and manage a bigger organization (based on hired labor) and more outside (credit, insurance, inputs supply etc.) contracts adapted to his specific needs; a risk-taking entrepreneur prefers riskier but more productive (specialized, high margin) ventures etc.

The *behavioral* factors such as individuals' bounded rationality and opportunisms have been identified as responsible for the transaction costs, and thus for the choice of organizational mode [Williamson, 1996]. They are widely studied in the insurance theory as a source for cheating by both sides of contract [Derrig].

The agents do not possess full information about the economic system (risks, price ranges and dynamics, trade opportunities, policy development) since collection and processing of such information is very expensive or impossible (multiple markets, future events, partners intention for cheating etc.). In order to optimize decision-making they have to spent on "increasing their imperfect rationality" (on data collection, analysis, forecasting, training, consultation) and selecting forms minimizing related risks/costs (internal organization, "selling out" risk etc.).

The agents are also given to opportunism and if there is an opportunity for some of the transacting sides to get non-punishably extra benefit/rent from the exchange he will likely to take an advantage of that[11]. A *pre-contractual* opportunism ("adverse selection") occurs when some of the partners use the "information asymmetry" to negotiate better contract terms. A *post-contractual opportunism* ("moral hazard") occurs when some counterpart takes advantage of impossibility for full observation on his activities (by another partner, a third-party) or when he takes "legal advantages" of unpredicted changes in exchange conditions (costs, prices, formal regulations etc.). The third form of opportunism ("free ride") occurs in development of large organizations where individual benefits are not-proportional to the individual efforts (costs) and everyone tend to expect others to invest in organizational development and benefit from the new organization in case of a success [Olson].

It is often costly or impossible to distinguish the opportunistic from the non-opportunistic behavior because of the bounded rationality - e.g. a farmer finds out that purchased seeds are not of high quality only during the harvesting time.

---

[11] If there was no opportunism only risks related to the bounded rationality would remain (natural, technical) and consequences easily recovered with the cooperation and in a mutual benefit (risk sharing) of all parties.

Therefore, the agents have to protect their rights, investments, and transactions from the hazard (risk) of opportunism through: ex-ante efforts to find reliable counterpart and design efficient mode for partners credible commitments; and ex-post investments for overcoming (through monitoring, controlling, stimulating cooperation) of possible opportunism during the contract execution stage [Williamson, 1996].

In the agri-food sector the opportunism is widespread before signing an insurance contract (not disclosing the real information for possible risks) or during the contract execution period (not taking actions for reducing damages when risky event occurs; consciously provoking damages in order to get insurance premium etc.). That augments considerably the insurance prices and restricts the utilization of insurance contracts by small enterprises. On the other hand, insuree often "discover" the pre-contractual opportunism of the insurers only after the occurrence of harmful event finding out that not all assurance terms (protected risks, extend of coverage of damages, ways of assessing damages, extra hidden costs) had been well explained and/or adapted to farmers needs [Bachev, 2010b].

For many kinds of farm related risks the markets evolve very slowly and/or the insurance services are practically inaccessible by the majority of small operators. What is more, for many important risks an insurance is not available "for purchase at all" – e.g. the risk of lack of market demand for farm products, the fluctuation of prices, possible opportunism of the counterparts etc. That is why farmers have to develop other (private, collective) modes to safeguard their investments and rights or lobby for a public intervention in the assurance supply.

The institutional environment ("rules of the game")[12] is important factor for the management choice. For instance, in many countries some forms of risk governance are fundamental rights (on food, labor, environmental security and safety) and guaranteed by the state; a public income support to farmers is "institutionalized"; environment and food safety standards could differ even between different regions in the same state etc. Furthermore, the (external) institutional environment considerably affects the level of transaction costs – e.g. in recent years tens of thousands of European farms and processors have been closed due to the impossibility to adapt to (invest for) newly introduced EU standards for quality, safety, environmental preservation, animal welfare, certification etc.

Principally, in the conditions of stable and well-working public regulation (regulations, quality standards, price guarantees, quotas) and the effective

---

[12] That is *formal* and *informal* rights and rules, and the system(s) of their enforcement [North]. They are defined by the (formal, informal) laws, tradition, culture, religion, ideological and ethical norms, and enforced by the state, convention, community pressure, trust, or self-enforcement.

mechanisms for laws and contract enforcement, a preference is given to the standard (spotlight and classical) market contracts. When rights and rules are not well defined or changing, and the absolute/contracted right effectively enforced, that lead to the domination of primitive form of risk management (subsistence farming, personalized and over-integrated forms) and the high vulnerability to diverse (natural, private, market, contractual, policy etc.) risks. The later was the case during the post-communist transition in East Europe characterized by the fundamental restructuring, the "rules change" and ineffective public enforcement, a high exposure to "new" (natural, market, entrepreneurial, private, contractual, institutional, international etc.) risks by the newly evolving private structures, unsustainable organizations, large gray economies, undeveloped or missing (agrarian credit, insurance, extension supply etc.) markets, individuals (e.g. thefts) and organized (e.g. providers of "security services") risk introduction devastating the private businesses and the household welfare [Bachev, 2010a].

The dimensional characteristics of the activity and transactions (the *combination* of uncertainty, frequency, assets specificity, and appropriability)[13] are critical for the management choice.

When *recurrence* of the transactions between the same partners is high, then both sides are interested in sustaining and minimizing costs of their relations (avoiding opportunism, sharing risk, building reputation, setting up incentive, adjustment, and conflict resolution mechanisms). Here continuation of the relations with a particular partner/s and designing a special mode for transacting has a high economic value and the costs for its development could be effectively recovered by frequent exchange. When a transaction is *occasional* (incidental) then the possibility for opportunism is great since the cheating side cannot be easily punished by turning to a competitor (losing future business).

When *uncertainty* surrounding transactions increases, then costs for carrying out and secure transactions go up (for overcoming information deficiency, safeguarding against risk etc.). Since bounded rationality is crucial and opportunism can emerge the agents will use a special private form diminishing transaction uncertainty – e.g. trade with origins; providing guarantee; using share-rent or output-based compensation; an obligatory collateral for providing a credit; participating in inputs-supply or marketing cooperative; complete integration.

The transaction costs get very high when *specific assets* for the relations with a particular partner are to be deployed. Here a costless alternative use of the specific assets is not possible (loss of value) if the transactions fail to occur, are

---

[13] First three factors are identified by Williamson [1981], and the forth added by Bachev and Labonne.

prematurely terminated, or less favorable terms are renegotiated (in contract renewal time before the end of the life-span of the specific capital). Therefore, the dependant investment/assets have to be safeguarded by a special form such as a long-term or tied-up contract, interlinks, hostage taking, joint investment, quasi or complete integration. Often, the latter is quite expensive, investment in the specific capital not made, and the activity/transactions cannot take place or occurs without (or loss of) comparative advantages in respect to the productivity [Bachev, 2011b].

If a high *symmetrical* (risk, capacity, product, timing, location etc.) dependency of the assets of the counterparts exists (a regime of "bilateral trade") there are strong incentives in the both parties to elaborate a special private mode of governance (e.g. interlinking the credit, inputs and insurance supply against the marketing of output). A special *relational contract* is applied when detailed terms of transacting are not known at outset (a high uncertainty), and a framework (the mutual expectations) rather than the specification of the obligations of counterparts is practiced. Here partners' (self)restrict from opportunism and are motivated to settle emerging difficulties and continue relations (a situation of frequent reciprocial trade).

When *unilateral* dependency exists (risk of unwanted "exchange", quasi or full monopoly), then the dependent side has to protect the investments against possible opportunism (behavioral uncertainty/certainty) through integrating transactions (unified organization, joint ownership, cooperative); or safeguarding them with an interlinked contract, exchange of economic hostages, development of collective organization to outstand asymmetrical dependency (for price negotiation, lobbying for Government regulations) etc.

The activity and transacting is particularly difficult when *appropriability of rights* on behavior, products, services or resources is low. Because of the bounded rationality, the costs for the protection, detection, verification, and a third-party (court) punishment of unwanted exchange extremely high. The agents would either over-produce (e.g. negative externalities) or under-organize such activity (positive externalities) unless they are governed by an efficient private or hybrid mode - cooperation, strategic alliances, a long-term contract, trade secrets, or a public order.

The progress in science and technologies significantly improves the risk management and facilitate the diversification of its form. For instance, the introduction of new (resistant) plant and livestock varieties; the mechanization and standardization of operations and products; the application of information, forecasting, monitoring, storage, and transportation technologies, all they improve significantly the risk management in agri-food chain [COST; Hefnawy]. The modern application of the science and technologies is also associated with the production and/exposure to the new type of risks – e.g. green-house gas emitions, genetic contamination, natural resource depletion, technical over-dependency etc.

Finally, the *natural environment and its evolution* are critical factors for the management choice. For instance, certain geographical regions (mountainous, river beds, tropics, etc.) are more prone then others for natural menace and risks like soil erosion, soil and water contamination, frosts, droughts, floods, pest attacks, diseases, wild animal invasions etc. What is more, evolution of the natural environment associated with a global worming, extreme weather, plant and animal diseases, drought, flooding and other natural disasters, is posing series of new challenges for the risk management in the agrarian and food sector [Hefnawy; OECD, 2011].

The identification of the *"critical factors"* of the risk management choice, the range of practically possible forms, and their efficiency (costs and benefits) for the individual agents, stages, subsectors, countries, food chains and public at large, is to be a subject for a special *micro-economic study.*

The *comparative analysis* is to be employed to select among the feasible forms the most efficient one reducing the overall risk to an *"acceptable"* level and minimizing the *total* (risk assurance and governance) *costs.* Most of the elements of the efficiency of the risk governance are hardly to quantify – e.g. the individuals' personal characteristics, the amount of the risk, the level of benefits and costs[14] associated with each mode etc. That is why a *qualitative (Discrete structural) analysis*[15] could be used. The later matches the *features of a risk* to be managed (the probability, significance, acceptance level, needs for collective action etc.) and its *critical (institutional, technological, behavioral etc.) factors* with the *comparative advantages* (the effective potential) of the *alternative modes* to inform, stimulate an appropriate behavior, and align the interests of associated agents, and to overcome, reduce, control, share, dispute, and minimize the overall costs of that risk.

In a *specific* market, institutional, technological and natural environment the effective risk governance choice will depend on the combination of the risk features (probability of occurrence, likely magnitude of damages) and the critical dimensions of the activity/transactions (appropriability, assets specificity and

---

[14] The "measurement problems" associated with the transaction benefits and costs are well specified [Bachev, 2011b]. They also prevent the utilization of the traditional (Neoclassical) models simply by adding a new "transacting", risk management etc. activity [Furuboth and Richter].

[15] The operationalisation of the Discrete Structural Analysis of the economic organization is done by Williamson [1981].

frequency). Figure 2 presents a matrix with the principle forms for the effective risk governance in agri-food sector.

Critical dimensions of activity				Appropriability				
				High				Low
				Assets Specificity				
				Low		High		
				Frequency				
Risk features				Low	High	Low	High	
Severity of damages — High	Probability/uncertainty — High	High		MCC	MCC	SC	VI	PO
		Low		MCC	SC	CO	CO	
	Low	Low		na	na	SC	VI	na
Low		High		MCC	MCC	TPI	VI	CO & TPI

M – free market; CC – classical (standard) contract); SC – special contract; VI – vertical (internal) integration; CO – collective organisation, TPI – needs for a third-party involvement; PO – needs for a public organisation.

Figure 2. Principle modes for risk governance in agri-food sector.

For instance, likely probable and low damaging risks combined with a small assets specificity and appropriability usually do not necessitate (motivate, economically justify) *any risk management.*

A high "standard" risk could be effectively managed through a *free market* mode such as a standard *(classical)* insurance, inputs supply, marketing etc. *contracts.*

Highly probable and damaging risks with a good appropriability and frequency of transactions between the same partners require a *special* (e.g. relational) *contract.* The later form is also appropriate for the risks surrounding with low uncertainty, high assets specificity and appropriability, and occasional character of the relations between the counterparts.

Principally, risks combined with high specificity, appropriability and frequency could be effectively managed though a *vertical integration* (internal risk management, contract forward or backward integration for risk sharing or mitigation).

Highly likely and menacing risks combined with a high assets specificity and a good appropriability call for a *collective organization* (cooperation, collective action). Moreover, such risk/costs sharing organization could be easily initiated and maintained since the condition of a high risk and assets dependency is in place.

A serious transacting risk exists when the situation of assets specificity is combined with a high uncertainty, low frequency, and good appropriability. The elaboration of a special governing structure for private transacting is not justified, the specific (risk reducing) investments not made, and the activity/restriction of activity fails to occur at an effective scale ("market and contract failure"). Here, a *third-part* (private, NGO, public) *involvement* in the transactions is necessary (assistance, arbitration, regulation) in order to make them more efficient or possible at all. The unprecedented development of the special origins, organic farming, systems of "fair-trade" are good examples in this respect. There is increasing consumer's demand (a price premium) for the organic, original, and fair-trade products associated with some forms of (natural, poor household, labor, quality etc.) risk management. Nevertheless the supply of the later products could not be met unless effective trilateral governance including an independent certification and control is put in place.

Similarly, for risks with a low appropriability a third party *(public)* intervention is necessary to secure the effective risk management. Moreover, while a high probability low danger risks need a *collective organization assisted by a third-party* ("quasi" public organization for risk sharing and mitigation), the high damaging risks necessitate a *public organization*.

Stages in the Analysis and Improvement of Risk Management

The *analysis* and the *improvement* of the risk governance in the agri-food chain is to include following *steps* (Figure 3):

First, identification of *existing* and *emerging* threats and risks in agri-food chain. The persistence of certain risks is a good indicator for ineffective management [Bachev and Nanseki]. The modern science offers quite reliable and sophisticated methods for assessing various risks *to* or *caused* by the agri-food chain [DTRA and IIBR; Trench et al.].

Second, specification of *existing* and *other feasible modes* of risks governance, and assessing their efficiency, sustainability and prospects of development.

The *efficiency* of individual modes shows the capability for risks detection, prevention, mitigation and recovery at lowest costs while the *sustainability* reveals the "internal" potential to adapt to socio-economic, technological and environmental changes and associated threats and risks. A holistic framework for assessing the efficiency and the evolution of governing modes is suggested by OECD [2011] and Bachev [2010a].

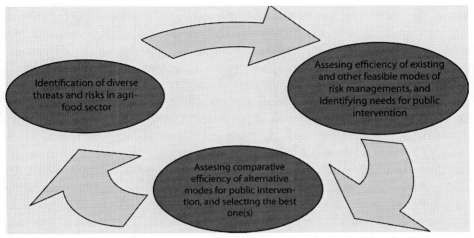

Figure 3. Analysis and improvement of risk management in agri-food sector.

That stage is to identify the *deficiencies* of dominating (market, private, and public) modes to solve the existing and emerging risks, and to determine the *needs for a (new) public intervention*. For instance, when appropriability associated with the transaction/activity is low, there is no pure market or private mode to protect from associated risks[16]. Emerging of a special large-members organization for dealing with low appropriability to cover the entire "social" risk would be very slow and expensive, and they unlikely be sustainable in a long run (free riding). Therefore, there is a strong need for a *third-party public intervention* in order to make protection of such risk possible or more effective – either pure public organization (e.g. public assurance for high damage natural or economic disasters) or "quasi public" mode (collective organization assisted/ordered by a third party) for high probable lower damaging risks (Figure 2).

Third, identification of the *alternative* modes for public intervention to correct (the market, private, public) failures, assessing their *comparative efficiency*, and *selection* the best one(s).

The comparative assessment is to be made on (technically, economically, politically) *feasible* forms as mode(s) minimizing the *total* risk management (implementing *and* transaction) *costs* selected. The analysis is to take into account the overall *private* and *social* costs – the *direct* and *indirect* (individual, third-party, tax payer, assistance agency etc.) expenses, and the *private* and *public*

---

[16] Respecting others rights or "granting" risk protection rights to others could be governed by the "good will" or charity actions (e.g. eco-sustainability movement initially evolved as a voluntary activity). In any case, the voluntary initiatives could hardly satisfy the entire social demand especially if they require significant costs.

transacting costs. The later often comprise a significant portion of the overall risk management costs and are usually ignored by analysts – e.g. costs for the coordination, stimulation, mismanagement of the bureaucracy; for the individuals' participation and usage of the public modes (expenses for information, paper works, payments of fees, bribes); the costs for community control over and for the reorganization of the bureaucracy (modernization and liquidation of public modes), and the (opportunity) costs of public inaction, etc.

Initially, the existing and emerging problems (difficulties, costs, risks, failures) in the organization of market and private governance have to be specified. The appropriate pubic involvement would be to *create institutional environment* for: making private investments less dependent, decreasing uncertainty surrounding market and private transactions, increasing intensity of exchange, protecting private rights and investments etc. For instance, the State establishes and enforces quality, safety and eco-standards, certifies producers, regulates employment relations, transfers management rights on natural resources etc., and all that increases the efficiency of market and private risk management.

Next, practically possible modes for increasing appropriability have to be considered. The low appropriability is often caused by unspecified or badly specified private rights and obligations. In some cases, the most effective government intervention would be to *introduce and enforce new private and groups (property) rights* – on diverse type of risks and its trading; on natural and biological resources; on food safety and clean environment; tradable quotas for products, inputs, emissions; on intellectual property, origins etc. That intervention transfers the organization of activity/transactions into market and private governance, liberalizes market competition and induces private incentives (and investments) in certain agrarian risk management.

In other instances, it is more efficient to put in place *public regulations* for risk minimization: for utilization of resources, products and services (e.g. standards for labor, product, and environmental safety); introduction of foreign species and GM crops, and for (water, soil, air, comfort) contamination; ban on certain inputs, products or technologies; regulations for trading ecosystem service protection; trade regimes; mandatory risk and eco-training and licensing of operators, etc.

In other instances, using the incentives and restrictions of the *tax system* is the most effective form for intervention. Different sorts of tax preferences are widely used to create favorable conditions for the development of certain (sub)sectors and regions, forms of organization, segment of population, or types of activities. For instance, the environmental taxation on emissions or products (inputs, outputs of production) is applied to reduce use or emissions of harmful substances; tax reductions are used to assist overcoming the negative consequences of natural disasters by private agents etc.

In some cases, *public support* to private organizations is the best mode for intervention. Programs for modernization, enterprise adaptation, income support, environmental conservation, public risk-sharing etc. are common in most countries around the world. For instance, in the USA farm crop insurance has emerged as the most important farm program while insurance payments to farmers are the largest source of farm assistance [Zulauf and Orden].

Often providing *public information, recommendations, and training* to farmers, entrepreneurs, residence, and consumers in risk management is the most efficient form.

In some cases, *pure public organization* (in-house production, public provision) is the most effective as in the case of critical infrastructure; food safety inspections; research, education and extension; agro-meteorological forecasts; border sanitary and veterinary control; recovery from the natural catastrophe etc.

Usually, the specific modes are effective if they are applied alone with other modes of public intervention. The necessity of *combined intervention* (governance mix) is caused by: the complementarities (joint effect) of the individual forms; the restricted potential of some less expensive forms to achieve a certain (but not the entire) level of the socially preferred risk prevention and mitigation; the possibility to get extra benefits (e.g. "cross-compliance" requirement for participation in the public programs); the specific critical dimensions of governed activity; the risk and uncertainty (little knowledge, experience) associated with likely impact of the new forms; the administrative and financial capability of the Government to fund, control, and implement different modes; and the dominating policy doctrine.

The level of effective public intervention (governance) also depends on the kind of risk and the scale of intervention. There are public involvements which are to be executed at *local* (ecosystem, community, regional) level, while others require *nationwide* governance. And finally, there are risk management activities, which are to be initiated and coordinated at *international* (regional, European, worldwide) level due to the strong necessity for trans-border actions or the consistent (national, local) government failures. Very frequently the effective governance of many problems and risks requires *multilevel* governance with a system of combined actions at various levels involving diverse range of actors and geographical scales.

The public (regulatory, provision, inspecting) modes must have built mechanisms for increasing the competency (decrease the bounded rationality, powerlessness) of the bureaucrats, beneficiaries, interests groups and public at large as well as restricting the possible opportunism (cheating, interlinking, abuse of power) of the public officers and stakeholders. That could be made by training, introducing new assessment and communication technologies, increasing transparency, and involving experts, beneficiaries, and interests groups in the management of public modes at all levels.

Generally, *hybrid modes* (public-private partnership) are much more efficient than the *pure* public forms given coordination, incentives, control and cost-sharing advantages. The involvement of the farmers, beneficiaries and interest groups increases the efficiency, decreases asymmetry of information, restricts opportunisms, increases incentives for private co-investment, and reduces management costs. For instance, the enforcement of most labor, quality, animal welfare, and environmental standards is often very difficult or impossible at all. Stimulating and supporting (assisting, training, funding) the private voluntary actions are much more effective then the mandatory public modes in terms of incentive, coordination, enforcement, and disputing costs [Bachev, 2010a].

If there is strong need for a third-party public involvement but the effective (government, local authority, international assistance) intervention in risk management is not introduced in a due time, then significant risks to individuals and public at large would persist while the agrarian "development" substantially deformed.

Dealing with many problems and risks in the agri-food sector/chain would require *multiform, hybrid, multilevel,* and *transnational* intervention, and therefore the appropriate *governance mix* is to be specified as a result of the comparative analysis. The later let improve the design of the (new) public intervention according to the specific conditions of the food-chain components in the particular country or region in terms of increasing security and decreasing costs.

Suggested new approach also let predict likely cases of the (new) public failures due to the impossibility to mobilize a political support and resources or ineffective implementation of otherwise "good" policies in the particular conditions. Since *public failure* is feasible, its timely detection permits foreseeing the persistence/rising of certain risks, and informing the local and international communities about the consequences.

The risk management analysis is to be made at *different levels* − the individual component (inputs supply, farm, processing, transportation, distribution etc.), regional, sub-sectors, food-chain, national, and international according to the *type of risks* and the *scales of collective actions* necessary to mitigate the risks. It is not a onetime exercise completing in the last stage with a perfect system of risk-management. It is rather a *permanent process* which is to improve the risk-management along with the evolution of socio-economic and natural environment, the individual and communities' awareness, and the modernization of technologies. Besides, the public (local, national, international) failure often prevails which brings us into the next cycle in the improvement of risk-management in the agri-food sector.

For the application of the suggested new approach, besides traditional statistical, industry etc. data, a *new type of data* are necessary for the diverse type of risks and the forms of governance, their critical factors for each agent, the level of related benefits and costs etc. Such data are to be collected through interviews with the agri-food chain managers, stakeholders, and experts in the area.

2. Contemporary Opportunities and Challenges for Agri-Food Risk Management

The modern agri-food chains involve millions actors with different interests, multiple stages, and divers risks requiring a complex, multilateral and multilevel governance at a large scale. For instance, in the EU the number of employed persons in the agri-food chain reaches 48 million working in almost 17 million different holdings and enterprises (Table 1) while final consumers comprises 500 millions[17].

Various existing and emerging (natural, technological, health, behavioral etc.) *threats and risks* along with the modern agri-food chains are well-identified [DTRA and IIBR; Eurostat, 2011a; Humphrey and Memedovic; OECD).

Table 1. Number of enterprises and persons employed in EU agri-food chain (1000)

Number		Agriculture	Food and beverages activities			
			Manufacturing	Wholesaling	Retailing	Services
		2007	2008			
Holdings and enterprises	EU - 27	13 700.4	267.9	275.1	1 060.2	1 448.4
	Bulgaria	493.1	5.1	5.4	31.5	19.2
Regular farm labor force and persons employed	EU - 27	26 669.4	4 725.0	2 001.5	7 369.7	7 316.5
	Bulgaria	950.0	106.5	44.9	102.0	92.0

Source: Eurostat, 2011a.

---

[17] figures get much bigger if we take into account the total number of the global agents involved in the EU agri-food chains – farmers, processors, importers etc. from around the world.

Risks	Modes of governance		
	market	private	Public
Natural disasters and extreme weather; Pests and diseases; Improper using pesticides and chemicals; Using contaminated water and soils; Improper animal health practices; Poor waste disposal; Using prohibited antibiotics; Using contaminated feeds; Animal-borne diseases; Improper handling and storage; Poor cooling system; Poor sanitation and hygiene; Using unhygienic containers, processing units, and transport facilities; Improper grading and packaging; Using prohibited food-additives;	Clientati-sation; Direct marketing; Informal branding; Insurance purchase; Organic production; Specific origins; Brands; Eco-system services; Special (quality, eco-) labeling; Outsourcing; Security services; Fair trade system; Standards insurance contract; Hedging with future price contacts	Improved inputs, technology, variety and structure of production; Product and income diversification; Self-insurance forms; Patronage and community insurance; Voluntary initiatives; Professional codes; Building (good) reputation; Guarantees; Private producers labels and brands; Private traders labels and brands; Private and collective origins and specialties; Private products recalls; Long-term contracts; Interlink contracts (inputs and service supply against marketing); Inputs and service cooperatives; Production cooperation; Joint-ventures; Internal audits; NGOs; Professional and consumer associations; Good Agricultural Practice; Good Hygienic Practice; Good Manufacturing Practice; Good Transport Practice;	Mandatory (products, process, labor, animal-welfare, environmental) quality and safety standards; Regulations/bans for using resources, inputs, technologies; Regulations organic farming; Quotas for emissions and using products/resources; Regulations for introduction foreign species/GMC; Regulations for plant and animal nutrition and healthcare; Licensing for using agro-systems and natural resources; Mandatory farming, safety, eco-training; Mandatory certifications and licensing; Compulsory food labeling and information; Public accreditation and certification; Mandatory records keeping and traceability coding; Public products recalls; Public food, veterinary, sanitary, border control; Public price and income support; Public preferential crediting; Public funding farms and processors adaptation; Public safety nets and disaster reliefs; Financial support to organic production, traditional and special products, private and collective actions; National GAPs, cross-compliance requirements; Public education, information, advise; Designating vulnerable/dangerous zones; Tax rebates, exception, breaks; Eco-taxation (emissions, products, wastes);

Figure 4. Continued on next page.

Risks	Modes of governance		
	market	private	Public
Inputs, resources and output contamination; Chancing social demands; Market price fluctuation; Market failures; Political and institutional instability; Ignorance of agents; Opportunistic behavior of counterpart, collation partner, a third party or public officer; Criminal intrusion; Terrorist attacks		Good Trade Practice; GLOBALGAP; Private and collective food quality and safety management systems; Certification; Licensing; Third-party verification; Inputs supply integration; Integration into processing and marketing; Franchises; Risk pooling and marketing cooperatives; Vertical integration; Consumers cooperatives	Public eco-contracts; Public food and security research/extension; Assistance in farmers, stakeholders, security cooperation; Public promotion/partnerships of private initiatives; Public food security monitoring, assessments, foresights; Public food reserves and buffer stocks; Public prevention and recovery measures; Public compensation of (private) damages; Disposal of (old) chemicals, degraded lands and water purification; Protected Designation of Origin, Protected Geographical Indication, Traditional Specialty Guaranteed; European Rapid Alert System for Food and Feed; EU policies, support and enforcement agencies (EFSA, ECDC, ECHA, CFCA, OSHA, EEA); International Standardization Organization (ISO 22000); UN (FAO, WHO) agencies interventions (Codex Alimentarius; Early Warning Systems; Crisis Management Centers); Bilateral and multilateral trading agreements/rules (WTO); National and international anticrime/antiterrorists bodies

Figure 4. Major risks and modes of governance along with modern agri-food chain.

Diverse *market* and *private* modes have emerged to deal with the specific risks driven by the ethics, competition, consumer demand, business initiatives, and trade opportunities – e.g. direct marketing, voluntary codes (professional and corporate social, labor, environmental etc. responsibility), industry standards, insurance schemes, guarantees, fair-trade, trade with brands, origins, organic and quality products etc. (Figure 4).

Furthermore, different *bilateral and multilateral private* forms are widely used to safeguard against the risks, explore the benefits, and facilitate the exchange – e.g. clientalisation, contractual arrangements, cooperation, complete backward or forward integration etc.

Special *trilateral forms* have evolved to enhance security and partners and consumers' confidence including an independent (a third-party) certification and inspection. Trade internationalization is increasingly associated with the *collective private* actions (standards, control mechanisms etc.) at a transnational and global scale (e.g. GLOBALGAP).

The property (security and safety) rights modernization, and the market and private "failures" brought about needs and modes for *public interventions* (assistance, regulations, provision) in the agri-food sector. Moreover, the scope and stringency of publicly-imposed rules expend constantly embracing new products, methods, dimensions (human, animal, plant, eco-health), hazards (GMC, nanotechnology, terrorism), and information requirements.

Furthermore, the globalization of exchange, and threats and risks increasingly require setting up a *transnational public order* (e.g. ISO, WHO, FAO, WTO etc.). For instance, there are common (traceability, precaution, communication) principles, (food, veterinary, phytosanitary, feed, environmental etc.) legislation, and implementing and enforcing agencies (such as EFSA, ECDC, ECHA) for the agri-food chains in the EU (including for imported products).

Consumers concerns about the food-safety risks significantly have increased after the major food-safety "events"/crisis in recent years (e.g. Avian flu; Mad-cow and Foot-and-mouth diseases; poultry salmonella; contaminations of dairy, berries, olive-oil; natural and industrial disasters impacts etc.).

For instance, since 2005 there has been an augmentation of the respondents "worrying about food-safety problems" in the EU and it comprise a significant share now (Figure 5); as much as 48% of the European consumers (in Bulgaria 75%) indicate that the consumed food "very or fairly likely" can damage their health etc. [Eurobarometer].

The number of cases and incidence rates of various foodborne and waterborne diseases is significant even in developed countries. For example, in the USA yearly 1 in 6 or 48 million people gets sick, 128,000 are hospitalized, and 3,000 die of foodborne diseases [CDC]. In the EU there are also a number of confirm cases of foodborne diseases having a high incidence rate, most notably Giardiasis (167,025), Campylobacteriosis (190,579) and Salmonellosis (134,606) [ECDC].

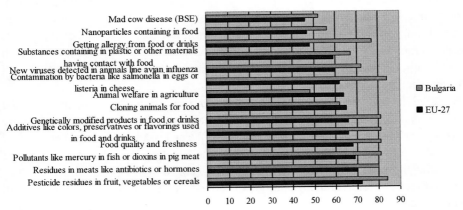

Source: Eurobarometer.

Figure 5. Indicate if you are worried in relation with following food-safety problems (% of respondents).

There are a number of *(new) opportunities* for the risk governance in the agri-food chain (Figure 6):

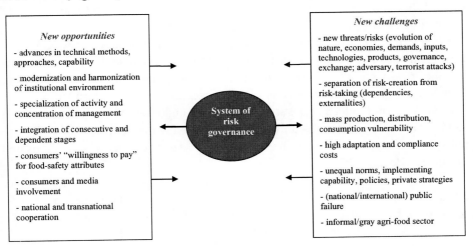

Figure 6. Opportunities and challenges for risks governance in agri-food chain.

First, the advances and the dissemination of the *technical* food-chain, training and risk-management *methods* (such as microbiological, genetic, electrical, laser, robotic, immunological, chemical and biosensors, nanotechnology, ICT etc.), the integral and food-chain *approaches,* and the research, monitoring, testing, decision, and foresighting *capability* for the risk-detection, assessment, prevention, and mitigation [COST; Trench at al.]. For instance, the advancements in detection, assessment and mitigation methods and technologies associated with the biological and the chemical risks have been presented at a recent international conference [DTRA and IIBR].

Second, the modernization and the *international* harmonization of the *institutional environment* (private, corporate, collective, NGOs, public food-safety and related standards, rules, enforcements etc.). For instance, the EU membership improves considerably the "rules of the game" in the new member states like Bulgaria; the market access rules, and/or the "corporate responsibilities" induce the agri-food sector transformation of exporting countries in Africa, Latin America and Asia etc.

Third, the considerable development of the *specialization* of activities (including in the risk-taking, monitoring, management) and the *concentration of (integral) management* in the food-production, processing, servicing, and distribution - centralized innovation and enforcement; time, scale, and scope economies; easy third-party control etc. For instance, the market share of the three largest food-retailers comprise between 27-91% in the EU states [Eurostat, 2011a]; the food-safety training, certification, inspection, and information are big international business [Humphrey and Memedovic] etc.

Forth, the quasi or complete *integration* of the food-chain's consecutive or dependent stages creating mutual interests, and the effective and long-term means for the risk-perception, communication, and management. For example, in Bulgaria the (raw) milk supply is closely integrated by the (dairy) processors through on-farm (collecting, testing) investments and interlink (inputs, credit, and service supply against milk-delivery) contracts with the stallholders, while the dairy marketing is managed by branding and long-term contracts – standards and bio-labels [Bachev, 2011a].

Fifth, the increasing consumers "willingness to pay" for the food-safety attributes such as chemical and hormone bans, safety and inspection labels, original and special products etc. [Trench at al.]. The later justify and make economically possible the paying-back of the costs for a special governance.

Six, the growing *consumers'* (representation, organizations) and the *media* involvement, and the *national* and *transnational* (information, technical, managerial, training, certification etc.) *cooperation* of partners and stakeholders improving agents choice, inducing public and private actions, enhancing risk-management communication, efficiency, and speed.

The modern development is also associated with a number of *(new)* *challenges* for the risk governance in the agri-food chain:

i.   the emergence of new threats, risks and uncertainty associated with the evolution of *natural environment* (e.g. climate change, water stress, "new" plant, animal and human hazards etc.) as well as the new human induced *economic, financial, food, food safety, water, environmental etc. crises* at large *(transnational, global) scales*. For instance, in the EU the household waste associated with the food (packaging, animal and vegetal wastes) is quite significant as merely its animal and vegetal components amounts to 23.8 million tones and comprises almost 11% of the all household waste[1], or 48 kg per capita [Eurostat, 2011b].

ii. the increasing new threats, risks and uncertainty connected with the *inputs, technologies,* and *products* differentiation and innovation – e.g. Fukushima nuclear accident severely affected the agri-food sector in Japan and beyond [Behdani]; there are uncertainties and safety concerns associated with the growing application of nanotechnologies and GMCs etc. [Eurostat, 2011a].

iii. the increasing specialization and concentration of activity and organizations which *separates* the *"risk-creation"* (incident, ignorance, opportunistic behavior) and the *risk-taking* (unilateral-dependencies, quasi-monopolies, spill-overs, externalities etc.). That makes the risk-assessment, pricing, communication, disputing, and liability through the (pure) market and private modes very difficult and costly. For instance, cheating, misleading, and pirating are common in the food-chain relations - high information asymmetry, detection, disputing, and punishment costs [Bachev, 2010a]. It is indicating that for the risk information consumers in the EU trust more to the "health professionals", "family and friends", "consumers associations", "scientists" rather than the "food producers" and "supermarkets and shops" (Figure 7).

iv. the widespread mass production, distribution, and consumption increases the *vulnerability* of the agri-food chain expending the scope and the severity of natural, incidental, opportunistic, criminal or terrorist risks. For instance, in the EU there has been a progressive number of the official notifications based on the market and non-member countries

---

[1] these levels and shares are believed to be underestimates.

controls, food-poisoning, consumer complaints, company own-checks, border screening and rejections approaching 8000 in 2009 [Eurostat, 2011a].

v. the increasing *adaptation* and *compliance costs* (capital, training, certification, documentation etc.) for the rapidly evolving market and institutional environment which delay or prevent the reformation of smaller farms and food-chain enterprises [Trench et al.; Bachev, 2010a]. For instance, in Bulgaria the dairy and meat processors adaptation to the EU standards have continued 10 years while two-thirds of them ceased to exist before the country accession to the EU in 2007 [Bachev, 2011a].

vi. the public and private food quality and safety standards and the efficiency of their enforcement differ considerably between the industries, countries, and regions [Humphrey and Memedovic]. That is a result of the *unequal norms* (e.g. GAPs, formal and informal rules) and the *implementing* and *enforcing capability*, and/or the deliberate *policies* or the private *strategies* (e.g. multinationals sell the "same" products with unlike quality in different countries). The "double/multiple standards" is responsible for the inequality of exchange, and the dissimilar threats and risks exposure of individual agri-food systems.

vii. the *wide spreading "public failures"* in the food-chain (risk) management – the bad, inefficient, delayed, under or over interventions; gaps, overlaps, infighting and contradictions of different agencies and rules; high bureaucratic costs; unsustainable and underfunding etc. For instance, the Bulgarian Food Agency and its Risk Assessment Center were established with a 5 years delay after joining the EU (in 2011); the EU Acquis Communautaire are still not completely implemented in the country (capability deficiency, mismanagement, corruption); trust to the EU rather than the national institutions prevails [Bachev, 2010a]. There are also numerous instances of the *international* assistance or governance *failures* when institutions are "imported" rather than adapted or designed for the specific local conditions [Bachev, 2010a].

viii. the production, marketing, and consumption traditions, the high food or governance costs, the will and capacity deficiency, all they are responsible for the persistence of a large risky *informal/gray* agri-food sector around the globe without an effective control, and substandard, fake, and illegitimate products and activities. For instance, merely one-third of the Bulgarian dairy farms comply with the EU milk-standards, only 0.1% possess safe manure-pile sites, a half of produced milk is home-consumed, exchanged or directly sold [Bachev, 2011a].

ix. the multiplying new treats and risks associated with the *adversary* (e.g. by a competitor) and the *terrorist* attacks, and the emerging *governing and exchange forms* (e.g. street-sells; internet, phone and mail-orders; shopping-trips etc.). All they require specific non-traditional risk-management methods and modes such as guards; policing; intelligence; multi-organizational and transnational cooperation etc.

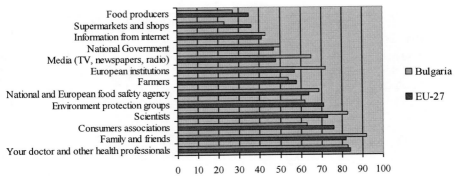

Source: Eurobarometer.

Figure 7. In case a serious food-safety risk is found I would trust for risk information to (% of respondents).

4. Assessing Risk Management in Bulgarian Dairy Sector

Modes and Efficiency of Governing Risks for Dairy Farms

Bulgarian dairy sector has been among the most significantly affected by the fundamental post-communist transformation after 1989 and the process of EU integration in recent year[2].

The major generic type of risks facing by the dairy farms and causing by the dairy sector are natural, market, private and societal (Figure 8).

The major natural risks for the dairy farms are:

— occasional or epidemic livestock, crop and labor diseases;
— invasion of wild animals (wolfs, bears) on farm livestock;
— bad meteorological conditions (extreme temperatures, hails, frosts);

---

[2] Bulgaria joints the European Union on 1 January, 2007.

– damages from pest and predators;
– natural disasters like floods, mudslides, fires, thunders etc.

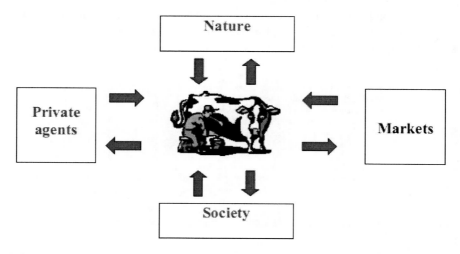

Figure 8. Generic types of Risk Faced and Caused by the Bulgarian Dairy Farming.

Most dairy farms use traditional methods to protect from the natural hazards: small-sized farm, more sustainable animal and crop varieties, appropriate livestock structure (more goats and sheep, few cows), private dogs and guards, production diversification, remoteness of plots, keeping "emergency fund" etc.

During the entire transition now the primitive technologies and agro-techniques have been widespread among the majority of farms. Due to the lack of knowledge, possibility and/or financial means the application of sustainable varieties, proper livestock care and diet, veterinary and extension services, chemical application and irrigation of lands have been very insufficient by most holdings [Bachev, 2012b]. For instance, the amount of fertilizers and pesticides used in agriculture has declined considerably, and their current per ha application is 22% and 31% of the 1989 level[3]; there is 21 folds decline in the water used in agriculture due to the considerable distortion of irrigation facilities and the high water price etc.

All these have contributed to degradation of farmlands and livestock capability having a harmful impact on livestock and crop yields, and farmers' income and welfare. Moreover, no adequate healthcare and feeding of animals,

---

[3] Now, N, P and K fertilizers are applied for 37.4%, 3.4% and 1.9% of utilized agricultural lands [MAF].

and irrigation and crop rotation have been introduced to adapt (counterbalance, resist to) the effects and risks of global climate change on farms [Bachev, 2012b]. During much of the post-communist transition the farms had no access to specialized insurance products since they were either unavailable or too expensive. *Agrarian insurance market* has been developing in the last few years but it is still not wide-used (Figure 9).

The larger farms[4] have stronger incentives to *sell the risk out* because they are highly specialized and in the case of hazardous event damages are quite significant.

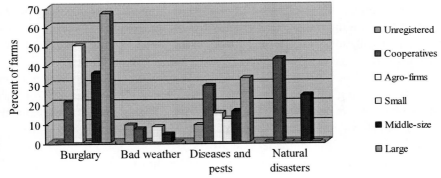

Source: interviews with farm managers.

Figure 9. Type of purchased insurance by Bulgarian dairy farms.

Besides, these enterprises possess bigger financial means to insure livestock, crops and related assets. In some cases, the big farms possess better positions to negotiate more favorable insurance terms than the bulk of the farms (big contracting power, economy of scale, available on farm experts or outside expertise).

Moreover, "purchase of insurance" is usually explicitly requested by the banks and/or public agencies for participating in diverse commercial and public support programs. The big commercial farms are the main recipients of such loans and grants and often unwillingly pay supplementary price (for insurance supply) to obtain the "interlinked" outside funding. In this case, related risk is carried by a specialized market supplier (insurance company rather than bank or public

---

[4] The average milk-cows per farm is 3.3, buffalo-cows 7.3, ewes 10 and she-goats 3.1. The holdings with 1-2 heads comprise around 80% of all cow farms (and 30% of the livestock) and 64% of the buffalos farms (and 11% of the livestock) in the country, while the share of ewes and she-goat holdings with up to 9 heads in total farms is accordingly 30% (83% of livestock) and 96% (67% of livestock) of all holdings [MAF].

agency) and debtor-farms are charged with extra costs to assure needed bank loan or public support.

The majority of farms cannot afford the purchase of risk insurance because of the high (unaffordable) premiums, unfavorable terms of insurance contracts (not-tailored to particular conditions of an individual farm), and low satisfaction from the services of commercial insurance providers (frequent disputes about the terms of contracts and extent of harms, lengthy delays of payment for damages etc.).

On the other hand, the insurance companies are reluctant to deal with the small farms because of the miniature size (high transacting costs, low profit), and the high possibilities for pre- and post-contractual opportunism. Consequently, a great part of farming resources and activities is not assured (insuring labor is practically absent, most animal, machineries and buildings are uncovered etc.), and a considerable majority of farmers bear the entire risk of failures.

Despite the potential efficiency (non-for-profit organization, members orientation, tailoring products to farms' needs) the collective modes for farm insurance have not evolved in the country. Here the high transaction costs for the initiation and development of a large member organization, and the conflicting interests of different farms impedes that process.

Moreover, an effective public intervention has not been undertaken to assist (initiate, support, legislate) farmers in organization of ("quasi-public", "quasi-private") mode for collective supply of agrarian insurance. Neither badly needed agrarian guarantee and/or compensation fund has been launched. Subsequently, a good part of the affected smaller and middle-size farms (having little internal capacity to bear yield failures and property damages) experience severe losses, and see the scale of their operations (assets, financial means) and welfare further decreased.

In the last years and especially after the country's EU accession the public veterinary, disease, technology etc. control and the emergency assistance to livestock holdings have been enhanced - e.g. isolation and distortion of endangered animals, compensation of farms etc. These measures aim at protecting against significant industry and/or public risk(s) from certain diseases and epidemics – e.g. mad cow disease, foot and mouth disease, avian influenza etc. They have been driven by the public concern for potentially huge economic losses for farms, related industries, export, and/or human health hazards.

Furthermore, some farms have got public aid to cover losses (or recover) from the recent natural disasters – animal diseases, floods, rainstorms, mudslides, and extreme droughts. The later modes have been incidental and affected mostly the larger operators having incentives and capability to deal with the complicated (and costly) bureaucratic procedures.

Finally, an effective public system for farmers' training and advise in important areas such as entrepreneurship, environmental and risk management, diversification etc. has not been established in the country.

Subsequently, most farms do not have proper internal and outside (market, collective, public) insurance against the natural risks and face constantly hazards and damages. Affected smaller and middle-size holdings experiences severe losses, and sees their assets, scale of operations, and welfare further decreased.

The market risk in dairy farming is mostly associated with:

- the high market uncertainty in terms of demand for milk, quality requirements, supply of critical inputs;
- the huge competition and price fluctuation;
- the (semi)monopoly condition in the inputs supply and marketing;
- the missing markets situation.

Unlike the natural risk, the market related risk cannot be assured by a purchase of insurance. Special governance is to be put in place to safeguard farmers' investments.

The emergence and persistence of the vast subsistence and part-time farming has been an effective mode to protect the household assets and labor in the conditions of great institutional and economic uncertainty [Bachev, 2010a]. During the transition period market and contract trade of owned capital was either impossible or very expensive - "missing" markets, high uncertainty, information asymmetry, opportunism, little job opportunities and security. There was also great uncertainty associated with the market supply of basic foods in terms of costs, stability, quality, origin etc.

The *internal family production* was the most effective way of protecting and getting return on the available household resources (labor, land, livestock, savings etc.). In some instances, a *group subsistent or market oriented farming* (partnership) between relatives or close friends developed to allow continues operation, part-time farming, effective concentration of resources, benefiting from the complementarily of partners' assets and skills, and exploration of economies of scale and scope.

Similarly, the missing market for the critical farm inputs and services was a major reason for the development and sustainability of the *production cooperatives*. The big interdependence and complementarities of the assets, and the "not-for-profit" and membership orientation, attracted many smallholders. Production cooperatives evolved as an effective (cheap, stable) form of supplying highly specific to the farms forage, mechanization service, essential inputs, storage, processing etc.

The larger farms integrate entirely the forage supply exploring the economies of scale and scope and safeguarding against the risk associated with the price, quality, time of delivery, and behavioral uncertainty of the outside procurement. Our survey demonstrates that all commercial farms secure a significant portion of needed forage for the livestock though own-production. Likewise, they own (rather than rent) the dairy animals, and all critical assets (milking equipment, barns, machineries) are either owned or protected through long-lease contracts.

Furthermore, private form to govern bilateral trade between the farms and the processor has been increasingly employed interlinking the supply of critical inputs (forage, cooling tanks etc.) with the marketing of output (Figure 10). The later diminishes considerably the risk from market inputs supply and marketing of output of dairy farms, and increases the incentives for productive investments.

The significant risks from the market supply of the critical labor and services are typically governed through a *private mode*. In dairy farming most managerial and technological knowledge and even "relationships" with the individual animals are highly farm-specific and extremely important for the productivity. Therefore, the critical activities are secured by family labor and permanent employment (management, everyday care for animals).

The "ineffective" or "missing" market for the general labor is a major source of risk in the sector preventing expansion of the farm size beyond the family borders. The limited and unreliable supply (mostly from the unqualified gypsy population), the inferior labor conditions, the low wages, and the needs for huge farm specific investment (long working hours, lack of holidays, specific knowledge on individual animals, land plots etc.) make it a problem to find and maintain needed hired labor. Reliance on family labor and friends as well as interlinking the labor supply with the "free" housing, land-leasing, food, other services, in some cases with property rights, are all common for the larger commercial farms.

A great majority of the dairy farms report facing significant risks in the milk marketing.

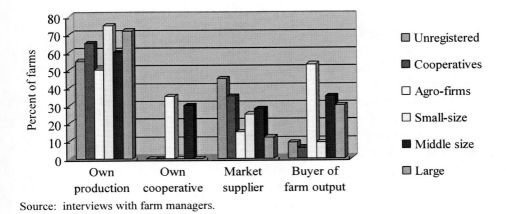

Source: interviews with farm managers.

Figure 10. Modes of forage supply in Bulgarian livestock farms.

Firstly, the price and quality competition increases all the time (including a cheap import of powder and fresh milk for processing, consumers goods). Recent assessment of the competitiveness has found that most dairy holdings are with low level of competitiveness [Koteva and Bachev]. Furthermore, all commercial farms want to see the milk price augmented in order to allow a modern production and capacity for competition.

Secondly, in some regions the farmers face monopolies experiencing a price-discrimination, delayed payments, not-fulfillment of contracted terms etc. The individual (smaller scale) producers cannot store fresh milk and/or transport it to a long distance (low market appropriability of rights, high cite and freshness dependency of the dairy farm). At the same time the incentives to cooperate between competing producers and neutralize the regional monopolies have been low (high transaction costs, opportunism of free-rider type).

Third, many smaller-scale dairy farms have been entirely ignored by the dominating large processors since they are not able to meet the quantity, quality and safety requirements, and command high transportation, training, and transaction costs. These farms have only available a restricted local fresh-milk market with insignificant demand from the minor processors, "street market" or direct delivery to individuals. In some milk-producing but remote areas the farmers experience complete missing market situation - no consumers and processors.

A main response of dairy farms has been *non-market orientation, reducing or ceasing out* dairy activity. For instance, comparing to 1990, the number of cows decreased by 39%, she-buffalos by 59%, and ewes by 73%; only for 2003-2005 the livestock holdings in the country diminished by 20% [MAF].

The effective private modes have also emerged to deal with the marketing risks. When a high capacity, quality, time of delivery, origin dependency with a particular buyer is in place then there are strong bilateral incentives for integration. Diverse modes for marketing arrangements are increasingly applied - long-term delivery contacts, price guarantees, premiums, interlinks etc. There are also few good examples for collective organizations of marketing with effective negotiating and enforcing relationships with the downstream partners.

A prospective mode for the protection of highly specialized and specific investments is organic and eco-production. The later comprises a few but growing number of farms and livestock closely integrated into a modern value chain in national and/or international scale[5].

There have emerged two independent associations of the dairy producers in the country. However, they attracted few farms because of the inefficiency in protecting producers' interests with processors and in lobbying for the public support. The sporadic attempts for "collective" actions of the milk producers (protests, milk pouring in cities, blocking highways etc.) have given no positive results. Consequently, there are huge income variation for different farms, regions, and years, and a constant reduction in the number of farms.

A *public mode* of production quotas for cow milk was introduced in 2007 aiming at diminishing the risk from market and income instability. The initial experience shows that the individual quotas exceed the nationwide ones and have not been able to eliminate the market risks. What is more, the established non-governmental Milk Board have not been able to secure the effective organization of producers, reconcile conflicts with the processors and lobby for the public support, and its functions have been marked by mismanagement, conflict of interests, and corruption.

In the last years, the strong income decline and protests of producers accompanied with increasing public demands for quality and safety in the sector have induced state subsidizing (national top-ups) for the dairy producers (Figure 11).

The later has not improved the deteriorating situation of the sector because of the delays of payments, insufficient scales to secure income growth, and predominately benefiting the large(r) producers.

---

[5] A case study for the evolution and the successful market integration of an organic dairy sheep farm is presented by Bachev and Tanic.

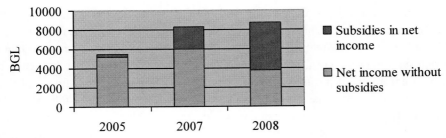

Source: MAF.

Figure 11. Evolution of income support in Bulgarian farms specialized in Grazing Livestock.

Diversification into sheep, goat, and buffalo productions (where no quotas exists) as well as into related (processing, restaurant, rural tourism, branding, marketing) and not related activity, is also taking a place as a risk reduction strategy of younger entrepreneurs.

The dairy farms experience major risks from the individuals and private agents such as:

– burglaries and other intrusions on the farm livestock, yields, and property;
– opportunistic behavior(s) in the contractual relations with the hired labor, inputs and service suppliers, buyers of output, and the coalition members in partnership and collective organizations;
– farming or another activity adversely affected the dairy holdings - pollution; unwanted "security services" etc.

There is not an effective *public system* (police, municipal guards, court) for the protection and the recovery of property, and for the punishment of offenders. The farmers are extremely vulnerable for thieves and organized crimes since most farm output and property is "in open", dispersed in wide areas and many locations.

The permanent risk for the agrarian property is widely assured by *private modes*. Our survey has found that the "costs for protection" for all type farms are significant in terms of time and resources spent, hired security guards and services, "payments for property protection and restoration" etc. Besides, the insurance coverage against burglary is most used market assurance of the bigger producers (Figure 9).

The high transitional uncertainty and insecurity (reputation is not important, difficulties to formulate and dispute contracts), the little contractual experience (difficulties to protect own interests), the impossibility to write a complete (labor, service supply) contract in farming and dispute contractual terms, the high cost for contract enforcement through the court system (inefficiency, corruption), all they are responsible for the considerable risk from contractual failure[6]. Not accidentally, most farm managers consider the "respecting laws and private contracts" as one of the most important factors for development of dairy farms (Figure 12).

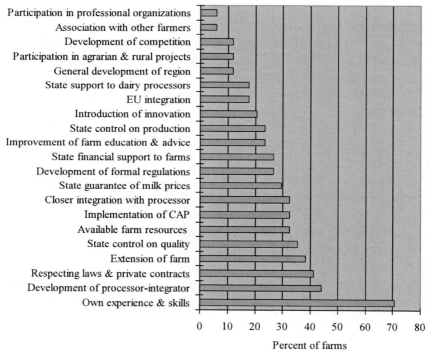

Source: Survey data from Plovdiv region.

Figure 12. Most significant factors for development of Bulgarian dairy farms.

In order to mitigate the risk from pre- and post-contractual opportunism the private modes are broadly employed. Since possibilities for opportunisms are

---

[6] Similarly to the market related risk no insurance for the protection from the "contractual risks" could be bought on market.

great (high information asymmetry, uncertainty, costs for supervision and direction) it is typical to use self-enforced own and/or family labor for all critical operations [Bachev, 2010a]. Therefore, the effective operation size in most dairy farms is determined by the available household labor. Small partnerships are practiced exclusively between relatives and friends where the costs for coordination, decision-making and motivation is low (here mutual goals and trust govern effectively relations).

In the large holdings, additional core labor is hired on the permanent basis and the output-based compensation, interlinking, social disbursements, supplementary services and paid holidays are further used to enhance motivation.

Similarly, a high-dependency from a particular buyer is effectively governed through reciprocal (rather than classical) contracts interlinking inputs, credit, extension etc. supply against the milk marketing.

The large *collective* (production, inputs supply, marketing, processing) *modes* are rare because of the diversified interests of farmers (different age, unlike size and type of operations, extent of diversification and market orientation); the bad perception associated with the "collective" forms (historical legacy, widespread mismanagement, low sustainability); the huge transaction costs for initiation and development; and the lack of appropriate legislation and incentives for association until recently.

There are situations where the dairy farms are badly affected by the harmful activities of other farms and industries influencing livestock welfare and behavior, causing pollution or other damages.

There are also cases of conflicts of interests over the limited natural resources with other agents. Most farmers have no means to defend against such hazards since the appropriate legislation is not in place (farmers has no rights) or it is difficult (costly) to protect and dispute assigned rights though existing forms (ineffective public enforcement, strong "private" pressure). Consequently, the farmers suffer considerable damages (on yields, produce quality, animal welfare etc.), perform bellow safety and quality standards, reduce or cease livestock activities.

The post-communist transition has been associated with the unprecedented changes in the institutional structure (social and institutional risks). There has been huge uncertainty about the directions and the kind of changes, and instability (dynamics, constant amendments, controversies) in the structure of rights, legislation, regulations, taxation, public organizations, authorities' responsibilities, public support mechanisms etc.

The new public administration has been ineffective, incompetent, unpredictable, and corrupted. Carrying out farming and business in such environment has been associated with significant risks and costs for studying, complying with, safeguarding from the formal regulations and the "informal rules" of the bureaucracy (authority).

Most livestock operation has been carried by numerous small-scale and primitive holdings often located within the residential borders. They contribute significantly to air, water and soils pollution, and discomfort of the local population. The conflicts between the farms and neighborhoods are common in recent years and bring about strong community demand (formal and informal pressure) to limit or relocate activities.

Carrying livestock activity is risky because of the frictions with the community and uncertainty/certainty about the potential need and costs for adaptation. That particular risk has been responsible for the low (investment) incentives for modernization in smaller (subsistent, semi-market, commercial) holdings. The later additionally contributes to a greater exposure to natural, market, and other type institutional risks.

A considerable risk for the most dairy farms has come from the uncertainty (presently "certainty") surrounding the modes of introduction of EU CAP in the country. Until accession there was not clear the pace and scale of implementation of the EU rules in the dairy sector of the country. The EU quality, hygiene, veterinary, environment, animal-welfare etc. standards were introduced in 2007 and there was a transition period for the adaptation to the new requirements (until end of 2009). In addition public measures have been implemented to support adaptation, modernization and market orientation of farms.

Nevertheless, there were merely 900 farms with 50000 cows meeting the EU raw-milk quality standards (0.5% of all cow-farms and 13% of cows in the country). At the same time, most holdings with milking cows (81%) had no milking installations and only 0.1% of the dairy farms were with safe manure pile cites [MAF].

The public support has been initiated and moved from zero to positive territories since 2007 – e.g. currently subsidies accounts for 27% of the net income in farms specialized in grazing livestock [MAF]. Nevertheless, the special public measures for the farm adaptation, market orientation and modernization has affected a tiny number of the dairy holdings (mostly large operators). Consequently, the greatest portion of farms had to move into informal sector and perform bellow the official quality and safety standards.

Our survey of the commercial dairy farms has found out that different type farms have unequal capacity for the adaptation to the new EU requirements. Most holdings have no sufficient potential for adjustment to the new institutional norms (Table 2). That is particularly truth for the small-scale unregistered producers which dominate the sector. Only a third of the dairy farms believe their production capacity corresponds to the modern requirements of competition, productivity, eco-performance and animal welfare. Merely one-seventh of the dairy farms have internal capacity and access to outside sources to fund the necessary investment associated with the adaptation to the new standards. Thus, most dairy farms are effectively at risk to be ceased since do not and cannot comply with the legal requirements.

Table 2. Share of farms with big and good capacity for adaptation to new EU requirements for dairy sector (per cent)

Farms capacity	Type of farms			Total
	Unregistered	Firms	Coops	
Extend of knowledge on new requirements	22.7	63.6	100	38.2
Available skills and knowledge for adaptation	22.7	54.5	100	35.3
Available production capacity	27.3	45.4		32.3
Improvement of quality and hygiene standards	36.4	72.7	100	50
Improving animal welfare	31.8	72.7		44.1
Improving environmental performance	31.8	54.5		38.2
Finding necessary investment	9.1	27.3		14.7

Source: survey data from Plovdiv region.

The planed "market orientation" of the huge (semi) subsistence farming has not taken place. Programmed funding with the National Plan for Agrarian and Rural Development under Measure 141 "Support for Restructuring of Semi-market Holdings" has been greatly underutilized (merely 15% of the target reached) because of the lack of interest and complicated bureaucratic requirements and procedures.

It is not feasible to envisage any improvement in the small (semi market and commercial) holdings due to the high costs for farm enlargement and adjustment to the new market and institutional environment (no entrepreneurial capital available, low investment and training capability of aged managers). Besides, most of the farm operators are old in age and have no successor willing to undertake the business. Since there is no existing or prospective market for a "whole dairy farm" in the country, the incentives for the long-term investments for farm modernization are absent.

Nevertheless, there will be technically and politically impossible to enforce the official standards in that enormous informal sector of the economy (especially during the period of the economic crisis and the lack of any alternative income opportunities in rural areas). Thus there is no significant immediate institutional risk for these farms and they will likely dominate the sector in years to come.

Modes of Governing Risks from Dairy Farms

Major risks to environment from dairy farms are associated with the pollution of soils, air and waters; unsustainable use of farmland and grasslands; and significant contribution to greenhouse-gas emissions.

Until recently the voluntary initiatives, private organizations, market driven modes (such as organic farming), and public intervention, all have had no significant importance for the protection of environment and governing eco-risks from the dairy farming [Bachev, 2012b]. The cross-compliance eco-requirement and a range of public eco-measures are introduced with the EU CAP implementation – eco-conditionality, eco-standards, eco-regulations, eco-education, financial support to eco-activities, organic farming, zones with eco-difficulties, market-orientation and diversification of farms etc.

As a (side or planed) results from the restructuring of farms and the production structures and methods there is considerable amelioration of surface and ground waters quality. Nevertheless, Nitrate Vulnerable Zones cover 53% of country's territory and 68% of utilized agricultural lands [MAF]. In drinking water, 5% of the analyses show deviation of N up to 5 times above appropriate level, while in water for irrigation in 45% of the samples N concentrations exceed contamination limit 2-20 folds [EEA]. The lack of effective manure storage capacity and sewer systems, and numerous illegal garbage locations in the rural areas, improper use of N fertilizers, crop and livestock practices, non-incompliance with rules for farming in water supply zones etc. all are responsible for that problem. What is more, decreasing amount of manure has been used for fertilization of merely 0.17% of the utilized farmlands in recent years.

Furthermore, erosion is a major factor for the land degradation as one-third of the arable lands are subjected to wind erosion and 70% to water erosion [EEA]. Deforestation, uncontrolled pasture, ineffective agro-techniques and crop rotation, plowing pastures, deficiency of anti-erosion measures are etc. contribute to that problem. In some regions overgrazing of the public (state, municipality) pastures by private and domestic livestock is a significant problem while in others the under-grazing poses sustainability problem.

A negative rate of fertilizer compensation of N, P and K intakes dominate in the country being particularly low for P and K [MAF]. In addition unbalance of nutrient components has been typical with application of 5.3 times less P and 6.7 times less K with appropriate N rate. Consequently, deterioration of agricultural lands comes as a result – the share of land affected by acidification increases, and thousands tons of N, P_2O_5 and K_2O are irreversibly removed annually from the soils.

There is a considerable reduction of GHG emissions from the agriculture since 1989 [EEA]. Nevertheless, agriculture has been the major ammonia source accounting for two-thirds of national emission as most NO_2 emissions comes from agricultural soils, manure management and burning of stubble fields. Similarly, the methane emission from agriculture represents about a quarter of the national, and the biggest portion of CH_4 comes from the fermentation from domestic livestock and manure management.

Consequently, there is a considerable risk to the nature and the amount and quality of the eco-system services related to the development of dairy farming in the country.

The livestock farming has been a significant risk to the public which is mostly associated with the quality, authenticity, and safety of livestock products; the livestock diseases causing considerable treat to human health; the new public, ethical etc. concerns about the environment preservation and improvement, animal welfare, keeping tradition etc.

Table 3. Control from the processor and the state on farms (% of farms)

Control on:	Processor	State body
Milk quality	94.1	52.9
Milk safety	47.1	17.6
Hygiene of production	58.8	44.1
Animal health	20.6	55.9
Forage for animals	11.8	35.3
Care for animals	8.8	35.3
Care for environment	8.8	41.2
Control is permanent	2.9	20.6
Sanctions and punishments are applied	38.2	8.8

Source: survey data from Plovdiv region.

All of that brings to life appropriate policies, regulations and support measures. There has been increasing pressure, control, and sanctions on the dairy farms both by the processors and the state for complying with the new requirements (Table 3). Most dairy farms had to make or are being undertaking significant changes related to the novel institutional requirements in order to sell milk (Figure 13).

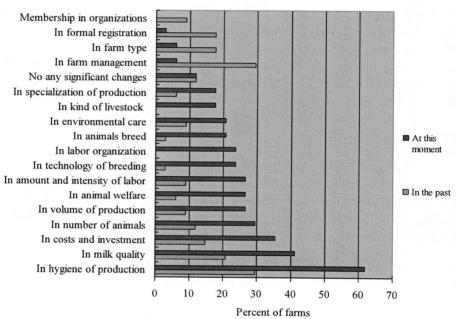

Source: survey data from Plovdiv region.

Figure 13. Changes to be made to sell milk to "Dimitar Madzarov" LTD.

Our surveys show that many of the specific EU regulations are not well-known by the implementing authorities and a great portion of farmers [Bachev, 2010a]. The lack of readiness, experiences and capability would require some time lag until the "full" implementation of the CAP in Bulgarian conditions. Besides, most farm managers have no adequate training and/or managerial capability, are old in age with small learning and adaptation potential. Therefore, there will be significant inequalities in application of the new laws and standards in diverse sectors, farms of different type and size, and various regions of the country.

The dairy farms pose considerable risks to other farms, individuals, private agents. There are many incidences for using others grasslands and crop yields, or otherwise damaging land and property by the dairy farmers. Some dairy holdings pose a serious risk for the comfort of individuals and others businesses (e.g. organic farms, recreation and tourism operators, water suppliers etc.). These risks are mitigated privately by the affected individuals and businesses through negotiating, monitoring, employing guards, or illegitimate means.

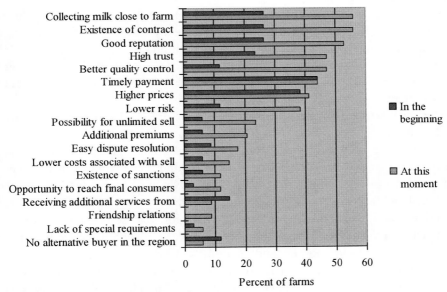

Source: Survey data from Plovdiv region.

Figure 14. Main reasons for selling milk to "Dimitar Madzarov" LTD.

The small-scale and semi-subsistence farms have been major milk suppliers to the dairy processors putting them in a big (capacity, cite, quality, origin, safety) dependency. Divers private modes are broadly used by the processors to deal with those risks.

We have identified an effective system for the governing risk in relations of "Dimitar Madzarov" LTD with more than 1000 small-scale milk suppliers from Plovdiv region [Bachev, 2011a]. In the last 10 years this dairy-processing company has developed a comprehensive system for the protection of interests and the coordination, stimulation, controlling, and conflict resolution with the farmers including: building a good reputation and trust, constant communications, regular group discussions of problems, training of farmers in new industry and institutional requirements, using written delivery contracts, significant relation-specific on-farm investments (in milk collecting, cooling, and controlling facilities and staff), permanent verification of the quality and the registration of delivered milk by each farm, punishment for the offenders, effective and regular payment mode, differential prices stimulating farm enlargement and increasing milk-supply, interlinking interest-free crediting against the marketing of milk, providing assistance to the farmers in construction and preparation public support projects, encouraging farms grouping etc.

Namely this special governance has contributed considerably for the tighter integration with the dairy farms, increasing efficiency of the bilateral relations, enhancing the farms' relation investments, and their adaptation to the company's requirements for milk quality and quantity (Figure 14). Involved farms consider the development of "Dimitar Madzarov" LTD as one of the most important factors for their own farm development (Figure 13).

The dairy farming has been responsible for the great risks to markets during transition now.

There was a deficiency in the quantity of different type milks during the market adjustments in the first years of the transition. The risks of insufficient supply and the price volatility were successfully overcome by the market (rather than failed public[7]) governance - opening up markets, development of market competition and demand. Up-to-date the risk for the consumers which is associated with the authentic quality, safety, origin of milk and dairy products has been a serious issue and informal (and illegitimate) market is considerable.

The introduction of the EU standards for milk production and trade is causing a new risk for the insufficient supply of local milk. The biggest dairy processors have been trying to overcome the shortages of quality local milk through processing imported fresh and/or powder milk. Nevertheless, they increasingly face another problem (risk) of the low consumer demand for dairy products based on the non-fresh milk.

In order to deal with that capacity and quality deficiency risk some processors are introducing specific modes for the risk governance – origin and quality guarantee, brand names, traditional and eco-products etc. The later has brought a variety of private modes for the governing vertical relations backwards with the supplying farmers, and upwards with the food chains, retailers, and importers [Bachev, 2011a].

---

[7] In 1990 there were numerous unsuccessful attempts to stabilize markets by controlling prices, banning import or export, introducing quotas and tariffs etc.

A public intervention is also undertaken aiming at modernizing and commercializing the dairy farms, and stimulating the production of dairy, local and eco-products – e.g. introduction and protection of rights on dairy products (e.g. special regulations for the Bulgarian yogurt and cheese), special traditional and organic products, subsidies for the modernization of farms and adaptation to the EU quality and safety standards, support for the market orientation, public training and advisory services to farmers etc.

Impact of EU CAP on Farms' Risk Management Capability

The EU integration and the implementation of CAP have affected positively the risk management capability of the commercial dairy farming in the country.

According to the considerable portion of the dairy farms managers the EU CAP implementation has had a good or significant impact on the income, efficiency, competitiveness and sustainability of their holdings (Figure 15). The positive effect of the new policies is especially great for the managerial efficiency of farms which improves their ability to govern diverse risks in the new conditions.

Nevertheless, a good proportion of the commercial dairy holdings managers assess as neutral or even negative the CAP impacts on different aspects of their farms development. The new policies measures affected particularly negatively the competitiveness, the economic sustainability, and the managerial efficiency of numerous dairy enterprises. That indicates for unchanged or deteriorating capability for risk management (lack of financial means, worsen ability to face and adapt to market competition) in some substantial part of the dairy farms as a result of the introduction of the EU policies.

Furthermore, there have been progressive trends in the development of dairy farms and their relations with other agents comparing to the period before EU accession (Figure 16).

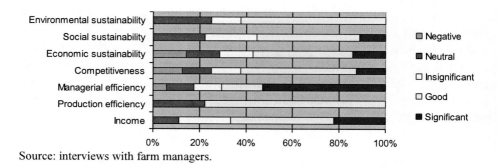

Source: interviews with farm managers.

Figure 15. Impact of EU CAP implementation on Bulgarian dairy farms.

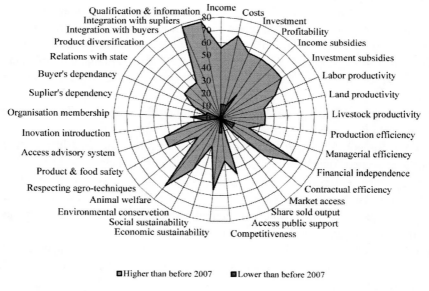

Source: interviews with farm managers.

Figure 16. Importance of dairy farms' indicators comparing to the period before EU accession (percent of farms).

More than a half of the holdings see an increased income, investment, subsidies, profitability, and economic sustainability after the EU integration. Two-third of them report higher costs, financial independence, and animal-welfare. Almost 78% of farms experience superior qualification and information, and bigger integration with the suppliers. All that is likely associated with decreased risks and improved risk management in the majority of commercial dairy holdings.

At the same time, more than 22% of dairy farms reports lower than before profitability and memberships in professional organization, and higher dependency from the buyers and processors. Every 11 out of 100 farms has got a poorer income, investment, managerial and contractual efficiency, competitiveness, innovation introduction, and economic sustainability, and a higher indebtedness and dependency from the suppliers comparing to the period before EU integration.

Therefore, a good portion of the dairy farms in the country have not improved or wakened their capability for risk management during the EU integration and CAP implementation.

Conclusion

The analysis of the modes, efficiency and challenges of risk management in agri-food chain let us withdraw a number of academic, business and policies recommendations:

First, the governance (along with the technical, information etc.) issues are to take a central part in the risk management analysis and design. The type of threats and risks, and the specific (natural, technological, behavioral, dimensional, institutional etc.) factors, and comparative benefits and costs (including third-party, transaction, time) are to be taken into account in assessing the efficiencies, complementarities and the prospects of alternative (market, private, public and hybrid) modes. The system of the risk management is to adapt/improved taking advantage of the number of the new opportunities and overcoming/defending against the evolving new challenges summarized in the paper.

Second, more hybrid (public-private, public-collective) modes should be employed given the coordination, incentives, control, and costs advantages. The (pure) public management of the most agri-food-chain risks is difficult or impossible (agents opportunism, informal sector, externalities). Often the introduction and enforcement of new rights (on food security, risk-management responsibility etc.), and supporting the private and collective initiatives (informing, training, assisting, funding) is much more efficient.

Third, a greater (public) support must be given to multidisciplinary and interdisciplinary research on (factors, modes, impacts of) the risk governance in the agri-food chain in order to assist effectively the national and international policies, the design of modes for public interventions, and the individual, collective and business actions for the risk management.

The analysis of the post-communist development of dairy farming has identified quite specific risk structures facing by and causing from this sector of Bulgarian agriculture. The huge market and institutional instability and uncertainty, and the high transaction costs, have blocked the evolution of effective market and collective modes for the risk protection. A great variety of private modes (internal organization, vertical integration, interlinking etc.) have emerged to deal with the significant natural, market, private, and institutional risks faced by the dairy farms and affected agents.

Diverse risks associated with the Bulgarian dairy farming were not effectively governed and persist during the transition now. That was a consequence of the ineffective public (Government, international assistance etc.) intervention to correct market and private sector failures in the risk governance. The later have had considerable negative impacts on the evolution of (size, productivity, sustainability of) the farms, the development of the markets, the structure of production and consumption, and the state of environment.

The EU integration and CAP implementation improved significantly the risk management capability of a great portion of commercial dairy holdings. At the same time, a good portion of the dairy farms have not improved or even wakened their capability for risk management in the new economic and institutional environment. Furthermore, certain risks related to the dairy sector "disappeared" due to the ineffective risk governance and declining dairy farming. That would lead to a further deformation in the development of dairy and related sectors unless effective public (regulations, assistance, control etc.) measures are taken to mitigate the existing problems and risks.

References

Babcock, B. (2004). *Economics of Risk Management in Agriculture*, Center for Agricultural and Rural Development. Iowa State University, www.card.iastate.edu/risk_management.ppt.

Bachev, H. (2010a). *Governance of Agrarian Sustainability,* New York: Nova Science Publishers.

Bachev, H. (2010b). Framework for Analysis of Agrarian Contracts, *Management Research and Practice* Vol. 2 Issue 1, 39-66.

Bachev, H. (2011a), Dairy Supply Chain Management in Bulgaria, *IUP Journal of Supply Chain Management*, 2, 7-20.

Bachev H. (2011b). Needs, Modes and Efficiency of Economic Organizations and Public Interventions in Agriculture, *Review of Economics and Finance*, 3, Academic Research Centre of Canada, 89-103.

Bachev, H. (2011c). Governing of Chemical and Biological Risks in Agri-food Sector: Modes, Efficiency, Challenges, in *Exploring Multidisciplinary Approaches to Chemical and Biological Defense*, Proceedings DTRA and IIBR Workshop, June 19-23, 2011, Eilat, Israel.

Bachev, H. (2012a). Risk Management in Agri-food Sector, *Contemporary Economics*, Volume 6, Issue 3.

Bachev H (2012b). Management of Agro-Ecosystem Services: Framework of Analysis, Case of Bulgaria, in *Advances in Environmental Research*. Vol.17, Ed. Justin A. Daniels, New York: Nova Science, 119-164.

Bachev, H. and M.Labonne (2000). *About Organization of Agrarian Innovations*. Montpellier: INRA.

Bachev, H. and S.Tanic (2011). Issues and challenges for farm and enterprise diversification and integration of small scale farmers into value chains in EECA, in *"Enabling Environment for producer-agribusiness linkages in EECA"*, ed. S.Tanic, FAO: Ankara.

Bachev, H. and T.Nanseki (2008), Risk Governance in Bulgarian Dairy Farming, Proceedings 12th Congress of the European Association of Agricultural Economists *"People, Food and Environments – Global Trends and European Strategies"*, 26-29 August 2008, Ghent, http://ageconsearch.umn.edu/bitstream/44136/2/240.pdf.

Barker, G. (2005). *Tools for assessing and managing food chain risks*, Presentation to RELU conference Rural Economy and Land Use: The Challenge for Research 19-21 Jan 2005, Birmingham http://www.relu.ac.uk/events/Jan05/Presentations/p4%20Barker.PDF.

Behdani, B. (2012). *Japanese Catastrophe and the Dark Side of Global supply Chains* http://www.nextgenerationinfrastructures.eu/images/Japanese%20Catastrophe%20and%20the%20Dark%20Side%20of%20Global%20supply%20Chains%20(1).pdf.

CDC (2011). Centre for Disease Control and Prevention, USA. http://www.cdc.gov/foodborneburden/2011-foodborne-estimates.html.

CIPS (2012). *Risk management in food supply chains*, CIPS, http://www.cips.org/Documents/Resources/Knowledge%20Summary/Risk%20Management%20in%20food%20supply%20chains.pdf.

Coase, R. (1937). The Nature of the Firm, *Economica* 4, 386-405.

Coase, R. (1960). The Problem of Social Costs, *Journal of Law and Economics* 3, 1-44.

COST (2009). *COST Foresight 2030, Benefiting from the Digital Revolution*, COST Workshop on Food Security, Final Report, June 30- July 2, 2009, Gent, Belgium.

Dani, S. and A. Deep (2010). *Investigating risk management capability within UK food supply chains.* http://lboro.academia.edu/SamirDani/Papers/ 1060574/Investigating_risk_management_capability_within_UK_food_sup ply_chains.

Deep, A. and S. Dani (2009). *Managing Global Food Supply Chain Risks: A Scenario Planning Perspective,* POMS 20th Annual Conference, Orlando, Florida U.S.A., May 1 to May 4, 2009. http://www.apec.org.au/docs// Supply%20Chain%20Risk%20Assurance/124_SCRA.pdf.

Derrig, R. (2002). Insurance Fraud.*The Journal of Risk and Insurance.* 69(3), 271-287.

DTRA and IIBR (2011). *Exploring Multidiciplinary Approaches to Chemical and Biological Defence* (2011), Proceedings, DTRA and IIBR Workshop, June 19-23, 2011, Eilat, Israel.

Furuboth, E. and R. Richter (1998). *Institutions and Economic Theory: The Contribution of the New Institutional Economics.* Ann Arbor: The University of Michigan Press.

Gerasymenko, N. and O. Zhemoyda (2009). *New Challenges for Risk Management in Agri-food Industry,* EAAE 113th Seminar, September 3-6, 2009, Chania, Crete, Greece http://econpapers.repec.org/paper/agseaa113/ 58019.htm

ECDC (2010). *Annual epidemiological report on communicable diseases in Europe 2010,* European Centre for Disease Prevention and Control.

EEA (2010). *State of Environment Report,* Executive Environment Agency, Sofia.

Eurobarometer (2010). *Food-related risks,* Special Eurobarometer 73.5.

EU (2009). *The Rapid Alert System for Food and Feed, Annual Report 2009,* European Commission.

Eurostat (2011a). *From farm to fork – a statistical journey along the EU's food chain,* Eurostat.

Eurostat (2011b). *Waste statistics,* Eurostat.

Hefnawy, M. (editor) (2011). *Advances in Food Protection Focus on Food Safety and Defense,* Springer.

Humphrey J. and O.Memedovic (2006), *Global Value Chains in Agri-food Sector,* Vienna: UNIDO.

Jaffee S., P. Siegel and C. Andrews (2008), *Rapid Agricultural Supply Chain Risk Assessment,* World Bank.

Koteva, N. and H.Bachev (2011). A Study on Competitiveness of Bulgarian Farms, *Economic Tought,* 7, 95-123.

Luning P., F. Devlieghere and R. Verhé (2006), *Safety in the agri-food chain*, Wageningen Academic Publishers.

MAF (2011). *Agrarian Report*, Ministry of Agriculture and Forestry, Sofia.

North, D. (1990). *Institutions, Institutional Change and Economic Performance.* Cambridge University Press, Cambridge.

OECD (2008). *Managing Risk in Agriculture: a Holistic Approach*, OECD.

OECD (2011). *Managing Risk in Agriculture Policy Assessment and Design*, OECD.

Olson M. (1969). *The Logic of Collective Actions: Public Goods and the Theory of Groups*. Harvard Univ. Press.

Olsson, A. and C. Skjöldebrand (2008). Risk Management and Quality Assurance Through the Food Supply Chain – Case Studies in the Swedish Food Industry, *The Open Food Science Journal*, 2008, 2, 49-56.

Ramaswami, R., S. Ravi, and S.Chopra (2008). *Risk management in agriculture*, Working papers IDEAS http://ideas.repec.org/p/ind/ isipdp/03-08.html

RPDRM (2012). Disaster Risk Management in food and agriculture, Rome Partnership for Disaster Risk Management http://home.wfp.org/ stellent/groups/public/documents/communications/wfp201794.pdf.

Schaffnit-Chatterjee, C. (2010). *Risk management in agriculture. Towards market solutions in the EU*, Deutsche bank Research http://www.dbresearch.com/PROD/DBR_INTERNET_ENPROD/PROD00 00000000262553.PDF.

Shepherd, R, G. Barker, S. French, A. Hart, J. Maule, and A. Cassidy (2006). Managing Food Chain Risks: Integrating Technical and Stakeholder Perspectives on Uncertainty, *Journal of Agricultural Economics*, Volume 57, Issue 2, pages 313–327.

Sporleder, T. (1992). Managerial Economics of Vertically Coordinated Agricultural Firms, *American Journal of Agricultural Economics*, Vo l 74, No 5, 1226-1231.

Trench P., C. Narrod, D.Roy, and M. Tiongco (2011), *Responding to Health Risks along Value Chain*, New Delhi: 2020 Conference Paper-5.

Weaver, R. and T. Kim (2000). *Contracting to Manage Risk in Food Supply Chains*, Paper presented at IAMA 2000 Meetings, April 2000, Chicago, Illinois http://www.icavresearch.org/wp-content/uploads/2009/12/weaver_ Kim00.pdf.

Williamson, O. (1981). The Economics of Organization. *The American Journal of Sociology* 87 (3), 548–577.

Williamson, O. (1996). *The Mechanisms of Governance*. New York: Oxford University Press.

Zulauf, C. and D.Orden (2012). US Farm Policy and Risk Assistance, The Competing Senate and House Agriculture Committee Bills of July 2012, Issue Paper No. 44, Geneve: International Centre for Trade and Sustainable Development.

In: Progress in Economics Research. Volume 27   ISBN: 978-1-62808-201-2
Editor: A. Tavidze   © 2013 Nova Science Publishers, Inc.

Chapter 2

TYPOLOGIES OF UNIVERSITY SUPPORT PROGRAMMES FOR SETTING UP SPIN- OFFS: UNITED KINGDOM VS. SPAIN

José María Beraza-Garmendia[*]
and Arturo Rodríguez-Castellanos[#]
[1]University of the Basque Country UPV/EHU, Escuela Universitaria
de Estudios Empresariales, San Sebastián, Gipuzkoa, Spain
[2]University of the Basque Country UPV/EHU, Facultad de
Ciencias Económicas y Empresariales, Bilbao, Bizkaia, Spain

Abstract

This study addresses two central research objectives: on the one hand, to identify the different models of spin-off support programmes to be found in British and Spanish universities, and to analyse their differentiated characteristics; on the other, to validate the models identified in the literature. The analysis was performed using data collected by way of a survey, targeted at the heads of university spin-off support programmes, to which we applied a statistic analysis.

[*] E-mail address: josemaria.beraza@ehu.es, Tel: +34 943015782, Fax: +34 943018360, Address: University of the Basque Country UPV/EHU, Escuela Universitaria de Estudios Empresariales, Plaza de Oñati 1, 20018 San Sebastián, Gipuzkoa, Spain.
[#] E-mail address: arturo.rodriguez@ehu.es, Tel: +34 946013709, Fax: +34 946013710, Address: University of the Basque Country UPV/EHU, Facultad de Ciencias Económicas y Empresariales, Avda. Lehendakari Agirre, 83, 48015 Bilbao, Bizkaia, Spain.

Firstly, we applied factorial analysis to identify the most significant variables explaining the characteristics of these programmes. Secondly, using the cluster analysis technique based on the variables identified, we classified the British universities on the one hand, and the Spanish ones on the other. Using Anova analysis we went on to describe the differentiated characteristics of each of the clusters found. This analysis enabled us to identify four significantly different types of spin-off support programmes in British universities and another four in Spanish universities. It also confirmed that programmes existed in the United Kingdom could be differentiated in terms of resources, university commitment, proactivity and selectivity; in the case of the Spanish universities, as well as these four variables, we also found differences in terms of experience and the number of spin-offs created. Among the various types of programmes identified, we found one in the United Kingdom and two in Spain that appear to be models for success. The study also confirms the importance of a favourable environment to the success of these programmes; however it does not confirm that the universities tend initially to follow a policy of low selectivity, as indicated in the literature.

1. Introduction

Studies on the mission of the university have placed increasing importance on transferring research results to the market as a source of development and competitiveness (Etzkowitz et al., 2000; Geuna, 1999; Mowery and Sampat, 2001; Shane, 2004). However, this is a complex interactive process (Lundvall, 2002), involving a wide variety of agents (Benner and Sandstrom, 2000; Etzkowitz et al., 2000; Okubo and Sjoberg, 2000). Conscious of the difficulties it poses, universities and governments have begun establishing policies for promoting this type of development (OECD 1999).

The creation of knowledge-based firms has become particularly important in recent decades (Autio, 1997; Callan, 2001; European Commission, 2002; Shane, 2004; Storey and Tether, 1998), bringing with it a proliferation of university support programmes for setting-up spin-offs (Golob, 2003; Helm and Mauroner, 2007; McQueen and Wallmark, 1991; Mustar, 1997; Schutte et al., 2001; Shane, 2004; UNISPIN, 1999). Nonetheless, there are considerable differences in the way the various programmes are structured and operate, in terms of their aims, strategies, functions and activities and the organisational structures and services they offer (Clarysse et al., 2002; Clarysse et al., 2005; Degroof, 2002; Degroof and Roberts, 2004; European Commission, 2002; Powers and McDougall, 2005a; Roberts and Malone, 1996; Smailes and Cooper, 2004; Wright et al., 2007).

In addition, many of these programmes are newly-founded and consequently have neither a solid organisational structure nor clearly identified activities

(Clarysse et al., 2005; Heirman and Clarysse, 2004). For this reason, different models of academic spin-off support programmes have been proposed (Clarysse et al., 2002; Clarysse et al., 2005; Degroof, 2002; Degroof and Roberts, 2004; Roberts and Malone, 1996).

Table 1. Main research on models of academic spin-off support programmes

Authors	Number of institutions analyzed	Countries	Method	Main results
Roberts and Malone (1996)	7 Universities and the British Technology Group	US and United Kingdom	Case study Interviews and secondary sources	Identification of spin-off process models; main dimensions of a supportive policy; and link between environment, policy and results
Powers and McDougall (2005b)	134 universities	US	Factorial and Regresión Jerárquica	Roberts and Malone (1996) model validation
Degroof (2002)	3 universities 2 research institutes 47 spin-offs	Belgium	Case study Interviews and secondary sources	Identification of spin-off process models, supportive policies and results in unfavourable contexts for entrepreneurship
Degroof and Roberts (2004)	6 universities 2 research institutes 47 spin-offs	Belgium	Case study Interviews and secondary sources	Identification of spin-off process models, supportive policies and results in unfavourable contexts for entrepreneurship
Clarysse, Lockett, Quince and Van de Velde (2002)	2 universities and 5 research institutes or others technology transfer institutions	Europe	Case study Interviews and secondary sources	Identification of spin-off support strategy models and results
Clarysse, Wright, Lockett, van de Velde and Vohora (2005)	43 universities, research institutes and others technology transfer institutions	Europe	Case study Interviews and secondary sources	Clarysse, Lockett, Quince and Van de Velde (2002) models validation

Source: Authors´review.

The main aim of this work is to identify the different models of spin-off support programmes to be found in British and Spanish universities, and to analyse their differentiated characteristics. Using data collected by way of a survey, targeted at the people in charge of university programmes for supporting the creation of spin-offs, a statistical analysis was performed applying univariate and multivariate techniques. Firstly, we have applied the technique of factorial analysis to identify the most significant variables explaining the characteristics of these programmes. Secondly, using the cluster analysis technique, we have classified the British universities on the one hand, and the Spanish ones on the other. Using a one-factor analysis of variance (Anova) we went on to describe the differentiated characteristics of each of the clusters found.

We believe that this study is of particular interest, since by comparing universities from two European countries with a different degree of experience in developing spin-off support programmes (extensive in the United Kingdom, quite recent in Spain) we can identify changes resulting from maturity amongst these programmes.

By identifying groups of universities with similar programmes we can characterise these groups and highlight differences between them, making it possible to set out guidelines to orient universities in ensuring that support for the creation of spin-offs is more effective.

The paper consists of an introduction and five other sections. In the second one, we review the literature on types of university spin-off support programmes, identifying the different models suggested by different authors. Third, we explain the research methodology used. Fourth, we perform a multivariate statistical analysis, using the cluster analysis technique, to identify the different existing models of spin-off support programmes in British and Spanish universities. Fifth, we make a descriptive statistical analysis to characterise each of the models identified and highlight its main differentiating features. In the sixth section, we summarises the main conclusions obtained.

2. Literature Review

We then proceed to review the main typologies of university support programmes for setting up spin-offs developed in the literature. This mostly consists of qualitative research based on case studies. The characteristics and results of these studies are shown in Table 1.

Roberts and Malone (1996) can be considered the pioneers in this area. For them, the two main dimensions of a policy of economic commercialization through the creation of spin-offs are *selectivity* and *support*, for each of which they distinguish two levels: high and low and they argue that there are only two viable models of support policy: low selectivity/low support and high selectivity/high support.

A low selectivity/low support policy means that many spin-offs are created to which little support is given. This policy reduces the costs of the process, ensuring that in the end a certain number of spin-offs can take hold. The choice of the projects eligible for support is left to external agencies (for example, venture-capital funds), which are seen as having greater experience and expertise in choosing possible "winners" and prevent possible conflicts of interest. This strategy makes sense in settings in which spinning-off is common practise and venture capital is in abundant supply.

In a high selectivity/high support policy, a small number of spin-offs is created to which a large degree of support is given, giving them large possibilities of success. This strategy is more likely in environments where spinning-off is more unusual and venture capital is scarce. In this context, a university wanting to develop a support policy has no choice but to take the place of the financial market, playing the role of a financial investor, and encouraging a culture of entrepreneurship. In less favourable environments, therefore, the spin-off process can follow a *technology push* strategy, in which the university must get involved in the process of selecting and supporting the spin-offs throughout all stages of the process.

To sum up, Roberts and Malone find from their field work that a variety of environments are related to spin-offs; that different policies of support are applied depending on the existing environment, and that different results are achieved, as shown in Table 2.

Table 2. Link between environment, policy and results, according to Roberts and Malone (1996)

Environments	Policy	Spin-off process	Results
Favourable	Low selectivity/low support	*Business pull*	More *spin-offs*
Unfavourable	High selectivity/high support	*Technology push*	Less *spin-offs*

Source: Based on Roberts and Malone (1996).

Powers and McDougall (2005b) seek to test Roberts and Malone's model empirically. To do this, they use a sample of 134 universities in the US and measure the results of each one's technology transfer, based on the number of initial public offers for companies using licences awarded by the university and the royalties obtained from the sale of products based on these licences.

The results of the analysis are inconclusive, since they only identify a positive relationship between the characteristics of the environment and the number of initial public offers and for public universities there appears to be a negative relationship between selectivity and the characteristics of the environment, considered as a whole, and the number of initial public offers. This latter result appears to confirm that, in the case of public universities, in an unfavourable environment, it is recommendable to pursue a high selectivity policy, and in a favourable environment to pursue a low selectivity policy.

Degroof (2002) analyses how an environment that is unfavourable to entrepreneurship affects the type of spin-offs created in the academic institutions. Based on a study of spin-off creation in five organisations of this type, he distinguishes two models for spinning off in this type of environment. One model is that pursued by the specialist research institutions and the other is more typical of universities.

The process used by the specialist research institutes has a long incubation period, lasting several years for technical incubation and up to a year and a half for business incubation. The new company is only incorporated when it can avail of protected technology, a business plan with strong market potential, a convincing business model to draw on and lastly an entrepreneurial team capable of leading the project with the help of venture-capital organisations, company directors from the industry and other advisers.

In contrast, the process pursued by universities does not normally include incubation or assistance in developing the business plan. The spin-offs are founded at a very early stage, when the project is still undefined and its primary asset is its scientific knowledge. As a result, in most cases the business is developed after the spin-off's incorporation, when it is already up and running as a firm.

The author goes on to relate the results of the study to Roberts and Malone's selection and support dimensions in the spin-off process and concludes that the process adopted by the specialist research institutes involves pursuing a high selectivity/high support policy, whereas the process identified in the universities involves a low selectivity/low support policy, thus contradicting Roberts and Malone's conclusions. However, the author notes this process is not static, but becoming increasingly more sophisticated as the institutions learn from their experience.

This approach sheds lights on one important practical aspect: the difficulty of establishing from the outset a high selectivity/high support policy in an environment that is unfavourable to entrepreneurship. Implementing such a policy requires considerable resources and skills, which may not exist in the universities; moreover, implementing them involves, among other factors, bringing about a considerable cultural and structural change.

Even in unfavourable environments, therefore, a university can start out in a position of low selectivity/low support and gradually move towards a position of greater selectivity and support, although it remains to be seen whether all universities are capable of following this path and at what speed.

Finally, Degroof (2002) notes that the sort of spin-off process pursued will have implications for the type of firm created. His study shows that in reality different types of companies are created by different types of research institutions, pursuing different processes. The specialist research institutes create *venture capital backed firms*[1], after a long process of incubation, whereas in the universities the companies created at an initial stage are mainly *lifestyle* spin-offs[2], although as the programmes gain greater experience, more growth-oriented spin-offs may emerge, particularly *prospector* spin-offs[3], if the environments are unfavourable to enterprise.

To sum up, Degroof (2002) notes that, in an unfavourable context for entrepreneurship, different research institutions use different support policies for the creation of spin-offs, following different creation processes and leading to spin-offs with different characteristics.

Using the institution-policy-process-spin-off link (see Table 3), it is possible to examine the influence of the institution and the process pursued on the creation of spin-offs.

---

[1] *Venture capital backed firms* start out with external capital from venture capitalists or venture capital firms. They normally have a patented innovating technology that can be used for different applications (a technological platform) and when set up they are still a long way from having a commercially viable product. They tend to have a large entrepreneurial team with little experience in management and industry; however, they usually bring experienced managers on board during the venture's first few years. These companies target significantly-sized international or global markets.

[2] *Lifestyle* spin-offs look for a market large enough to provide the founder and his/her family with a comfortable lifestyle, support job creation or retain employment in the new company's local area. They are characterised by having low capitalisation, capital owned by people connected to the founder, low management capacity and little or no growth orientation. They are ultimately survival-oriented.

[3] Prospector spin-offs are growth-oriented, but in an environment that is unfavourable to enterprise, where the university provides no support. As a result, they are spun off at an early stage with no solid business model, and their main base is the founders' scientific knowledge. They are characterised by their moderate growth-orientation, an intermediate level of capitalisation, and capital owned by people closely connected to the founder, as well as some external investor that is not a venture-capitalist. As time passes, they gain management experience and skills, enabling them to determine the specific business model and grow faster.

In 2004, the same author, working with Roberts, published a study using a larger sample taken from the same environment, in which they refined the previous analysis, distinguishing four archetypes of spin-off policies pursued by the research institutions: absence of a proactive spin-off policy; minimalist support and selectivity; intermediate support and selectivity and high support and selectivity. The first three are implemented by universities, whereas the fourth is characteristic of specialist research institutes.

They also note that the spin-off policy implemented has implications for the growth potential of the spin-off ventures created. Policies that involve no or minimal support and selectivity, lead to spin-offs that can be classed as traditional non growth-oriented SMEs[4].

Table 3. Institution-policy-process-spin-off link in unfavourable contexts for entrepreneurship, according to Degroof (2002)

Institution	Policy	Process	*Spin-off*
Specialist research institutes	High selectivity/ high support	Long incubation	*Venture capital backed*
University	Low selectivity/ low support	Anything or little incubation	*Lifestyle o prospector*

Source: Based on Degroof (2002).

Table 4. Institution-policy-process-spin-off link in unfavourable environments for entrepreneurship, according to Degroof and Roberts (2004)

Institution	Policy	Process	*Spin-off*
Specialist research institutes	High selectivity/ high support	Long incubation	*Venture capital backed*
University	Intermediate selectivity/ intermediate support	Little incubation	*Prospector*
University	Minimalist selectivity/ minimalist support	Anything incubation	*Lifestyle*
University	Absence of selectivity/ support	Anything incubation	*Lifestyle*

Source: Based on Degroof and Roberts (2004).

---

[4] Equivalent to the lifestyles.

A policy of intermediate support and selectivity creates growth-oriented spin-offs in gestation[5]), characterised by the fact that in their initial stage they follow the traditional SME model, but with the intention of finding an opportunity with greater growth potential. A high support and selectivity spin-off policy creates growth-oriented ventures[6].

To sum up, Degroof and Roberts (2004) confirmed Degroof's earlier conclusions; in an unfavourable context for entrepreneurship, different research institutions can utilize different spin-off policies, go through different creation processes and, in consequence spin off ventures of different characteristics. Using the institution-policy-process-spin-off link (Table 4), it is possible to examine the influence of the institution and the process followed on spin-off creation.

For their part, Clarysse et al. (2002), Clarysse et al. (2005) and Wright et al. (2007) explored the different strategies employed by European research institutions for spinning out companies.

They argue that research institutions can have different objectives which are reflected in the results of their activities. They analyse the extent to which these institutions differ when it comes to organising and managing spin-off activities, the resources needed to undertake these activities appropriately, and whether the differences in organisation and management lead to different types of spin-off.

They identify three possible missions of research institutions in this respect: the creation of self-employment oriented spin-offs, the creation of economically profitable spin-offs and the creation of exit-oriented spin-offs.

The mission of a research institution is to stimulate the creation of self-employment oriented spin-offs when the objective is to create employment and enhance development in a depressed region. Alternatively, it can set itself the mission of stimulating the creation of economically profitable spin-offs. Finally, the mission of stimulating the creation of exit-oriented spin-outs arises when the aim is to create businesses capable of generating high returns for investors.

They go on to make an in-depth analysis for each of the institutions selected of the different activities into which a proactive spin-off process can be broken down, following Degroof's division by stages (Degroof, 2002): opportunity search and awareness creation; management of intellectual property, project selection, incubation and business plan development; and funding and control of the spin-out process after start-up of the spin-out company.

They also make an in-depth analysis in each of these institutions of the resources needed to perform the spin-off process, drawing a distinction between

---

[5] Equivalent to the prospectors.
[6] Equivalent to the venture capital backed.

human, networking, and financial, physical, technological and organisational resources.

Taking into account the aims pursued, the activities developed and the resources used, they initially distinguish three models of support for the creation of spin-offs: the *low* or *self-selective* model, the *supportive* model and the *incubator* or *protective* model.

In the *low selective* model the aim is to generate as many spin-offs possible. To this end, the purpose is to stimulate in particular entrepreneurial initiative, with an analysis of the economic or financial potential of the initiatives being relegated to second place. This means that the main activities are opportunity search and awareness creation. The key resource is the presence of an experimented entrepreneur acting as an administrator who can raise awareness among students, researchers and teachers and enhance ease of access to public funds for the projects. The aim of this model is to create as many spin-offs as possible; these may be based not only on only technology, but also on skills developed within the university. Hence many companies are created, but only a few have the ambition to grow, and even fewer to actually succeed. In short, the companies created can be classed as *lifestyle* spin-offs.

In the *supportive* model, the aim is to create companies with economic potential and a will to grow, although they may not initially have a validated business plan. In this model, management of intellectual property and business plan development are essential, and there needs to be a financially independent organisation whose activities receive support from the university management. Public and private funding is also needed to allow the projects to develop in the initial stages. In this model, spin-offs are an alternative option for getting value from the technology. The basis for the creation of the spin-off is therefore the existence of a protectable technology that can create a competitive advantage; purely knowledge-based consulting firms do not tend to be supported. The aim is to create spin-offs with an ambition for growth (albeit this ambition may not be proven at the time of the start-up), which will set up in the immediate territorial area of the institution, foster regional development and forge links with the institution that will encourage industry relations. Consequently, fewer spin-offs are created than in the previous model. Companies created in this model can be classed as *prospector* spin-offs.

The *incubator* model seeks to create solid companies that attract venture capital, with the result that venture capital organisations are involved in them from the outset. In this case, in addition to the activities set out for the previous models, funding activities are of particular importance. Applying this model requires a research group that enjoys international recognition in a given technology. In addition, the technology transfer unit must be capable of incubating the project, facilitating the recruitment of outside managers, attracting international venture capital from the initial stages and forming the base of the company's intellectual property. This model also views the creation of spin-offs to be one possible means of marketing the research results. A spin-off will be created only if a broad and strong enough portfolio of patents can be built. It must therefore be clear from the outset that the spin-off is growth-oriented. Venture capitalists are attracted from the start; indeed, the research institution creates its own venture capital fund. Companies created along these lines can be classed as *venture capital backed* spin-offs.

In a later work, extending the study sample, the authors identified two further categories, differing from the three previous models: *resource deficient* organisations and *competence deficient* organisations.

Table 5. Objective-policy-activity-resource-spin-off-results link, according to Clarysse et al. (2002), Clarysse et al. (2005) and Wright et al. (2007)

Objective	Policy	Key activity	Key resource	*Spin-off*	Results
Self-employment oriented spin-offs	Low selectivity/ low support	Awareness	Entrepreneur manager	*Lifestyle*	Many *spin-offs*
Economically profitable spin-offs	Intermediate selectivity/ intermediate support	Management IP and business plan development	Independent organisation	*Prospector*	Intermediate number of *spin-offs*
Exit-oriented spin-offs	High selectivity/ high support	Funding	Recognized research groups	*Venture capital backed*	Few *spin-offs*

Source: Based on Clarysse et al. (2002), Clarysse et al. (2005) and Wright et al. (2007).

In the *resource deficient* group they include spin-off programmes which have ambitious goals, but lack the necessary resources to achieve them. The lack of resources is reflected, firstly, in the fact that the programmes do not have enough financial resources to act autonomously and invest in the spin-offs; secondly, in the fact that the staff do not have either the *expertise* or the necessary contact networks to carry out the activities required; and, thirdly, in a lack of support from the research institution's management. Because of these deficiencies, such programmes are positioned as being weak support and are therefore incapable of achieving the aims initially set out. These spin-off objectives tend to be based on successful examples from the surrounding environment, but they do not have the same resources, leading to unsatisfactory results. Research institutions classed in this group tend to lack a critical mass in number of researchers in some technological areas.

The *competence-deficient* group includes spin-off programmes that have the necessary resources to implement some of the three previous models, but lack the skills needed to perform the necessary activities. This group shows what can happen if a support programme is endowed with a large quantity of resources to establish *supportive* or *incubator* models, but lacks the necessary knowledge to integrate these resources in a way that will generate the required skills, which can only be developed over time. Some of the cases in this group are in a situation that could be described as of "transition" from one model to another. They have decided to change model, but are in an intermediate situation, because they lack the skills required to achieve the anticipated results of the new model.

To sum up, these authors note from their field work that different research institutions can have different objectives, use different policies of support for the creation of spin-offs, carry out different activities, use different resources, generate spin-offs of different characteristics and obtain different results. The objective-policy-activity-resources-spin-offs-results link (Table 5) shows the influence of the objectives on spin-off creation.

Summing up, we draw the following conclusions from the literature: firstly, there is no single model for a spin-off support policy; secondly, the two main dimensions of a policy of support for this type of company are selectivity and support; thirdly, it is very important that the universities, based on environment-specific conditions, know what their objectives are and clearly set out what resources and activities are required to achieve these objectives; and fourthly, establishing a high support and high selectivity policy requires considerable resources to which many universities rarely have access on an individual basis; and even if they can, they may require a certain period of time to develop the necessary skills to utilise these resources efficiently.

Below we present the model used as a starting point for the empirical study, the questions asked in the questionnaire used as the basis for this study, and the process employed for gathering and processing the information.

3. Methodology

3.1. Starting Model

Several authors have used a linear approach to describe the spin-off process and its various stages (Clarysse et al., 2005; Degroof, 2002; Golob, 2003; Hindle and Yencke, 2004; Pirnay, 2001; Reitan, 1997; Roberts and Malone, 1996; Shane, 2004; Vohora et al., 2004). There is, however, no consensus as to the number of stages, what they should be called and at what point the process begins.

In designing the empirical study we have used as our basis a model of the linear process[7] of valorisation via spin-off which distinguishes between six successive stages: promoting an entrepreneurial culture, searching for and detecting ideas, evaluating ideas, developing projects, setting-up companies, consolidating value creation.

The model also identifies the university's level of involvement in the different stages (Pirnay, 2001), as shown in Figure 1.

This figure shows that the university's involvement is indispensable in the first stages of the process of spin-off creation, thereafter becoming gradually less important. This does not mean that the university cannot be involved in the final stages, but that there are other agents (financial institutions, science and technology parks, business incubators, etc.) that can favour their development more effectively and efficiently.

3.2. Questions

This empirical study used information taken in a survey on a series of variables related to resources and results, activities, organisational structure, the university's relations with the spin-offs, how long the programmes have been in place and the success achieved.

As stated, in selecting the questions used in the research, we used the model of the linear process of valorisation via spin-offs shown in Figure 1. This model sets out the various stages a university needs to consider in supporting the creation of spin-offs, with particular emphasis on stages and activities at which the

---

[7] Although the division of the spin-off process into six successive stages aids understanding of the process, it should not be taken to imply our complete acceptance of the linearity of the innovation process, since the real situation is more complex. The various phases in the process do not occur in an ordered consecutive sequence, one after another, but normally involve relations of reciprocity and interdependence.

university's direct intervention can be decisively important. These can be grouped analytically into three basic stages: promotion of entrepreneurial culture; search for and detection of ideas; and evaluation and valorisation[8] of ideas. To these three stages we have added a further two sections corresponding to general information and the creation of spin-offs.

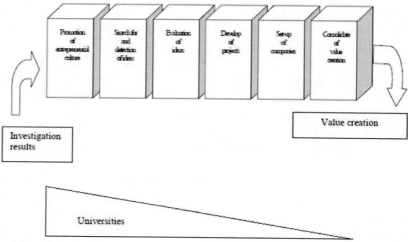

Source: Adapted from Pirnay (2001).

Figure 1. Process of valorisation through creation of spin-offs: stages of the process and university's involvement.

The boundary between these three stages is sometimes blurred, since there is a certain overlap between the different areas. Nonetheless, we feel that this division is useful as an analytical outline for deciding on the questions to be asked and indicating what aspects of the support programme they reflect.

The questions included in each of the five sections are described below.

3.2.1. General Information

The university itself is the most important element in the support programmes, as a source of marketable research results (Polt et al., 2001). For this reason, as well as the identifying data, three additional questions were included in

---

[8] The term "valorisation" refers to the different forms of involvement of the university, as an institution, and of the people from whom the idea comes, in developing the project and setting up the spin-off.

the survey[9]: the type of body performing the spin-off set-up support activities; the number of people in that body; and the activities related to this type of company carried out at the university.

3.2.2. Promotion of Entrepreneurial Culture

In unfavourable conditions for entrepreneurship, a prerequisite for creating spin-offs is the promotion of an entrepreneurial culture amongst university personnel (Jack and Anderson, 1999; Klofsten, 2000; Pirnay, 2001; Trim, 2003, Henry et al., 2005). Four questions were included in the survey for this reason: the university's level of commitment to promoting entrepreneurial culture; the actions being taken to promote this culture; the number of people that will benefit from these activities and the degree of success obtained.

3.2.3. Search for and Detection of Ideas

Commercially exploitable ideas deriving out of university research do not normally arise spontaneously (Siegel et al., 2003; McDonald et al., 2004; Shane, 2004). Four questions were included in the survey for this reason: the university's level of proactivity in searching for and detecting ideas; the actions carried out to search for and detect ideas; the source of the entrepreneurial ideas and the degree of success obtained.

3.2.4. Evaluation and Valorisation of Ideas

The ideas initially detected need to be assessed to determine whether they meet a series of prerequisites for viable commercial exploitability (Wright et al., 2004). Likewise, the university, as an institution, and the people from whom the idea comes must support the project in order for it finally to become a spin-off (Baxter et al., 2004; Vohora et al., 2004). Nine questions were included in the survey for this reason: the use of a specific methodology for evaluating and exploiting ideas; the use of external personnel in technological assessment; the use of external personnel in market assessment of the idea; the profile of these personnel; who assumes the leadership in promoting the spin-off; the role generally taken in the spin-off by the research group from which the idea originated; the number of exploitable ideas detected over a one-year period; the percentage of these ideas that are positively evaluated and, finally, the percentage of positively evaluated ideas that lead to the creation of a spin-off.

---

[9] The questionnaire can be viewed at www.ehu.es/entreprenari.

3.2.5. Creation of Spin-Offs

The ideas detected and supported lead to the creation of spin-offs, which can be of varying types and have varying degrees of success (Clarysse et al., 2005), and with which the university can have different links (Lockett et al., 2003). Nine questions were included in the survey for this reason: number of spin-offs created over the last five years; type of spin-offs created; average length of time from detection of the marketable idea to creation of the spin-off; most common source of financial resources; university's stake in the spin-off's capital; university's involvement in its management; survival rate of this type of company; percentage of firms that fail before three years and, finally the year in which the university began activities to support spin-off creation.

3.3. Sample and Data Collection

The study population comprises European universities in general, and Spanish and British universities in particular, that perform some type of activity involving spin-off creation.

The system used to identify the study population and select the sample was as follows: firstly, we searched in Google for a list of European universities, classified by countries; secondly, we visited the websites of each of these universities one by one; thirdly, we identified the body responsible for spin-off set-up support activities[10]; and finally we identified the persons in charge of these bodies: name, position, telephone number and e-mail address.

Altogether a total of 74 universities were identified in the UK and 255 in the rest of Europe (not including Spanish universities). We sent these universities a letter of presentation by e-mail, inviting them to fill out the online questionnaire[11]. Replies were received from 25 universities in the United Kingdom and 42 universities elsewhere in Europe, representing a response rate of 34% and 17%, respectively. In the case of Spanish universities, the letter of presentation was sent to practically all universities with a Technology Transfer Office (TTO), the great majority of which were public universities. 35 replies were received, representing

---

[10] We tried to identify a body specifically devoted to supporting the creation of spin-offs; if none could be found, we looked for the body responsible for technology transfer activities or failing that, the body responsible for research/innovation/corporate relations.

[11] The information-gathering process ran from the beginning of November 2005 to the end of February 2006.

a response rate of 58%. Altogether, a total of 389 letters were sent, and 102 replies were received, representing a response rate of 26%[12].

We then proceeded to discard universities with a certain number of incomplete replies or those that might be considered atypical[13], finally obtaining a database comprising a total of sixty-five universities, of which eighteen were in the UK, twenty-three in Spain and twenty-four elsewhere in Europe[14]. The rate of complete replies is therefore 17% for the sample as a whole, 24% for British universities, 38% for Spanish universities and 9% for other European universities.

The data thus obtained were statistically analysed using univariate and multivariate techniques. In this work we started by classifying universities in the UK and in Spain, using the cluster analysis technique to group them based on the most significant variables that explain the characteristics of the programmes of support to the creation of university spin-offs, previously identified by applying the factorial analysis technique. We then describe the differentiated characteristics of each of the clusters in the United Kingdom and in Spain, by means of a descriptive statistical analysis. Finally, we compared the clusters identified in the two countries.

4. Multivariate Analysis

4.1. Factorial Analysis: Obtaining Representative Substitute Variables

We used the database drawn from the information obtained to make a factorial analysis to determine the most significant variables explaining the characteristics of the university spin-off support programmes.

Using this technique we proceeded first of all to identify factors. To do this, we used the *Principal Components Analysis* data reduction method. To determine the number of factors to be extracted, we used the *latent root criterion* technique. We then calculated the contributions of each variable to the different factors and

---

[12] Not all universities that replied to the questionnaire answered all the items. Specifically, eleven universities replied to few items and twenty-four furnished no information on spin-off creation. Thus only 67 of the 102 universities in the sample replied to all or practically all items.

[13] Two Spanish universities were discarded as atypical for two reasons: firstly, they stated that they created a much higher number of spin-offs than the other universities; secondly, they were the only private universities in the sample.

[14] The twenty-four universities in the rest of Europe were in the following countries: Italy (7), France (5), Germany (3), Netherlands (2), Ireland (2), Austria (1), Belgium (1), Bulgaria (1), Estonia (1) and Sweden (1).

selected the variables that contributed most too each one, in order to identify the variables that most appropriately described the university spin-off support programmes, and use them in the subsequent cluster analysis.

Table 6. Most significant variables classified according to the stages of the process of exploitation by spin-off

General information	Number of people who are part of the body. Relative importance of the promotion of entrepreneurial culture. Relative importance of search for and detection of ideas.
Promotion of entrepreneurial culture	Success in the promotion of entrepreneurial culture.
Search for and detection of ideas	Importance of monitoring of the projects undertaken by research groups. Importance of monitoring of business design/project competitions. Relative importance of "Others" in the origin of ideas.
Evaluation and valorisation of ideas	Relative frequency of postgraduate-PhD students as leaders in promoting spin-offs. Relative frequency of external personnel hired as leaders in promoting spin-offs. Appropriate for research groups to provide technological consultancy to the spin-offs. Percentage of ideas detected over a one-year period that are positively evaluated. Percentage of positively evaluated ideas that lead to the creation of a spin-off.
Creation of spin-offs	Percentage of knowledge-based spin-offs. Percentage of "Other" spin-offs. University´s involvement in the spin-off´s management. Percentage of spin-offs that dies before 3 years.

Forty-seven variables were originally used in this study, all the quantitative variables in the survey; and by applying the *latent root criterion* the final solution chosen was that formed by sixteen factors[15]. In order to improve the solution, a Varimax rotation was used. This solution preserves 78.652% of total variability.

We then selected the variables with the greatest load for each factor[16], as representative of each of the factors. In this way, we managed to group the original quantitative variables that are intended to represent different aspects corresponding to the different stages of support in the creation of spin-offs, into sixteen variables.

Table 6 shows these variables classified according to the different phases of the process of exploitation by spin-off.

4.2. Cluster Analysis: Typology of University Support Programmes for Setting Up Spin-Offs in the Universities of United Kingdom and Spain

Once the most significant variables had been detected, we have classified the British universities on the one hand, and the Spanish ones on the other using the cluster analysis technique. The distance used was the *Euclidean distance squared*[17], following standardisation or typification of the variables by transforming them into *Z scores* with a mean of 0 and a typical deviation 1.

The clusters were formed using hierarchical clustering and *Ward's method*.

There is no objective or standard procedure for determining the final number of clusters, and in this case the clustering coefficient criterion does not give clear results, since it does not experience relevant changes when the number of clusters is varied.

We therefore opted for obtaining various different cluster arrangements, and checking whether there were significant differences between the clusters obtained, in order to verify whether a real differentiation can be seen between the different spin-offs programmes analysed.

To this end, we used the one-factor analysis of variance (Anova), taking the variable containing the information on the cluster to which each university belongs as an independent variable or factor and each of the variables included in

---

[15] In our case, the value of the determinant of the correlation matrix is practically zero. Likewise, Bartlett's sphericity test rejected the null hypothesis that the matrix of correlations is an identity matrix with a significance level of 1%. Factorial analysis is therefore a relevant technique for analysing these variables.

[16] The corresponding tables are available on request.

[17] The squared Euclidean distance is the measurement of distance recommended for the centroid and Ward cluster analysis methods.

the analysis (the sixteen most significant variables identified in the previous sub-section) as dependent variables.

The results of the analysis are shown below.

4.2.1. Typology of University Support Programmes for Setting Up Spin-Offs in British Universities

Figure 2 shows the process of hierarchical agglomerative clustering in a dendogram. Four clear clusters can be seen, although a three-cluster arrangement might also be appropriate. *A priori*, therefore, three- or four-cluster arrangements appear to most closely match the situation in the UK *vis-à-vis* spin-off programmes.

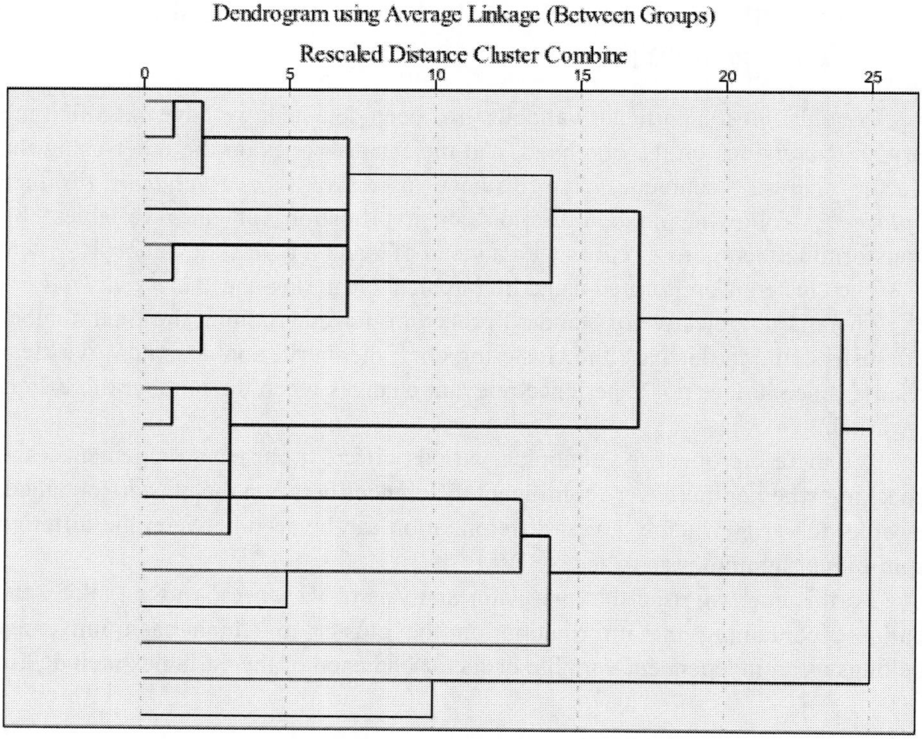

Figure 2. British universities. Dendogram.

The next task is therefore to determine the final number of clusters to be formed. In our case, the largest increase in the *agglomeration coefficient* comes in the step from three to two clusters $(18.08\%)^{18}$. Based on this criterion, therefore, a three-cluster arrangement might seem the most appropriate.

However, given that there is no major increase in absolute or percentage terms in the *agglomeration coefficients*, we have chosen to test out various different cluster arrangements and then decide which is the most suitable based on the behaviour of the variables.

We therefore considered arrangements with two, three and four clusters and checked whether there were significant differences between them, in order to determine whether there was a real differentiation between the different spin-off programmes under analysis. The results obtained in the one-factor analysis of variance (Anova) show that there are a number of variables with significant differences that are practically the same for the three- and four-cluster arrangements and that these differences are smallest for the two-cluster arrangement. We have therefore opted for the four-cluster arrangement, since it allows greater differentiation between the programmes, without proving excessive[19].

Thus, in the four-cluster arrangement (Table 7), seven variables have significant differences[20]: "number of people who are part of the body", "relative importance of search for and detection of ideas", "importance of monitoring of business design/project competitions", "Relative importance of "Others" in the origin of ideas", "appropriate for research groups to provide technological consultancy to the spin-offs", "percentage of ideas detected over a one-year period that are positively evaluated" and "percentage of "Other" spin-offs".

These results suggest the following characterisation of the clusters obtained.

Cluster 1 (eight universities), has few staff devoted to spin-off support; it considers organisation and monitoring of business design/project competitions to be important; it is relatively unselective, and therefore has a large percentage of ideas detected that are rated positively, and mainly supports the creation of technology-based spin-offs.

Cluster 2 is in turn made up of five universities which also have few staff devoted to spin-off support; however, unlike the previous one, they are selective, and therefore have a small percentage of ideas detected that are positively rated, and support both the creation of technology- and knowledge-based spin-offs.

Cluster 3 (two universities) also has few people devoted to spin-off support; they devote important efforts to searching for and detecting ideas.; they also consider organisation and monitoring of business design/project competitions to be important; entrepreneurial ideas mainly have their origin in "others"; they are

---

[18] Cluster record table available on demand.

[19] Two- and three-cluster Anova analyses available on demand.

[20] With a significance level of at least 10%.

less selective than the universities of Clusters 2 and 4, but more selective than those of Cluster 1, and mainly support the creation of technology-based spin-offs, but also "other" spin-offs.

Table 7. British universities. Descriptive statistics of the representative variables showing significant differences between the four clusters[a]

Variables	1		2		3		4	
	Mean	St. dev.	Mean	St. dev.	Mean	St. dev.	Mean	St. dev.
Number of people who are part of the body	1.38	0.51	(–) 1.00	0.00	(–) 1.00	0.00	(+)3.67	0.57
Relative importance of search for and detection of ideas	24.38	7.28	20.00	7.90	(+) 32.50	3.53	(–) 11.67	7.63
Importance of monitoring of business design/project competitions	(+) 4.00	0.53	(–) 2.20	0.83	(+) 4.00	0.00	3.00	1.00
Relative importance of "Others" in the origin of ideas	(–) 0.00	0.00	1.80	4.02	(+) 40.00	21.21	(–) 0.00	0.00
Appropriate for research groups to provide technological consultancy to the spin-offs	3.75	1.03	3.20	1.30	(–) 1.50	0.70	(+)4.00	1.00
Percentage of ideas detected over a one-year period that are positively evaluated	(+) 3.00	0.92	(–) 1.80	0.44	2.50	0.70	2.33	0.57
Percentage of "Other" spin-offs	(–) 0.00	0.00	(–) 0.00	0.00	(+) 25.00	35.35	7.67	10.8

[a]The cluster marked with a (+) or (–) has the highest or lowest mean for the corresponding variable.

Finally, Cluster 4 corresponds to three universities that have more people devoted to spin-off support; they devote little effort to searching for and detecting ideas; on the contrary, they devote important effort to spin-off support; for them the ideal situation is for the research group in which the idea originated to provide technological advice to the spin-off; they are more selective than universities in Clusters 1 and 3, but less selective than those of Cluster 2; they support the creation of technology-based spin-offs and to a lesser extent knowledge-based spin-offs.

4.2.2. Typology of University Support Programmes for Setting Up Spin-Offs in Spanish Universities

As for the results of the cluster analysis performed on the Spanish universities, the dendogram (Figure 3) shows the existence of two clear clusters, although three- and four-cluster arrangements might also prove suitable.

In order to determine the final number of clusters, in this case the largest increase in the *agglomeration coefficient* comes in the step from three to two clusters (13.59%) and from two to one (15.31%)[21]. According to this criterion, then, a two- or three-cluster arrangement might be considered most appropriate.

However, given that, as in the case of the British universities, there is no major increase in absolute or percentage terms in the *agglomeration coefficients*, we have chosen to test out various different cluster arrangements and then decide which is the most suitable based on the behaviour of the variables.

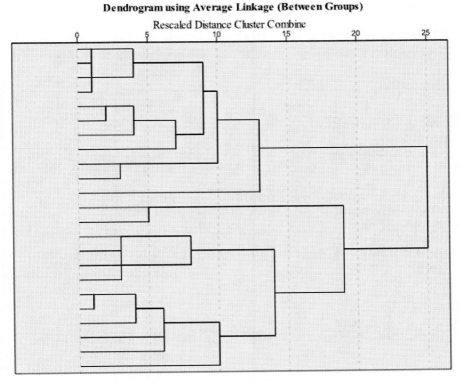

Figure 3. Spanish universities. Dendogram.

---

[21] Cluster record table available on demand.

Thus, two-, three- and four-cluster arrangements have been calculated and checked whether there were significant differences between them, in order to determine whether there was a real differentiation between the different spin-off programmes under analysis. The results obtained in the one-factor analysis of variance (Anova) show that there is a similar number of variables with significant differences for the different cluster arrangements (i.e., two, three and four clusters), we have therefore opted for the four-cluster arrangement, since it allows greater differentiation between the programmes, without proving excessive. Thus, in the four-cluster arrangement (Table 8), six variables have significant differences[22]: "number of people who are part of the body", "importance of monitoring of business design/project competitions", "percentage of ideas detected over a one-year period that are positively evaluated", "percentage of positively evaluated ideas that lead to the creation of a spin-off", "percentage of knowledge-based spin-offs" and "university's involvement in the spin-off's management".

Table 8. Spanish universities. Descriptive statistics of the representative variables showing significant differences between the four clusters[a]

Variables	1		2		3		4	
	Mean	St. dev.	Mean	St. dev.	Mean	St. dev.	Mean	St. dev.
Number of people who are part of the body	1.09	0.30	(–) 1.00	0.00	(+) 4.00	0.00	(–) 1.00	0.87
Importance of monitoring of business design/project competitions	(–) 2.45	1.12	3.50	1.51	(+) 5.00	0.00	4.00	0.81
Percentage of ideas detected over a one-year period that are positively evaluated	1.64	0.67	(+) 3.17	1.16	(–) 1.50	0.70	2.50	0.57
Percentage of positively evaluated ideas that lead to the creation of a spin-off	(–) 2.00	0.00	(+) 3.67	1.03	(–) 2.00	0.00	2.25	0.5
Percentage of knowledge-based spin-offs	(–) 14.18	13.09	37.67	10.6	(+) 40.0	28.28	32.00	14.2
University's involvement in the spin-off's management	1.09	0.30	(–) 1.00	0.00	(–) 1.00	0.00	(+) 2.25	0.50

[a]The cluster marked with a (+) or (–) has the highest or lowest mean for the corresponding variable.

---

[22] With a significance level of at least 10%.

These results suggest the following characterisation of the clusters obtained.

Cluster 1 is made up of eleven universities with few staff devoted to spin-off support; they are selective, with the result that a low percentage of ideas detected are rated positively and spun off; they mainly support the creation of technology-based spin-offs; and they do not intervene in the running of the spin-offs.

Cluster 2 is in turn made up of six universities which also have few staff devoted to spin-off support; however, unlike the previous one, they are not very selective, meaning that a large percentage of ideas detected is positively rated and spun off; they support the creation of both technology- and knowledge-based spin-offs, and do not intervene in their running.

Cluster 3 (two universities) includes universities that have more people devoted to spin-off support; they consider organisation and monitoring of business design/project competitions to be very important; they are selective, with the result that only a relatively small percentage of ideas detected are positively rated and spun off; they support the creation of spin-offs of both types, technology- and knowledge-based, and they do not intervene in their running either.

Finally, Cluster 4 is formed by four universities that have fewer people devoted to spin-off support; they consider organisation and monitoring of business design/project competitions to be important; they are less selective than the universities in Clusters 1 and 3, but more selective than those in Cluster 2; they also support the creation of technology- and knowledge-based spin-offs; unlike the other clusters, they *do* intervene in the running of the spin-offs.

5. Characterisation of Spin-Off Support Models

Having identified the clusters and the variables with significantly different means, we should now explain in more detail the characterisation of the clusters identified in the United Kingdom, on the one hand, and in Spain, on the other, as representatives of different models or types of spin-off creation support, comparing and contrasting them, to highlight possible similarities and differences.

For the purposes of this characterisation, we are first going to use all the quantitative variables included in the survey that show significant differences between clusters, as well as two new variables not included: return on RandD and number of patents. The reason for including these two variables is as follows: given the somewhat subjective nature of cluster analysis and in order to ensure the validity and practical relevance of the solution obtained, it is recommendable to incorporate variables that have not been used to form the clusters, but which are known to vary in value from one another, as is the case with the two variables chosen; moreover, both are relevant in this respect, as we show below.

RandD activity is one of the factors most used and most often cited in the literature amongst inputs related to the university business creation process. The variable included in the analysis was, specifically, return on RandD for academic year 2002-2003 in each of the universities, expressed as a percentage of return on RandD of the university with the greatest income.

At the same time, patent applications by universities are an indicator of university RandD results and their commercial orientation. While not all academic spin-offs are based on patented knowledge, a relationship can also be expected between the number of patents and the business creation process in the universities. However, in some cases the number of patent applications by the universities varies greatly from one year to another. For this reason, the variable used in the analysis was the average number of patent applications during the period 2002-2005 in the case of British universities, and 2000-2005 in the case of Spanish universities.

Secondly, starting from a smaller number of variables with significant differences between the clusters identified in the UK and Spain, we shall characterise the profiles of these clusters. Specifically, the six variables used in this characterisation are as follows[23]:

- The *age* of the spin-off support activities as an indicator of experience and, consequently, of availability of the necessary skills to carry out the activities required.
- The *number of people* in the body, as an indicator of the resources available to the spin-off support programme.
- The university's *commitment* to promoting an entrepreneurial culture, as an indicator of integration of entrepreneurial vision into the university's strategy and, consequently, in the day-to-day activity of the organisation.
- *Proactivity* in searching for and detecting ideas, as an indicator of capacity to detect possibilities for commercialisation of the knowledge generated in the university from an early stage.

---

[23] There are significant differences in all these variables among Spanish universities. In the case of the British universities, on the other hand, there are no significant differences in seniority and the number of spin-offs created. Indeed, in the United Kingdom the "year spin-off support activities started" variable is 1998, 25, 1997, 2, 1997, 5 and 1998, 67 for the clusters 1, 2, 3 and 4, respectively; the "mean number of spin-offs created between 2000 and 2004" variable has values of 2.4, 1.73, 0.8 and 3.37 for the clusters 1, 2, 3 and 4, respectively.

- *Selectivity*, as an indicator of the university's rigour in selecting the results of research capable of being commercialised via a spin-off[24].
- The *number* of spin-offs created, as an indicator of the results of the support programmes.

5.1. Characterisation of Spin-Off Support Models in British Universities

Table 9 shows the means of all the quantitative variables obtained in the survey for each of the clusters of spin-off support programmes in British universities with significant differences[25].

Table 9. British universities. Means of all variables with significant differences in clusters[a]

Variables	1	2	3	4	Total
Number of people who are part of the body	1.38	(–) 1.00	(–) 1.00	(+) 3.67	1.61
Relative importance of search for and detection of ideas	24.38	20.00	(+) 32.50	(–) 11.67	21.94
University commitment to the promotion of entrepreneurial culture	3.63	(–) 3.00	4.00	(+) 4.67	3.67
Importance on promoting the preparation of the business plan in final-year assignments	2.13	(–) 1.20	(+) 4.00	1.67	2.00
Importance on the provision of information services	3.88	(–) 2.60	(+) 4.00	3.33	3.44
Number of people benefiting from these activities	1.50	(–) 1.20	1.50	(+) 3.33	1.72
Proactivity in searching for and detecting ideas	3.75	(–) 2.60	(+) 4.00	2.67	3.28

---

[24] This variable has not been included in the survey, but has been obtained indirectly from the "percentage of ideas detected that are positively rated" and "percentage of positively rated ideas that are spun off" variables". A smaller selectivity value means that a large percentage of positively-rated ideas detected are spun off, and therefore, that the corresponding cluster pursues a low-selectivity policy; inversely, a lower selectivity value means that a small percentage of positively-rated ideas detected are spun off, and therefore, that the corresponding cluster pursues a high-selectivity policy.

[25] With a significance level of at least 10%.

Table 9. Continued

Variables	1	2	3	4	Total
Importance of monitoring of business design/project competitions	(+) 4.00	(–) 2.20	(+) 4.00	3.00	3.33
Relative importance of "Others" in the origin of ideas	(–) 0.00	1.80	(+) 40.00	(–) 0.00	4.94
Success in searching for and detecting ideas	3.50	(–) 2.20	3.50	(+) 3.67	3.17
Relative frequency of "Others" as leaders in promoting spin-offs	12.25	(–) 1.80	(+) 55.00	45.00	19.56
Appropriate for research groups to take shareholdings in the spin-off	3.88	4.00	(–) 2.50	(+) 4.33	3.83
Appropriate for research groups give technology to the spin-off in Exchange for royalties	(+) 3.88	3.00	(–) 1.50	2.33	3.11
Appropriate for research groups to provide technological consultancy to the spin-offs	3.75	3.20	(–) 1.50	(+) 4.00	3.39
Number of ideas detected over a one-year period	2.13	(–) 1.20	(+) 3.50	3.33	2.22
Percentage of ideas detected over a one-year period that are positively evaluated	(+) 3.00	(–) 1.80	2.50	2.33	2.50
Percentage of "Other" spin-offs	(–) 0.00	(–) 0.00	(+) 25.00	7.67	4.06
Average of patents	14	(–) 11	19	(+) 34	17
% RandD	36	(–) 14	32	(+) 46	30

[a]The cluster marked with a (+) or (–) has the highest or lowest mean for the corresponding variable.

Figure 4 shows the profiles of the four types of programmes identified in British universities according to the six variables with significant differences indicated above.

Taking as our reference, firstly, all the variables with significant differences and, secondly, only the six mentioned above, we go on to describe the profiles of each of the four types of programme identified[26]:

Type 1: has relatively high RandD activity, but a small number of people devoted to spin-off support; their commitment to promoting an entrepreneurial culture is intermediate; these are proactive universities and they have a certain degree of success in searching for and detecting ideas; they give importance to monitoring business design/project competitions, but the number of ideas detected

---

[26] Clearly, this description refers to the date of the survey.

is relatively small; for them a relatively ideal situation is for the research group where the idea originated to be involved in the spin-off in a variety of ways; they rate a large percentage of the ideas detected positively; they generate an intermediate number of spin-offs, mostly technology-based.

To sum up, universities of this type have relatively little experience in spin-off support, have few resources for the task and little commitment from the university, they are quite proactive in searching for and detecting ideas and implement a low-selectivity policy; as a result, they generate an intermediate number of spin-offs, mostly technology-based.

Type 2: universities with a relatively low RandD activity that have a small number of people devoted to spin-off support; their commitment to promoting an entrepreneurial culture is also limited, and their activities therefore benefit a small number of people; they place very little importance on promoting the preparation of the business plan in final-year assignments and the provision of information services; they are very proactive and have little success in searching for and detecting ideas; in addition, they place little importance on monitoring business design/project competitions; consequently, the number of ideas detected is very limited; for them a relatively ideal situation is for the research group where the idea originated to take a shareholding in the spin-off; unlike the previous type, they give a positive rating to a small percentage of ideas detected; consequently they generate a smaller number of spin-offs, with an major trend towards knowledge-based spin-offs.

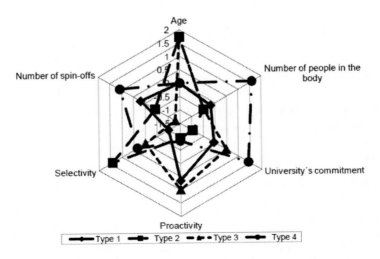

Figure 4. British universities. Profiles of the four types of programme.

Therefore, this type is characterised by having somewhat more experience in spin-off support; they also have few resources available for this task and less commitment by the university; they are not proactive in searching for and detecting ideas, but they follow a high-selectivity policy; as a result, they generate a smaller number of spin-offs, both technology- and knowledge-based.

Type 3: show an intermediate level of RandD activity; universities of this type also have a small number of people devoted to these programmes; they devote significant effort to searching for and detecting ideas; their commitment to promoting an entrepreneurial culture is high; however, their activities benefit a limited number of people; they place considerable importance on promoting the preparation of the business plan in final-year assignments and the provision of information services; they are the most proactive, but have an intermediate degree of success in searching for and detecting ideas, and place great importance on monitoring business design/project competitions, with the result that the number of ideas they detect is relatively high; entrepreneurial ideas mainly have their origin in "others"[27] and the spin-offs are also led by "others"[28]; for them the ideal situation is for the research group where the idea originated not to be involved in the spin-off; they give a positive rating to an intermediate percentage of ideas detected, and nonetheless, generate a very limited number of spin-offs[29], mainly technology-based but also "others"[30].

In short, this type shows somewhat more experience in spin-off support, has few resources for this task and enjoys somewhat more commitment from the university; they are quite proactive in searching for and detecting ideas and follow a policy of intermediate selectivity; however, they generate the least number of spin-offs, mostly technology-based, but with a significant proportion of "others".

Type 4: corresponds to universities with a relatively large degree of RandD activity, which have a large number of people devoted to spin-off support; they spend little effort on searching for and detecting ideas.; their commitment to promoting an entrepreneurial culture is very high, with the result that their activities benefit a large number of people; they are not very proactive but are

---

[27] Refers to degree students and former students.

[28] Refers in this case, mainly, to personnel from technology transfer offices, or business development managers employed by the university.

[29] This cluster has a somewhat contradictory profile, since it declares a commitment to promotion and an entrepreneurial culture and is proactive in searching for and detecting ideas, detecting a large number of ideas without being very selective; however it generates a very small number of spin-offs. One possible explanation might be that it seeks to encourage start-ups more than spin-offs. This would be reflected in the greater frequency of "others" both in the source of the ideas and in the leadership and type of spin-offs created.

[30] No university in the UK has given details on the type of spin-offs included in "Others".

relatively successful in searching for and detecting ideas, and place intermediate importance on monitoring business design/project competitions; the number of ideas they detect is comparatively high; spin-offs are led mainly by "others"; for them the ideal situation is for the research group where the idea originated to have a shareholding and offer advice in technological strategy in the spin-off; they give a positive rating to an intermediate proportion of the ideas detected; they generate a relatively high number of spin-offs, with an important trend towards technology-based, but also knowledge-based ones.

Consequently, this type of programme has somewhat less experience in spin-off support, but has many resources for this task and enjoys considerable commitment from the university; it is not very proactive in searching for and detecting ideas.[31] and follows a policy of intermediate selectivity; as a result, it generates a larger number of spin-offs, mostly technology-based, but with a significant proportion of knowledge-based spin-offs.

5.2. Characterisation of Spin-Off Support Models in Spanish Universities

Table 10 shows the means of all the quantitative variables obtained in the survey for each of the clusters of spin-off support programmes in Spanish universities with significant differences[32].

Table 10. Spanish universities. Means of all variables with significant differences in clusters[a]

Variables	1	2	3	4	Total
Number of people who are part of the body	1.09	(–) 1.00	(+) 4.00	(–) 1.00	1.30
University commitment to the promotion of entrepreneurial culture	3.18	(–) 2.83	(+) 5.00	4.00	3.39
Number of people that benefit of these activities	(–) 1.55	1.67	(+) 4.50	3.25	2.13
Proactivity in searching for and detecting ideas	(–) 3.00	3.33	(–) 3.00	(+) 4.00	3.26
Importance of monitoring of business design/project competitions	(–) 2.45	3.50	(+) 5.00	4.00	3.22
Number of ideas detected over a one-year period	1.55	(–) 1.00	1.50	(+) 3.00	1.65

---

[31] This statement needs to be qualified, since it is the cluster that gives most importance to the activity of monitoring the research groups' projects and the one that has been most successful in searching for and detecting ideas.

[32] With a significance level of at least 10%.

Table 10 (Continued)

Variables	1	2	3	4	Total
Percentage of ideas detected with a positive evaluation	1.64	(+) 3.17	(−) 1.50	2.50	2.17
Percentage of ideas detected over a one-year period that are positively evaluated	(−) 2.00	(+) 3.67	(−) 2.00	2.25	2.48
Percentage of technology-based spin-offs	(+) 83.45	62.17	(−) 60.00	68.00	73.17
Percentage of knowledge-based spin-offs	(−) 14.18	37.67	(+) 40.00	32.00	25.65
University´s involvement in the spin-off´s management	(−) 1.09	(−) 1.00	(−) 1.00	(+) 2.25	1.26
Year in which the university began activities to support spin-off	(+) 2002	1999	(−) 1995	1999	2000
Average number of spin-offs created between 2000 and 2004	(−) 1.57	3.33	3.40	(+) 9.73	3.61
Average of patents	(−) 6.23	6.92	(+) 21.50	14.00	9.09
% IandD	29.64	(−) 25.50	58.00	(+) 66.50	37.43

[a]The cluster marked with a (+) or (−) has the highest or lowest mean for the corresponding variable.

Figure 5 shows the profiles of the four types of programmes identified in Spanish universities according to the six variables with significant differences indicated above.

The profiles of each of the types of programme identified are described below, as with the British universities[33]:

Type 1: made up of universities with a relatively small level of RandD activity, which have spin-off programmes started up recently and have a small number of people devoted to spin-off support; their commitment to promoting an entrepreneurial culture is limited, and their activities therefore benefit a limited number of people; they are not very proactive in searching for and detecting ideas; they place little importance on monitoring business design/project competitions and the number of ideas they detect is therefore limited; they give a positive rating to and spin off a small percentage of the ideas detected; they generate few ventures, mostly technology-based, and intervene little in their running.

This type of programme therefore has little experience in spin-off support, has few resources for this task and enjoys little commitment from the university; it is not very proactive in searching for and detecting ideas and follows a high selectivity policy; as a result, it generates a limited number of spin-offs, mostly technology-based.

Type 2: has major similarities with the previous type and, to a lesser extent, with Type 4. It includes universities with a relatively low degree of RandD

---

[33] Clearly, this description refers to the date of the survey.

activity, that started up spin-off programmes some years ago and have a small number of people devoted to this work; their commitment to promoting an entrepreneurial culture is likewise limited; however, they are quite proactive in searching for and detecting ideas; in addition, they place quite a large degree of importance on monitoring business design/project competitions; however, the number of ideas detected is very limited; unlike the previous type, they give a positive rating to and spin off a large percentage of the ideas detected; they generate an intermediate number of spin-offs, with a significant proportion of knowledge-based ones, but they do not intervene in their running.

Consequently, this type of programme has more experience in spin-off support, has few resources for this task and has less commitment from the university; it is somewhat more proactive in searching for and detecting ideas, but follows a low selectivity policy; as a result, it generates a larger number of spin-offs, mostly technology-based, but with a larger proportion of knowledge-based spin-offs.

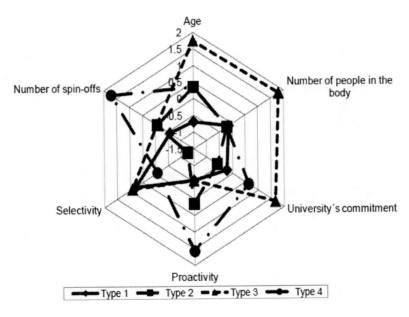

Figure 5. Spanish universities. Profiles of the four types of programme.

Type 3: universities with a relatively high degree of RandD activity, that have spin-off programmes started up quite a few years ago, and have a relatively large number of people devoted to supporting these programmes; their commitment to promoting an entrepreneurial culture is very high, and their activities therefore benefit a large number of people; they appear not to be very proactive in searching for and detecting ideas[34]; they place great importance on monitoring business design/project competitions, but the number of ideas they detect is relatively small; they give a positive rating to and spin off a small percentage of ideas detected; they generate an intermediate number of companies, with a significant proportion of knowledge-based ones, and they do not intervene in their running.

In short, this type of programme has a lot of experience in spin-off support, has plenty of resources for this task and enjoys great commitment from the university; it is not very proactive in searching for and detecting ideas and follows a high selectivity policy; however, it generates a comparatively high number of spin-offs, mostly technology-based, but with a larger proportion of knowledge-based ones than the previous type.

Type 4: also has a relatively high degree of RandD activity; universities included in this profile have spin-off programmes started up some years ago, although they have a small number of people devoted to them; their commitment to promoting an entrepreneurial culture is also high, and their activities therefore benefit a large number of people; they are very proactive in searching for and detecting ideas and place great importance on monitoring business design/project competitions, with the result that the number of ideas they detect is relatively high; they give a positive rating to and spin off an intermediate percentage of ideas detected; they generate a large number of spin-offs –though their rate of mortality is also high– with a large proportion of knowledge-based ones, and they tend to intervene in their running.

Summing up, this type of programme has more experience in spin-off support, has comparatively limited resources for the task, but enjoys considerable commitment from the university, and is very proactive in the search and detection of ideas and follows a low selectivity policy; as a result, it generates a major number of spin-offs, mostly technology-based, but with a larger proportion of knowledge-based spin-offs.

5.3. Comparison between Models

From the characterisation above and from a comparison between the means of the six variables cited where there are significant differences in the clusters

---

[34] This statement needs to be qualified, since it is the cluster that gives most importance to the activities of monitoring the research groups' projects and competitions of ideas/creation of spin-offs; and the one that has been most successful in searching for and detecting ideas.

(Tables 9 and 10), we may deduce certain similarities between the spin-off support models identified in the two countries. Thus, British types 4 and 2 have a very similar profile to Spanish types 3 and 1 respectively: British Type 3 shows some similarities with Spanish Type 4, and British Type 1 stands in an intermediate position between Spanish types 4 and 2.

Thus, British programmes of Type 4 and Type 3 in Spain are more successful, but also share other characteristics: they have many resources for performing their task and have a considerable commitment from their respective universities; they appear to prefer a policy of low proactivity in searching for and detecting ideas[35], and one of intermediate selectivity (or high, in Spanish universities) with regard to the ideas detected that are eventually spun off; they create the largest number of companies (or an intermediate number in Spain), with a high survival rate[36]. The policy followed by this cluster is close to the model of *intermediate support and selectivity* suggested by Degroof and Roberts (2004) and to the model of *support* suggested by Clarysse et al. (2002), Clarysse et al. (2005) and Wright et al. (2007), whose aim is to create companies with economic potential and growth ambition.

In contrast, British Type 2 programmes and Spanish Type 1 show that it is difficult to establish from the outset a policy of high proactivity/high selectivity/high support, since following this policy requires considerable resources and skills that are not always available. Although universities of this type have opted from the beginning for a high selectivity policy, their low proactivity limits the number of spin-offs achieved. These results appear to contradict the conclusion of Degroof (2002), whereby universities will initially be forced to start with a low selectivity/low support policy, to move gradually towards a position of greater selectivity and support.

Spanish Type 4 programme is another successful model. Although it does not devote many resources to this task, it enjoys the commitment of its university, and appears to opt for a policy of high proactivity in searching for and detecting ideas, and of low selectivity of the ideas detected that are eventually spun off. In

---

[35] As stated above, this statement needs to be qualified, since these are the types of programme that give most importance to the activity of monitoring the projects of the research groups; and the ones that have been most successful in searching for and detecting ideas.

[36] The "percentage of spin-offs that fail in under three years" variable has not been included in the characterisation of the profiles of the four clusters since there are no significant differences in this variable. This variable has values of 18.75, 17, 10.5 and 11.67 for the British clusters 1, 2, 3 and 4, respectively; and 4.55, 21, 12.5 and 24.5 for Spanish clusters 1, 2, 3 and 4, respectively.

addition, it appears to follows a policy of low support for spin-off projects, given that it is the type with the lowest mean time from idea detection to spinning-off[37].

The net result is the creation of a relatively large number of companies, but with a lower survival rate. The policy pursued by this group of universities appears to be close to the model of *low selectivity* proposed by Clarysse et al. (2002), Clarysse et al. (2005) and Wright et al. (2007), whose aim is to generate the largest possible number of companies.

In order to achieve this, they try to stimulate entrepreneurial initiative and do not concern themselves as much with the economic or financial potential of the initiatives.

British Type 3 programme has a similar profile to the previous one when it comes to resources, commitment and proactivity, but somewhat more selectivity and support; as noted, the result is that it generates a small number of spin-offs, though they have a high rate of survival.

Finally, Spanish Type 2 programme appears to show that some spin-off programmes are resource-deficient or competence-deficient. Among other factors, the lack of resources is reflected in the fact that the support of the university administration is lacking; and the lack of competences is reflected in the absence of the skills needed to carry out the activities required. Although universities of Type 2 appear to be somewhat proactive, they provide limited support and pursue a policy of very low selectivity, thus managing to create a relatively large number of spin-offs, though with a low survival rate. These results appear to confirm the conclusions of Clarysse et al. (2002), Clarysse et al. (2005) and Wright et al. (2007).

For its part, British Type 1 programmes stand somewhere half-way between Spanish programmes 2 and 4. This type enjoys a certain commitment from the university, and appears to opt for a quite proactive policy in searching for and detecting ideas, and one of low selectivity of the ideas detected that are finally spun off. The result is the creation of a smaller number of companies with a more limited survival rate than in Spanish types 2 and 4.

---

[37] The "mean time between detection of the idea and spinning-off" variable was not included in the characterisation of the profiles of the four clusters since this variable does not display significant differences. This variable has values of 1.82, 1.67, 2.5 and 1.5 for clusters 1, 2, 3 and 4, respectively.

Conclusion

Great importance has been given to the creation of knowledge-based ventures over the last decade, and in keeping with the idea of the university's "third mission", this has led to a proliferation in spin-off support programmes. In this paper we have set out to identify the different models of support programme that exist in universities in Spain and in the United Kingdom. In doing so, we have applied multivariate statistical analyses –particularly the cluster analysis technique– to the results of a survey of the people in charge of these types of programme. Having identified the models of support programme, we performed a statistical analysis to characterise them clearly. This enabled us to reach a series of conclusions, summarised below.

We identified four clusters of spin-off support programmes in British universities, differing in their degree of resources, university commitment, proactivity and selectivity; likewise, in Spanish universities we have identified another four clusters of spin-off support programmes, differing in the same variables, but also in terms of experience and the number of spin-offs created; all of these variables are identified by the literature as determining their characteristics and results.

The results obtained show certain similarities between the types of programmes found in Spain and in the United Kingdom, although in the latter we have not identified a set of universities that is close to the *low selectivity* model. Thus, British Type 4 has major similarities with Spanish Type 3 in terms of resources, university commitment and proactivity, although it is somewhat less selective and creates a larger number of spin-offs.

British Type 2 is similar to Spanish Type 1 in terms of resources, university commitment, proactivity and number of spin-offs created, but is somewhat more selective. British Type 1 stands between Spanish types 4 and 2; it is similar to them in terms of resources and selectivity, but has a greater university commitment, proactivity, and number of spin-offs created than Type 4, and conversely, less commitment, proactivity and number of companies created than Type 2. Finally, British Type 3 is similar to Spanish Type 4 with regard to resources, university commitment, proactivity and selectivity; however, it differs notably in the number of companies created.

These results confirm that universities pursue different spin-off support policies, utilise different spin-off creation processes and generate different numbers of companies of different characteristics, as various authors have indicated (Clarysse et al., 2002; Clarysse et al., 2005; Degroof and Roberts, 2004; Wright et al., 2007).

British programmes of Type 4 and Spanish 3 appear to be successful models, implementing a policy that comes close to the *intermediate support and selectivity* model proposed by Degroof and Roberts (2004) and the *supportive* model proposed by Clarysse et al. (2002), Clarysse et al. (2005) and Wright et al. (2007), whose aim is to create companies with economic potential and a growth ambition.

In contrast, British Type 2 and Spanish Type 1 show that it is difficult to establish a policy of high proactivity/high selectivity/high support from the outset; nonetheless, the fact that numerous universities pursue such a policy appears to contradict Degroof's assertion that universities will initially be obliged to start with a low selectivity/low support policy, to move gradually towards a position of greater selectivity and support.

Spanish Type 4 appears be another successful model, pursuing a policy close to the model of *low selectivity* proposed by Clarysse et al. (2002), Clarysse et al. (2005) and Wright et al. (2007), whose aim is to generate the greatest number of companies possible. To this end, such universities try to stimulate entrepreneurial initiative and do not concern themselves as much with the economic or financial potential of the initiatives.

Finally, Spanish Type 2, and, to a lesser extent, British Type 1, appear to show that some spin-off support programmes lack resources or competences, apparently confirming Clarysse's conclusions.

Moreover, the typology of the spin-off support programmes identified in this work enables us to make some recommendations for improving the least successful models in universities in the UK and Spain.

Type 2 programmes in the United Kingdom and Type 1 in Spain must devote a greater quantity of resources and strengthen their competences. Universities that adopt such programmes appear to be clear on the support policy they wish to pursue, but lack the resources and competences needed to put them into practice.

If they are to improve their results, therefore, they need to devote a greater quantity of resources to their programmes, and strengthen their competences through training and hiring of specialist personnel, as well as by establishing collaboration networks with external agents specialising in each of the activities in the process. One alternative for universities lacking sufficient scale could be to group together to create joint spin-off programmes.

Type 1 programmes in the UK and Type 2 in Spain must prioritise the establishment of the support policy they wish to pursue.

Although universities that adopt such programmes might seem to be pursuing a policy with a certain degree of proactivity in searching for and detecting ideas and low selectivity of the ideas detected that are finally spun off, it actually appears to be the lack of necessary resources and competences that leads them to pursue this policy. They must first of all establish the support policy they wish to apply, and it is therefore essential to have prior commitment from the university management.

Finally, the results obtained in this paper enable us to offer two additional observations.

Firstly, British Type 4 programmes and Spanish types 3 and 4 –i.e., the "successful models"– have the greatest return on RandD and the greatest number of patents. These results are in consonance with the literature, which sees RandD activity as one of the factors related to the business creation process in the universities; at the same time, they also show that patent applications by universities are an indicator of the results of university RandD and its commercial orientation.

Secondly, with one exception, universities with these "successful models" are found in regions with above-average innovation behaviour for their respective countries (Hollanders, 2007).

An innovating environment, therefore, appears to have a positive effect on the characteristics and results of university spin-off support programmes, in these two countries at least. This result backs the literature's insistence on the importance of a favourable environment to the success of spin-off programmes (European Commission, 2002; Hague and Oakley, 2000; Wright et al., 2007), but it also calls into question Roberts and Malone's assertion that a policy of high support/high selectivity is more likely in unfavourable environments[38].

References

Autio, E. (1997). New technology-based firms in innovation networks symplectic and generative impacts. *Research Policy*, 26(3), 263-281.

Baxter, C., Wing, P., Anderson, B., and Kayll, S. (2004). Selection, recruitment and development of the spinout management team. In: K. Tang, A. Vohora

---

[38] This last statement needs to be qualified, since when the authors speak of a favourable setting, they are referring to the US, and more specifically to universities such as MIT and Stanford, which continue to be an international reference point for spin-off support programmes. However, these two cases are atypical, even in America.

and R. Freeman (Eds.), *Taking Research to Market: How to build and invest in successful university spinouts* (pp. 88-100). London: Euromoney Institutional Investor Plc.

Benner, M. and Sandstrom, U. (2000). Institutionalizing the Triple Helix: Research Funding and norms in the Academic System. *Research Policy,* 29(2), 291-301.

Callan, B. (2001). Generating Spin-offs: Evidence from across the OECD. *Science Technology Industry review,* 26, 13-56.

Clarysse, B., Lockett, A., Quince, T., and Van de Velde, E. (2002). Spinning off new ventures: a typology of facilitating services. Brussels: Institute for the Promotion of Innovation by Science and Technology in Flanders.

Clarysse, B., Wright, M., Lockett, A., Van de Velde, E., and Vohora, A. (2005). Spinning out new ventures: a typology of incubation strategies from European research institutions. *Journal of Business Venturing,* 20(2), 183-216.

Degroof, J.-J. (2002). Spinning off new ventures from research institutions outside high tech entrepreneurial areas. (Ph.D. dissertation). Massachusetts Institute of Technology. Massachusetts.

Degroof, J.-J. and Roberts, E. B. (2004). Overcoming weak entrepreneurial infrastructures for academic spin-off ventures. Cambridge: MIT Industrial Performance Centre, Working Paper Series MIT-IPC-04-005. http://web.mit.edu/ipc/publications/pdf/04-005.pdf.

Etzkowitz, H., Webster, A., Gebhardt, C., and Cantisano, B. R. (2000). The future of the university and the university of the future: Evolution of ivory tower to entrepreneurial paradigm. *Research Policy,* 29(2), 313-330.

European Commission (2002). University spin-outs in Europe: Overview and good practice. Luxembourg: Office for Official Publications of the European Communities.

Geuna, A. (1999). The Economics of Knowledge Production. Funding and the Structure of University Research. Cheltenham: Edward Elgar Publishing Limited.

Golob, E. R. (2003). Generating spin-offs from university-based research: an institutional and entrepreneurial analysis. (Ph.D. dissertation). The State University of New Jersey. New Jersey.

Hague, D. and Oakley, K. (2000). Spin-offs and start-ups in UK universities. London: Committee of Vice-Chancellors and Principals of the Universities of the United Kingdom.

Heirman, A. and Clarysse, B. (2004). How and Why do Research-Based Start-Ups Differ at Founding? A Resource-Based Configurational Perspective. *Journal of Technology Transfer,* 29(3/4), 247-268.

Helm, R. and Mauroner, O. (2007). Success of research-based spin-offs: State-of-the-art and guidelines for further research. *Review of Managerial Science*, 1(3), 237-270.

Henry, C., Hill, F. and Leitch, C. (2005). Entrepreneurship education and training: can entrepreneurship be taught? Part I. *Education + Training*, 47(2), 98-111.

Hindle, K. and Yencken, J. (2004). Public research commercialisation, entrepreneurship and new technology based firms: an integrated model. *Technovation*, 24(10), 793-803.

Hollanders, H. (2007). 2006 European Regional Innovation Scoreboard (2006 RIS). European Commission, DG Enterprise. http://www.proinnoeurope. eu/ScoreBoards/Scoreboard2006/pdf.

Jack, S. L. and Anderson, A. R. (1999). Entrepreneurship education within the enterprise culture: Producing reflective practitioners. *International Journal of Entrepreneurial Behaviour and Research*, 5(3), 110-125.

Klofsten, M. (2000). Training entrepreneurship at universities: a Swedish case. *Journal of European Industrial Training*, 24(6), 337-344.

Lockett, A., Wright, M. and Franklin, S. (2003). Technology Transfer and Universities´ Spin-Out Strategies. *Small Business Economics,* 20(2), 185-200.

Lundvall, B. A. (2002). The University in the Learning Economy. DRUID Working Paper n° 02-06.

Mcdonald, L., Capart, G., Bohlander, B., Cordonnier, M., Jonson, L., Kaiser, L., Vonortas, N. S. (2004). Management of intellectual property in publicly-funded research organisations: Towards European Guidelines. Luxembourg: Office for Official Publications of the European Communities.

Mcqueen, D. H. and Wallmark, J. T. (1991). University Technical Innovation: Spin-offs and Patents in Göteborg, Sweden. In: A. M. Brett, D. V. Gibson and R. W. Smilor (Eds.), University Spin-off Companies, Economic Development, Faculty Entrepreneurs, and Technology Transfer (pp. 103-115). Savage, Maryland: Rowman and Littlefield Publishers, Inc.

Mowery, D. C. and Sampat, B. N. (2001). University Patents and Patent Policy Debates in the US, 1925-1980. *Industrial and Corporate Change*, 10(3), 781-814.

Mustar, P. (1997). Spin-off enterprises. How French academics create hi-tech companies: the conditions for success and failure. *Science and Public Policy*, 24(1), 37-43.

OECD (1999). University Research in Transition. Paris: OECD Publications.

Okubo, Y. and Sjoberg, C. (2000). The Changing Pattern of Industrial Scientific Research Collaboration in Sweden. *Research Policy*, 29(1), 81-98.

Pirnay, F. (2001). La valorisation économique des résultats de recherche universitaire par création d'activités nouvelles (spin-offs universitaires): Propositions d'un cadre procédural d'essaimage. (Ph.D. dissertation). Université du Droit et de la Santé - Lille 2. Lille.

Polt, W., Rarner, C., Gassler, H., Schibany, A., and Schartinger, D. (2001). Benchmarking Industry Science Relations: the role of framework conditions. *Science and Public Policy*, 28(4), 247-258.

Powers, J. B. and Mcdougall, P. P. (2005a). University start-up formation and technology licensing with firms that go public: a resource-based view of academic entrepreneurship. *Journal of Business Venturing*, 20(3), 291-311.

Powers, J. B. and Mcdougall, P. P. (2005b). Policy orientation effects on performance with licensing to start-ups and small companies. *Research Policy*, 34(7), 1028-1042.

Reitan, B. (1997). Fostering technical entrepreneurship in research communities: Granting scholarships to would-be entrepreneurs. *Technovation*, 17(6), 287-296.

Roberts, E. B. and Malone, D. (1996). Policies and structures for spinning off new companies from research and development organizations. *RandD Management*, 26(1), 17-48.

Schutte, F., Van der Sijde, P. and Van Tilburg, J. (2001). Entrepreneurship Skills and Incentives. *Science Technology Industry Review*, 26, 143-164.

Shane, S. (2004). Academic Entrepreneurship. University Spinoffs and Wealth Creation. Cheltenham: Edward Elgar Publishing Limited.

Siegel, D., Waldman, D. and Link, A. (2003). Assessing the impact of organizational practices on the productivity of university technology transfer offices: An exploratory study. *Research Policy*, 32(1), 27-48.

Smailes, B. and Cooper, S. (2004). Academic enterprise and sustainable wealth-creation. In: K. Tang, A. Vohora and R. Freeman (Eds.), Taking *Research to Market: How to build and invest in successful university spinouts* (pp. 21-30). London: Euromoney Institutional Investor Plc.

Storey, D. J. and Tether, B. S. (1998). New technology-based firms in the European Union: an introduction. *Research Policy*, 26(9), 933-946.

Trim, P. R. J. (2003). Strategic marketing of further and higher educational institutions: partnership arrangements and centres of entrepreneurship. *The International Journal of Educational Management*, 17(2), 59-70.

UNISPIN (1999). Good practice guide. Enschede: University of Twente.

Vohora, A., Wright, M. and Lockett, A. (2004). Critical junctures in the development of university high-tech spinout companies. *Research Policy*, 33(1), 147-175.

Wright, M., Birley, S. and Mosey, S. (2004). Entrepreneurship and University Technology Transfer. *Journal of Technology Transfer*, 29(3/4), 235-246.

Wright, M., Clarysse, B., Mustar, P., and Lockett, A. (2007). Academic Entrepreneurship in Europe. Cheltenham: Edward Elgar Publishing Limited.

In: Progress in Economics Research. Volume 27   ISBN: 978-1-62808-201-2
Editor: A. Tavidze   © 2013 Nova Science Publishers, Inc.

Chapter 3

THE NETHERLANDS: SOCIAL ECONOMIC IMPLICATIONS FROM AN INTELLECTUAL CAPITAL PERSPECTIVE

Carol Yeh-Yun Lin[1] and Jeffrey Chen[2]

[1]National Chengchi University, Taipei City, Taiwan
[2]Accenture, US

Abstract

Despite the wide breadth of literature concentrating on policy implications for social and economic issues, few articles have examined the linkage between tangible economic results and intangible national intellectual capital (NIC). This chapter is an examination of the co-evolution between tangible and intangible factors in the Netherlands in order to understand the underlying influence that intellectual capital has on the economy.

Intellectual capital at a national level consists of human capital, market capital, process capital, renewal capital, and financial capital. The dataset utilized captures a six-year time period from 2005 to 2010.This time frame is of particular interest as it spans the phases before, during, and after the 2008 global financial crisis. Using this dataset, this chapter examines the co-development of the intangible national intellectual capital and tangible GDP per capita (ppp).

In this manner, we present a holistic picture of the Dutch national intellectual capital landscape and perform year-on-year trend analysis. Next, we place the Netherlands within the context of 48 countries and compare the Dutch national intellectual capital trend against that of others. This allows for comparison and contrast of the Netherlands with other major countries to provide valuable insight for future social economic policies.

Data analysis shows that there is a high correlation between the intangible national intellectual capital and the economic success as well as the speed of recovery following the 2008 global financial crisis. The result leads to the conclusion that countries with high levels of intellectual capital develop better resilience and ability to weather crisis. The Netherlands is one such example. This study is part of a growing number of studies that focuses on intellectual capital and its impact on modern societies and economies.

Macroeconomic information reported in this chapter showed that the Dutch government navigated the country through the crisis relatively well. NIC related graphs and statistics also indicate that the Netherlands was able to not only maintain but even advance its short-term NIC international competitiveness. However, its long-term NIC has room for improvement. Its top ten NIC ranking among 48 countries may have played a role in facilitating its national development and helped withstand the financial turmoil.

Keywords: National intellectual capital, intangible assets, national well-being, economic development, the Netherlands

Introduction

There is a wide breath of economic literature and data analyzing every facet of the world economy. For the Netherlands, the situation is no different as institutions and government bureaus publish yearly projections and reviews of the country's economic outlook. In particular, over the past several years, there has been a particular emphasis on the notion of sustainability of economic and societal development in these publications.

The phrase "sustainable outlook" has garnered increasing attention after the 2008 global financial crisis as countries, including the Netherlands, sought to maintain the pace of their economic development amidst the free-falling world economy. Even now, at the time of this writing in the year 2012, the aftermath of the financial crisis continues to plague certain countries across the globe. As such, it is valuable to reflect upon the events of the past several years in order to understand the reasons behind the crisis and potential policy implications for the future.

What sets our study apart from the rest of the literature on the subject of the social economic implications of the financial crisis is that we approach this subject from the perspective of National Intellectual Capital (NIC). In particular, we closely examine the links between the tangible economic results and the intangible intellectual capital factors that come into play. In such a manner, we explain the co-evolution trends between tangible and intangible factors in order to understand the underlying influence that NIC has on the economy.

In the wake of the financial crisis, academics pointed out the inability of the conventional financial systems to detect the risks that led to this crisis (Reavis, 2009). In particular, areas such as non-transparent information disclosure and a lack of sufficient granularity in economic development data were singled out as key factors (Enoch, Moore and Zhou, 2011). In addition, the traditional metrics do not take into account factors such as intangible assets and capital that play an important role in determining the values and risks behind proper decision making (Reavis, 2009). What we present here in this chapter is an alternative way using an alternative set of metrics to evaluate the performance of a nation's economy.

It is our deep belief that national intellectual capital, albeit intangible, can provide valuable insight regarding future policy and strategy formulation. NIC can, and should, be used as a complement to the traditional metrics as a means of analyzing and assessing the health of a particular economy.

Intellectual capital at a national level consists of human capital, market capital, process capital, renewal capital, and financial capital (Lin and Edvinsson, 2011: 2). In this study, we mainly use a national intellectual capital dataset that spans the time period from 2005 to 2010 in order to examine the various components of intellectual capital in the phases before, during, and after the 2008 financial crisis. In this manner, we will examine the Netherlands in seven different areas including:

1) Global competitiveness
2) Economic status before and during the 2008 global financial crisis
3) The co-development of various types of national intellectual capital with GDP per capita (ppp)
4) The change of international competitiveness in national intellectual capital over the six years
5) Beyond the global financial crisis
6) Future prospects and challenges
7) The implications of national intellectual capital on the well-being of the Netherlands that policy makers can take into consideration.

In addition to specifically examining Dutch NIC, we will also place the Netherlands within the context of 48 countries and some selected countries to compare Dutch NIC trend against that of others. This allows for comparison and contrast of the Netherlands with other major countries to provide valuable insight for future social economic policies.

Economic Background

Before examining the details of Dutch national intellectual capital, it is important to present an economic context to form a basis for the dataset and further discussion. The national intellectual capital dataset that will be presented in the following sections spans from 2005 to 2010. In this section, we will briefly use macroeconomic statistics to give a background of the Dutch economy spanning the phases before, during, and after the 2008 global financial crisis. As such, a short description of the Netherlands' journey through the crisis becomes necessary to fully understand the context behind the NIC data.

Throughout the past few decades, the Dutch economy has been noted for its stable industrial relations, moderate unemployment and inflation, sizable current account surplus, and important role as an European transportation hub. In addition, its GDP per capita has remained roughly in line with that of the upper half of OECD countries (OECD, 2012b). The country has also been one of the leading European nations for attracting foreign direct investment and is one of the four largest investors in the U.S. (CIA, 2012). Up until the 2008 global financial crisis, the Netherlands experienced a remarkable 26 years of uninterrupted economic growth. Yet, due to its small domestic market and dependency upon foreign trade and financial services, the country was hit hard by this wave of financial turmoil (Enoch, Moore and Zhou, 2011).

National statistics from the year 2009 showed that its export of goods and services amounted to about 80% of GDP; almost twice the European average. In addition, total foreign claims to Dutch banks amounted to over 300% of GDP and exposure of Dutch banks to the United States' financial instruments was 66% of GDP (Masselink and Noord, 2009). As such, the Dutch economy in 2008 and 2009 was structured in such a way that made it inherently sensitive to changes in world trade and the international financial market.

At the start of the crisis, the unemployment rate in the Netherlands was the lowest in Europe at around 3% (Euro area average was 10%) and government debt was also relatively low at around 45% of GDP (Masselink and Noord, 2009). Despite the worldwide outbreak, the negative effects of the financial crisis did not become apparent until late 2008 when economic growth started to slow before coming to a halt in the second quarter of 2009 (Masselink and Noord, 2009).

Fortunately, the relatively good starting position made it possible for the Dutch government to undertake massive operations in order to stabilize financial markets. In total, about US$134 billion (EUR 90 billion, or 15% of the GDP) was spent on rescue operations (Masselink and Noord, 2009). The Netherlands' low unemployment rate, labor hoarding, and reduced-hour schemes also played a role in mitigating the impact of the crisis on private consumption.

Even with such measures, decisive government intervention and stimulus packages, the global crisis still led the Netherlands into deep recession (OECD, 2010a). Particularly, the Dutch financial system was hit hard due to its banks' high exposure to U.S. securitized mortgages and the tightening of the inter-bank funding market (Enoch, Moore and Zhou, 2011). In addition to the U.S. financial instruments, the Dutch banks also had a high degree exposure to Eastern European countries that were heavily impacted by the crisis (Masselink and Noord, 2009). Furthermore, Dutch households and businesses were relatively dependent upon bank loans, making them vulnerable to changes in the credit conditions. In 2007, total indebtedness of households in the Netherlands amounted to approximately 120% of the GDP, compared to Germany's 64%, France's 49%, and Belgium's 47%. Also, bank loans to corporations amounted to 83% of the GDP, compared to around 60% of the GDP in Germany, France, and Belgium (Masselink and Noord, 2009).

In order to rectify the downturn and put the Netherlands back on a sustainable path for the future, the Dutch government launched three economic stimulus packages, starting in November 2008,totaling US$17.3 billion, or approximately 2% of the GDP (US Department of State, 2012). Based on an OECD (2010a) report, the measures were largely implemented on the spending side and focused on four main pillars, including: maintaining employment (reduced working time scheme, retraining and job-search assistance, a debt assistance program for newly unemployed, etc.); shifting forward a number of planned public investment projects (monument restoration; coastal works; waterways; maintenance and construction works; maintenance and construction of road, bridge, youth centers and schools, etc.); providing liquidity to companies (relaxation of rules on carrying over losses from 2008, broader R&D tax rebates, abolishing the air flight tax, energy investment tax credits, various tax cuts for SME's, etc.); and supporting "economic sustainability" – various environmentally-motivated measures, including investments in energy efficiency and a car scrapping scheme.

As a result of all these actions, the Dutch economy started to show a significant rebound in exports with 2.75% quarter-on-quarter growth in the third quarter of 2009 (Masselink and Noord, 2009). Along with this, the economy exited recession in mid-2009 as effects of the fiscal stimulus, easier monetary policy, improved financial conditions and an emerging recovery in world trade (OECD, 2010a).The fiscal policy response was generally well designed, but as a result the deficit widened significantly and fiscal sustainability deteriorated (OECD, 2010b).

Global Competitiveness

Global competitiveness is a measure of how well a nation is doing relative to other world economies. To gain a general picture of the global competitiveness of the Netherlands in recent years, we have taken the summary statistics from the World Economic Forum's annual Global Competitiveness Index (GCI) from 2005-2012. In this way, we aim to present a general context of how the Netherlands progressed in relation to the rest of the world in broad terms.

The GCI index is relatively robust, for it takes into account the 12 distinct pillars[1] containing basic requirements, efficiency enhancers, and innovation factors that contribute to a nation's overall economic strength. The development of a total 142 countries was split into three stages in which different factors play the dominant role in determining the outcome of a country's economy. Stage 1, Stage 2, and Stage 3 are respectively characterized by being factor, efficiency, and innovation driven (Schwab, 2011).The Netherlands was categorized as a Stage 3 innovation-driven country.

From the statistics presented in Figure 1, it can be seen that the global competitiveness of the Netherlands fluctuated within a range of four rankings; bottoming out at 11 in 2005-2006 and peaking at 7 in 2011-2012. The country's recovery from the second half of 2009 is reflected from its continuous GCI ranking advancement in the last two periods. Relative to the rest of the world, the Netherlands remained a strong position and continues to be within the top 10 internationally in terms of global competitiveness.

The following four figures provide a quick overview of the impact of the 2008 global financial crisis, namely real GDP growth per capita, total general government debt, unemployment rate, and consumer price inflation during 2005 to 2011 based on the IMD (International Institute for Management Development) databank. Figure 2 shows that the Netherlands had a relatively sharp real GDP decline in 2009; however the economy rebounded swiftly in 2010. The 2009 decline reflects the drastic impact of the financial crisis on its export-led economy and the rebound explains the revival of international trade in 2010. Yet, with the global slowdown in the second half of 2011 due to lingering EU sovereign debt problems, the GDP of the Netherlands experienced a minor decline to 0.70% growth.

---

[1]The 12 pillars include: institutions, infrastructure, macroeconomic environment, health and primary education, higher education and training, goods market efficiency, labor market efficiency, financial market development, technological readiness, market size, business sophistication, and innovation.

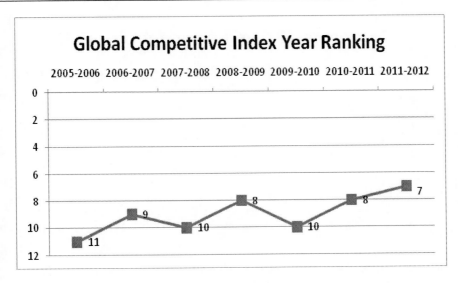

Figure 1. GCI Index ranking of the Netherlands from 2005-2012.

Figure 3 indicates that the Netherlands had modest general government debt percentage GDP before the financial crisis, with a low 45.29% in 2007.However, its debt level has continuously increased since 2008, reflecting the financial burden and the after effects of its stimulus packages.

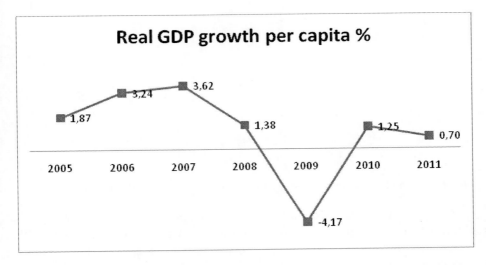

Figure 2. Real GDP growth per capita for the Netherlands from 2005-2011.

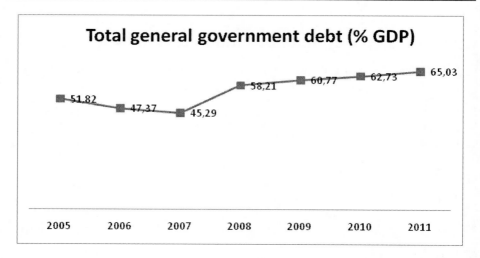

Figure 3. Total general government debt (% of GDP) of the Netherlands from 2005-2011.

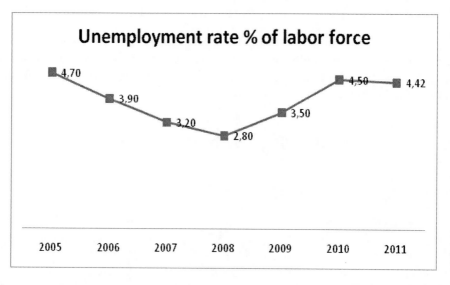

Figure 4. Unemployment rate percentage of labor force in the Netherlands from 2005-2011.

Figure 4 shows the unemployment rate of the Netherlands over seven years, with continuously reducing rate from 2005 to its lowest point of 2.80% in 2008. That is, the Netherlands were in very good shape in terms of its labor market. With the unfolding of the financial crisis, its unemployment rate rose in 2009 and plateaued in 2010 at 4.5%. In 2011, the rate had a slight decline but remained at a relatively high level in comparison to 2008. Even though the Netherlands experienced a rising unemployment rate after the financial crisis, the percentage is still lower than the EU average of 10%.

Figure 5 shows that the consumer price inflation (CPI) of the Netherlands peaked in 2008. In 2009 and 2010, its CPI was at a very low percentage, pointing to the likely possibility that the government stimulus plan took effect.

In the wake of the 2008 financial crisis, the most alarming signal was the rising general government debt there. Government finances should be brought under control to comply with the rules of its Stability and Growth Pact in order to secure fiscal sustainability (OECD, 2012a). Improving fiscal sustainability will also enable the government to focus on boosting employment and productivity in the years to come.

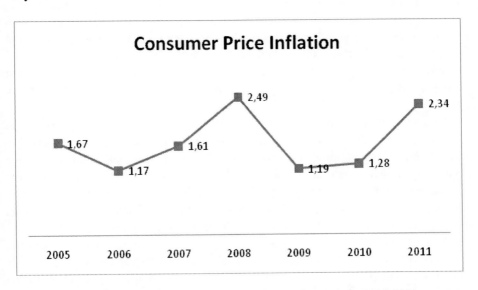

Figure 5. Consumer price inflation of the Netherlands from 2005-2011.

National Intellectual Capital Development

In this section, we first briefly introduce the concept of national intellectual capital (NIC), then present the development of NIC in the Netherlands over the six-year timeframe, afterwards graphically display the relationship between each individual component of NIC with GDP per capita (ppp). Furthermore, we describe the Netherlands' relative positions of long-term and short-term intellectual capital in comparison with countries with similar level of NIC ranking. In addition, we explain the dynamics of NIC for three time periods (2005-2006, 2007-2008, and 2009-2010) to present a comprehensive overview of how NIC correlates and relates to tangible economic conditions.

Definition of NIC

Intellectual capital is defined as "knowledge, information, intellectual property, and experience that can be put to use to create wealth." In addition, intellectual capital also functions as the roots for future earning capabilities (Edvinsson & Malone 1997; Stewart, 1997). In the context of global competition, these features, including educational system, international trade, infrastructure, and renewal capability, can all affect national competitiveness. Countries rich in knowledge-intensive activities will be winners in terms of future wealth creation (Bounfour & Edvinsson, 2004; Stahle & Pöyhönen, 2005). In this manner, NIC can be further broken down into major components of human capital, market capital, process capital, renewal capital, and financial capital (Lin & Edvinsson, 2011: 18).

Human capital includes a population's total capabilities as reflected in education, knowledge, health, experience, motivation, intuition, entrepreneurship and expertise. In addition, the presence of a highly-skilled labor force, the availability of scientists and engineers, and female participation in the labor force are also good indicators. Human capital provides the resources for the development and cultivation of other areas of intellectual assets (such as R&D and training), as the human factor is the most important link in the process of value creation.

Market capital refers to the general assets embodied in the nation's relationship with the international market. It is the aggregate of a country's capabilities and successes in providing an attractive, competitive solution to the needs of its international clients, a country's investment and achievements in foreign relations, coupled with its exports of quality products and services (Bontis, 2004). The assets in this area include customer or national loyalty, openness to globalization, flexibility and adaptability, resilience of economy, as well as the satisfaction expressed by strategic customers and national trading partners.

Process capital is the cooperation and flow of knowledge that requires structural intellectual assets, such as information systems, hardware, software, and databases. It also includes national infrastructure such as transportation, information technology skills, communications and computerization, technological readiness and telecom services, personal computers, cellular subscribers, knowledge transfer, a legal environment for entrepreneurship, a minimum number of days to start a business, and the quality management system. Such structural intellectual assets sustain and increase the output of human capital.

Renewal capital refers to a nation's capabilities and real investments made in an effort to increase its competitive strength in future markets, which, in turn, encourages future growth. Renewal and development assets include investments in research and development, patents, trademarks, start-up companies, the number of scientific publications, the number of patents registered in the US, EPO (European Patent Office) patent applications, total expenditure on R&D, and capacity for innovation.

Financial capital is regarded as the bottom line national economic performance, generally represented by the GDP or GNP for the past few decades.

Together, these 5 types of capital collectively makeup the NIC measurement model in this study. The individual indicator in each category of intellectual capital is described in detail in Appendix 1. This model has been statistically proven for its validity and reliability. The definitions of the indicators are listed in Appendix 2.

National Intellectual Capital of the Netherlands

This section introduces the NIC of the Netherlands in various forms, containing overall NIC and five component capitals, the relationship between each individual capital and GDP per capita (ppp), long-term and short-term NIC, and the dynamics of NIC in three time periods. To put Dutch NIC in context, the Netherlands ranks 12th in human capital, 4th in market capital, 10th in process capital, 13th in renewal capital, 7th in financial capital, and 10th in overall NIC among 48 major countries (Lin, Edvinsson, Chen and Beding, 2013). That is, the Netherlands was mainly within the world's top ten in terms of intangible NIC during this period.

Overall National Intellectual Capital and the Five Component Capitals

To have a general picture of overall NIC before, during and after the financial crisis, Figure 6 shows the Dutch sums of the five component capitals year by year, from 2005 to 2010. The world average NIC is also plotted for comparison purposes. The figure indicates that Dutch NIC is higher than the world average and maintains its level even during and after the 2008 financial crisis. That is, its intangible NIC is relatively stable and did not fluctuate much due to external economic shocks.

Figure 7 shows the five component capitals in the same graph. National human capital represents a nation's investment in nurturing qualified human resources, such as higher education enrollment, skilled labor, and public expenditure in education. Human capital is a long-term oriented NIC (Lin and Edvinsson, 2011: 323), which takes time to develop and is not susceptible to external impact. From the figure, human capital in the Netherlands shows continuous improvements despite the external economic shock experienced from late 2008 to the first half of 2009.

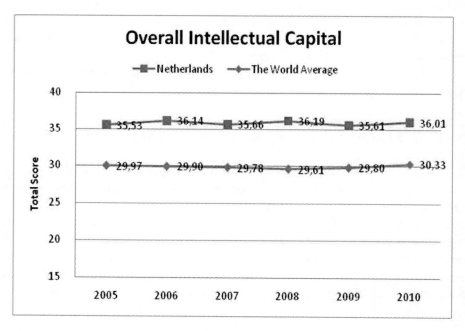

Figure 6. National Intellectual Capital (NIC) of the Netherlands and the world average from 2005 to 2010.

National market capital mainly refers to the general assets embodied in a nation's relationship with the international market, such as cross-border ventures, globalization, and the export of goods. Figure 7 indicates that Dutch market capital experienced two small declinesin2007 and 2009. However in 2010, the level of its market capital exceeded that of 2005, representing a good recovery after the financial crisis.

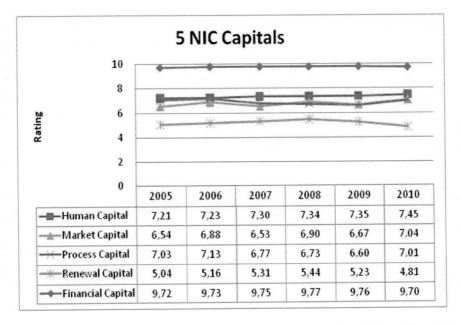

Figure 7. Human capital, market capital, process capital, renewal capital, and financial capital in the Netherlands from 2005 to 2010.

National process capital represents the infrastructure required for building a prosperous society, such as capital availability, mobile phone subscribers, and government efficiency. Figure 7 also shows that Dutch process capital experienced two small declines in 2007 and 2009.In 2010, the level of process capital returned to its pre-crisis level in 2005.

National renewal capital represents the capability of R&D and innovation, such as R&D spending, scientific articles, and patents. Figure 7 indicates that Dutch renewal capital started declining in 2009. That is, after the financial crisis, the Netherlands becomes comparatively weak in its renewal capability.

Financial capital is representative of GDP per capita (ppp) in US dollars transformed to a score on a scale of 1-10. The process of score transformation is explained in Appendix 1.Financial capital of the Netherlands did not have much variation over the six years, representing its relative stable economic performance (in the pool of 48 countries) even during the financial crisis.

The Relationship between Each Individual Capitaland GDP per Capita (PPP)

We investigate the relationship between each individual component capital and economic growth by using the following six figures (Figures8-13). The graphs have four dimensions: The X axis changes from graph to graph (NIC, human capital, market capital, process capital, and renewal capital), the Y axis however is a fixed dimension of GDP per capita (ppp) in US dollars (hereafter termed GDP); the color shade represents renewal capital with red denoting higher levels of renewal capital, and the bubble size denotes the population of an economy. Figure 8 is the relationship between NIC and GDP for all 48 countries. Figures9 to 13 display the co-development of the intellectual capital-GDP relationship over the six-year timeframe for the Netherlands. Since the financial capital score is calculated from GDP, there is no need to plot its relationship against itself. In the figures, 2005 is the starting point tagged with the name of the Netherlands, and the end point is 2010.

In particular, Figure 8 is plotted to clearly show a full picture of the relationship between NIC and GDP for 48 countries in year 2010. The strong positive correlation indicates that the higher the NIC the higher the GDP. Consequently, enhancing NIC is definitely a strategic issue that deserves the attention of national policy makers.

Plotting data from all 48 countries, Figure 9 shows the formation of the NIC and GDP co-development continuum from the bottom-left to the upper-right. The path of the Netherlands falls in the upper-right part of the continuum. What this shows is that the Netherlands exhibited higher NIC and higher GDP than most of the countries in our study, with a NIC ranking of 10 and a financial ranking of 7 among the 48 countries. The path also shows the country's continuous GDP growth (vertical progression) and its small improvement in NIC (horizontal progression).

Figure 10 shows the "human capital–GDP" continuum formation of the 48 countries and the co-development path of the Netherlands. The path also falls in the upper right part of the continuum, with clear vertical progression. That is, the Netherlands had a continuous GDP growth even though its human capital (ranked 12th) did not exhibit much variation over the six years.

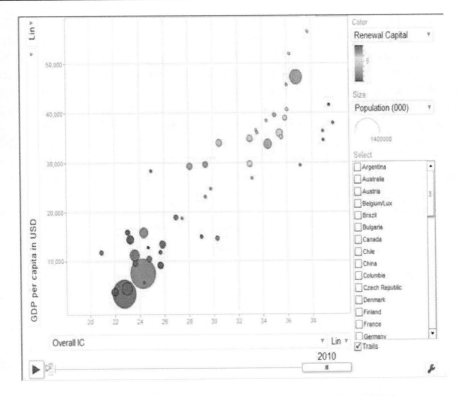

Figure 8. NIC vs. GDP per capita (ppp) for 48 countries in 2010.

The "market capital-GDP" formation of Figure 11 shows that there is no clear continuum like the last two figures as the data points spread further apart, indicating that the correlation between market capital and GDP is not high for these 48 countries as a whole. The market capital-GDP co-development path for the Netherlands is at the upper-right part of the graph, representing the fact that the country exhibits better market capital (ranked 4th) and GDP than most countries.

Figure 12 shows the "process capital–GDP" co-development of the Netherlands with the 48 countries in the background. Again, it can be seen that the figure exhibits a belt-shaped continuum. Although its path is still at the upper-right of the continuum, its process capital declined over the six years. In 2010, Dutch process capital was still below its pre-crisis levels.

Figure 13 shows the Netherlands in relationship to two country-clusters with different formations. In the lower-left corner of mostly less developed countries, there is a continuum with relatively strong correlation between renewal capital and GDP. That is, the higher the renewal capital, the higher the GDP growth for less developed countries. In the upper-right corner, data of the mostly well-developed countries spread out further, which indicates that the correlation between renewal capital and GDP is weak. In other words, countries with higher renewal capital are not necessarily countries with good GDP growth for developed countries. From this, it can be seen that two trends emerge–one showing strong correlation between renewal capital and GDP for less-developed countries and the other showing weak correlation for well-developed nations. The renewal capital and GDP co-development path of the Netherlands is in the lower-left part of the circle cluster, meaning other advanced countries have better renewal capital than the Netherlands, even though their GDP growth is not as good as that of the Netherlands. This finding provides a direction for the Netherlands to contemplate regarding its national development.

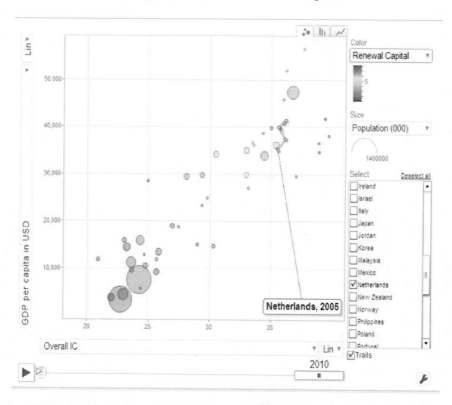

Figure 9. The co-development of NIC and GDP per capita (ppp) for the Netherlands from 2005 to 2010.

It is important to note that while the NIC scores give an absolute performance measure in particular areas, these numbers must be placed in a relative context with the rest of the world in order for the results to have any practicality. As such, the background countries are used as a reference point for the Netherlands to locate its world position and start the discussion on future NIC development.

Long-term and Short-term National Intellectual Capital

In addition to the six figures above that show the relationship of each individual capital with GDP, Figures 14 and 15 further plot the relationships between human capital and renewal capital, as well as between market capital and process capital. Based on our study (Lin and Edvinsson, 2011: 324), the combined increase in human capital and renewal capital would lead to a nation's long term development; whereas the combined increase in market capital and process capital might result in more immediate economic development. To present their relationships, the following two figures map the four capitals on a coordinate with all 48 countries at the background so that readers will know the relative position of the Netherlands.

In this section, the development paths of long-term and short-term NIC for the Netherlands will be placed side-by-side against Israel, Norway, and the U. S. The rationale of selecting these three countries is to explore the Netherlands' NIC competitiveness in comparison with countries in similar NIC level. Israel, the U. S., Iceland, Norway, and the Netherlands have NIC ranking of 6, 7, 8, 9 and 10, respectively (Lin et al., 2013). Iceland is not included for comparison due to missing data for 2007 and 2008 because of its financial system meltdown. Such comparison is an attempt at setting a reference point for comparison in order to translate the numerical statistics into actionable policy implications for future competitiveness.

Human capital is the very foundation that supports other types of capital development. For example renewal capital relies on good human capital. Figure 14 shows the co-development of human capital and renewal capital, representing long-term NIC. Israel and the U.S. have both high human capital and renewal capital, and Norway has higher human capital than renewal capital. The Netherlands is relatively weak in both human capital and renewal capital compared to these three countries. In addition, its renewal capital declined after the financial crisis and did not regain its pre-crisis level in 2010. This figure indicates that if the Netherlands would like to be more competitive in long-term NIC, its human capital and renewal capital need to be improved. These two capitals take time to develop and achieve, as human capital is based on unpredictable human performance and renewal capital is the end result of good human capital. Therefore, their development should be planned as early as possible.

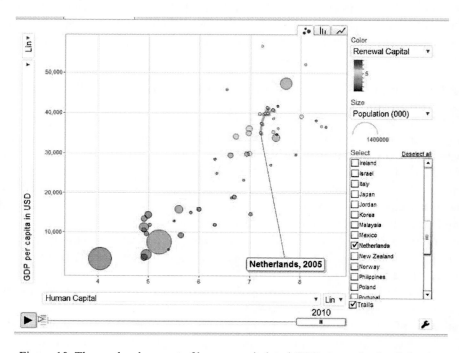

Figure 10. The co-development of human capital and GDP per capita (ppp) for the Netherlands from 2005 to 2010.

Figure 15 shows the co-development of market capital and process capital, representing short-term NIC. Different from the last figure, the Netherlands had higher market capital and higher process capital than the other three countries in 2010, even though its development regressed during the financial crisis.

Dynamics of National Intellectual Capital in Three Time Periods

The illustrations and graphs in the previous two sections describe the internal progression of NIC in the Netherlands over the six years (Figures 6 to 7) and the development path of various capitals (Figures 9 to 13). The ranking changes that will be introduced in this section represent external competitiveness. Ranking, by and large, is a zero-sum game in which the advance of one country simultaneously marks the decline of another.

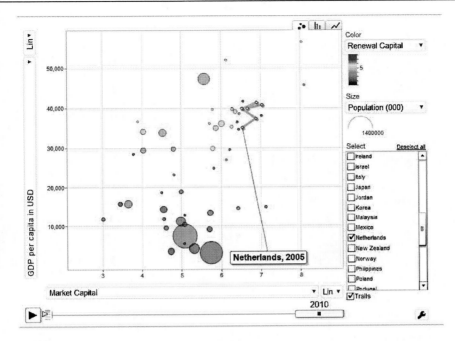

Figure 11. The co-development of market capital and GDP per capita (ppp) for the Netherlands from 2005 to 2010.

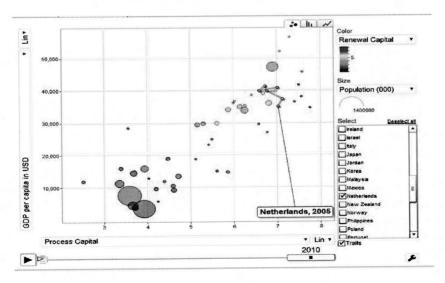

Figure 12. The co-development of process capital and GDP per capita (ppp) for the Netherlands from 2005 to 2010.

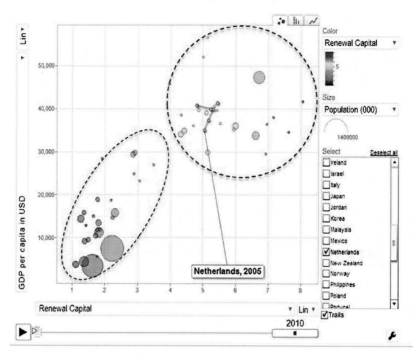

Figure 13. The co-development of renewal capital and GDP per capita (ppp) for the Netherlands from 2005 to 2010.

In order to probe the dynamics of NIC change before and after the financial crisis, we plotted Figures 16 and 17based on Table 1 in three time periods: 2005-2006, 2007-2008, and 2009-2010. To have a clearer presentation, we separate the data in two sets. The first set contains capital scores and ranking changes inhuman capital, market capital, and process capital in Figure 16. The second set exhibits capital scores and ranking changes of renewal capital, financial capital, and average NIC in Figure 17.

The figures are mapped based on the mean capital scores and ranking changes of each period. Ranking changes are next to each capital score and copied from the bold-faced ranking difference of columns 2, 5, 7, and 9 of Table 1. In looking at the human capital ranking difference (-2, 1, -3, -2) for example, the first ranking change of"-2," representing the difference between the 3rd (2009-2010) and 1st (2005-2006) period, is plotted at 2005; the ranking change of "1," representing the difference between the 2nd period (2007-2008) and 1st (2005-2006), is plotted at 2007; the ranking change of "-3," representing the difference between the 3rd period (2009-2010) and 2nd (2007-2008), is plotted at 2009; and the last ranking change of "-2," representing the difference between the 3rd period (2009-2010) and six-year average ranking, is plotted at 2010. Special attention can be paid to the negative numbers, which indicate that the level of a particular capital was higher before than after the financial crisis.

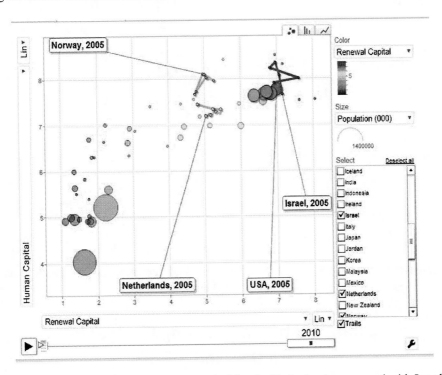

Figure 14. Human capital vs. renewal capital for the Netherlands compared with Israel, Norway, and the U.S.

From Figure 16 and Table 1, the Netherlands' human capital ranking change of -2, 1, -3, -2 shows its international competitiveness in human capital was modestly affected by the financial crisis. On the contrary, the all positive market capital ranking change of 4, 3, 1, 1 reflects its relative strength in international trade even during and after the financial crisis. Its gaining market capital ranking throughout the financial crisis indicates that other countries were not able to withstand the impact as the Netherlands did in terms of market capital. That is, the Netherlands became even more competitive in market capital after the financial crisis. The process capital ranking change of 2, 3, -1, 1 also shows its relative resilience during and after the financial crisis.

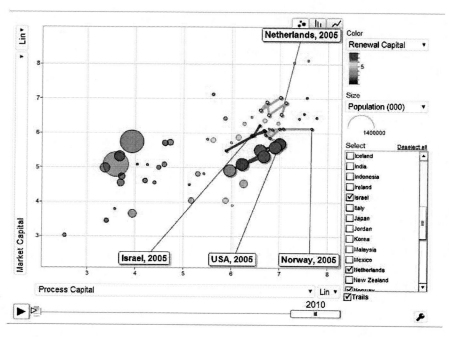

Figure 15. Market capital vs. process capital for the Netherlands, compared with Israel, Norway, and the U.S.

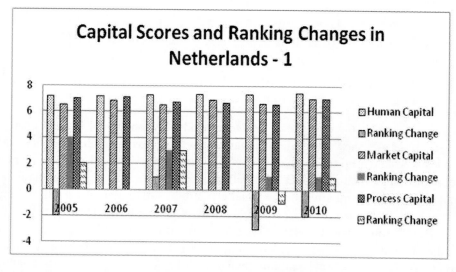

Figure 16. Human capital, market capital, process capital and ranking changes in the Netherlands.

Table 1. Ranking Changes in Three Time Periods for the Netherlands

	(1st period– 3rd period) Difference#1	1st period 2005-2006 Ranking	2nd period 2007-2008		3rd period 2009-2010		2005-2010 average NIC48 ranking	
			Ranking	Diffeence	Ranking	Difference	NIC 48 Ranking	Difference
Human Capital	-2	12	11	1	14	-3	12	-2
Market Capital	4	7	4	3	3	1	4	1
Process Capital	2	11	8	3	9	-1	10	1
Renewal Capital	-3	12	11	1	15	-4	13	-2
Financial Capital	2	8	7	1	6	1	7	1
NIC	2	11	7	4	9	-2	10	1

\# Remarks:
- The second column compares the 3rd (2009-2010) period ranking with the 1st (2005-2006) period ranking.
- The fifth column compares the 2nd (2007-2008) period ranking with the 1st (2005-2006) period ranking.
- The seventh column compares the 3rd (2009-2010) period ranking with the 2nd (2007-2008) period ranking.
- The last column compares the most current 3rd period ranking (2009-2010) with the original six-year average NIC48 ranking.

Figure 17 and Table 1 reveal the Netherlands' weakness. Its renewal capital ranking change of -3, 1, -4, -2 shows the country's weakest intangible asset. After the financial crisis, the Netherlands still did not resume its six-year average ranking and thus lost its international competitiveness in renewal capital. On the contrary, the financial capital ranking change was all positive, even though its government debt and deficit increased because of stimulus packages. For NIC, the ranking change of 2, 4, -2, 1 is relatively positive. Particularly, the last ranking change of "1" indicates that after the financial crisis (2009-2010), the Netherlands has gained one rank over its six-year average ranking and increased its international competitiveness in NIC.

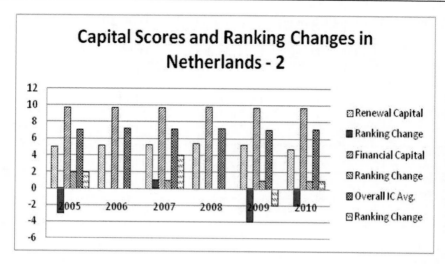

Figure 17. Renewal capital, financial capital, average NIC and ranking changes in the Netherlands.

Beyond the 2008 Global Financial Crisis

This section briefly explains the economic situation of the Netherlands after the 2008 global financial crisis. The Dutch economy recovered slowly in 2010 with an annual growth rate of 1.8% and 1.6% in 2011, mainly benefiting from increased exports and growth in Germany. In 2010, exports increased by 12.8% and imports by 11.7%, while in 2011 the figures were 18.5% and 19.67%, respectively. With the escalation of the international trade in 2010, the Dutch trade surplus grew to US$57 billion. During the financial crisis, short-time work scheme and expanded opportunities for employers to offer temporary contracts helped mitigate the impact of the country's unemployment (OECD, 2012b). In addition, labor productivity increased from the 3.1% in 2009 to 3.5% in 2010; however it then decreased to 2.25% in 2011, and is expected to be 1.75% in 2012 (US Department of State, 2012).

Nevertheless, the financial institutions that received government aid in the midst of the crisis have paid back almost all the loans. An exception is the nationalized ABN Amro Bank, as it will not be re-privatized before 2013 (US Department of State, 2012). For the banking sector, the non-performance loan ratio remains at manageable levels (less than 3% of total loans), with liquid assets more than short-term liabilities. Profits appear to be recovering in 2010, with a return on equity (ROE) of 7% for the sector through 2010 (Enoch, Moore and Zhou, 2011).

The Dutch deficit was 5.4% in 2010, which improved to 4.2% in 2011, and is projected to be 4.5% in 2012. However, the government debt increased rapidly from 45.5% in 2007 to 62.8% in 2010 and to 64.4% in 2011 (US Department of State, 2012). The economic decline of the Netherlands was mostly due to lower foreign trade. In addition to the reducing spending level of the Dutch consumers and investors, growth was also negatively impacted by restrictive budgetary policies (CPB, 2011). The foreseen downturn would require further cuts and reforms in order to strengthen the economy. To fight against increasing government debt and to reach the planned fiscal balance in 2015, the Dutch government announced a spending cut ofUS$26 billion by 2015 (OECD, 2011b; US Department of State, 2012). The largest austerity measures were implemented, including the downsizing of government (US$8.5 billion), cutting back on income transfers, child daycare, and rent subsidies (US$6.1 billion). There are also other significant cutbacks on defense, culture, and innovation subsidies (US Department of State, 2012). In total, the cabinet would make extra cuts of up to US$14.2 billion (€10 billion) to balance the government's books (Dutch News, 2011) and the consolidation plan will amount to aroundUS$26 billion (€18 billion) or 3.3% of GDP by 2015 (OECD, 2011b).

Although the Dutch recovery seemed to be well under way, the economy contracted in the second half of 2011. Domestic demand weakened as lasting financial problems made investors and consumers more cautious and damaged the solvency of pension funds (OECD, 2011b). In December 2011, the Netherlands Bureau for Economic Policy Analysis and the Chairman of the Executive Board Rabobank Netherlands announced that the Dutch economy was in recession again (CPB, 2011; Rabobank, 2012). The escalation of the debt crisis in the Eurozone has increasingly weighed on consumer and business sentiment. The central bank of the Netherlands reported that the economy contracted in the third quarter of 2011 (Dutch News, 2011) and predicted that the Dutch economy would come to a virtual halt in 2012, with GDP growth falling to 0.2% and unemployment rising to 5.3% (Dutch News, 2011). Overall, growth is set to remain below potential throughout 2012-13, and unemployment would rise further (OECD, 2012c). For 2013, the projection incorporates additional consolidation of about 1.5% of GDP to meet the Maastricht deficit target (less than 3%). To secure fiscal sustainability, planned measures to curb aging-related spending growth in the area of pensions and health care were considered (OECD, 2012c).

The Netherlands is expected to see growth resume only slowly, implying further increases in unemployment in the short term. In 2010 to 2014 and beyond, the financial sector faces considerable regulatory intrusion. In particular, the Basel III proposal by the Basel Committee on Banking Supervision will boost capital requirements and liquidity ratios (EIU, 2010). According to the Netherland Rabobank (2012), during the period from 2013 to 2017, real GDP growth is expected to average 1% – markedly lower than in the pre-crisis years – and consumer confidence will remain fragile. In addition, companies will be less inclined to invest, partly because it may take years before the European debt crisis is solved.

Future Perspective and Policy Implications

As of late 2012, even though Euro areas are in a recession again, the positive influence of this financial crisis is it provides an ideal opportunity for a country to examine the soundness of its economic system, the effectiveness of national responses, and the profoundness of national governance.

The world will be different after this unprecedented and swift global financial crisis. Radical changes are occurring in the global banking landscape, business models are being revised, the balance of power is shifting in the markets, and new rules are being negotiated – with certain parties taking a hard line (Doerig, 2009). Definitely, some countries will learn from the experience and emerge to be more resilient, some will continue their structural reforms to build their future strengths, and some may still be burdened by their chronic problems. After this financial crisis, there are prospects as well as challenges. The prospects and challenges to be described hereunder are meant to provide points of thought or discussion and are not an exhaustive list.

Prospects

In 2011, Dutch financial soundness has improved compared to 2008. The medium-term expenditure framework has been planned and strict adherence was monitored to facilitate implementation of the consolidation plan for a better recovery (OECD, 2011b). DNB (De Nederlandsche Bank) was making intensive and well-focused efforts to redress earlier shortcomings with the result that all large banks maintain capitalization buffers well above minimum requirements. The capital augmentation and general return to profitability has positioned the banks well to meet higher Basel III requirements (Enoch, Moore and Zhou, 2011).

To further reform the financial system, the government has adopted an objective-based "twin peaks" supervisory model for coping with the increasingly blurred conventional credit/insurance/securities boundaries. Under this model, DNB became a single prudential supervisor for all financial institutions (banks, insurance companies, investment firms, pension funds, and securities firms) as one peak. The second peak is the Authority for Financial Markets (AFM), which was created as supervisor responsible for conduct-of-business supervision with a strong focus on market behavior and consumer/investor protection (Enoch, Moore and Zhou, 2011). This model was based on the view that the objective of prudential supervision is to safeguard financial stability, while the objective of conduct-of-business supervision is to protect consumers. With micro and macro prudential oversight concentrated in one institution, DNB has the ability to take a systemic overview, which allowed it to react quickly and decisively to address the crisis. This structure also grants DNB power to appoint, instruct and dismiss official administrators on the basis of qualitative and quantitative triggers (Enoch, Moore and Zhou, 2011).

After the financial crisis, exit from state support was proceeding as planned and remains broadly appropriate, as several financial institutions have partially repaid the government following successful capital issuances (Enoch, Moore and Zhou, 2011). To improve deficit and government debt, the Dutch government started to withdraw the stimulus, reduce public administration costs, raise the retirement age in the state pension system, cut health care, and implement higher property taxes (OECD, 2010a). The plan expects a minimum of 0.5% of GDP improvement per year, until a structural balance is reached (OECD, 2010a). If a fiscal surplus is expected to take place every year over the medium term, 50% of the surplus will be used for paying off public debt and 50% will be used for tax reliefs (OECD, 2011).

In addition, the Dutch economy has well-grounded service industries for further development. For example, the Dutch asset management sector is large, modern and well managed. Besides pension funds, a considerable range of investment funds is available, including equity funds, bond funds, real estate funds, hedge funds, mixed funds and others. At end of 2009, investment funds (excluding pension funds and insurers) had assets under management of US$475 billion with the largest fund allocations in shares and other securities (EIU, 2010). In addition, the government strives to improve the investment environment in the Netherlands with the corporate tax rate of 25.5%, which is well below the EU average. Dividend tax has been reduced from 25% to 15%. The Netherlands also offers participation exemption and a 30% tax break for highly qualified foreign employees (QFinance, n. d.).

For natural resources, in 2009 the Netherlands was the second-largest producer and the second-largest net exporter of natural gas in Europe (both after Norway). The port city of Rotterdam is one of the world's major centers for crude oil imports, trading, refining, and petrochemical production. It is also Europe's largest port in terms of cargo tonnage (Heritage, 2012; US Department of State, 2012). The Netherlands' goal is to become a gas "roundabout" for the Western Europe, meaning a hub that gathers natural gas from various sources (including the North Sea, Algerian and Qatari liquefied natural gas, and Russia), and then distributes it via pipeline to continental Europe (US Department of State, 2012).

Furthermore, Dutch government works closely with industry and nongovernmental organizations to reach environmental targets. The country welcomed the EU's 2008 directive to cut greenhouse gas (GHG) emissions 20% from 1990 levels and increase power derived from renewable sources to 20% by 2020. The Netherlands has a binding national target to reduce emissions in sectors not covered by the EU emissions trading system by 16% in 2020. It also has a binding national target of 14% in 2020 for renewable energy (US Department of State, 2012).

The Dutch economy has benefited from globalization via stronger international trade and higher foreign direct investments. Continued globalization would push companies to become more innovative and search for new activities and markets. To further this process, the government is actively reforming policies for the business sector (OECD, 2012a).

In the Netherlands, when people were asked to rate their general satisfaction with life on a scale from 0 to 10, they gave a *7.5, higher than the OECD average of 6.7 (OECD, 2012d)*. Main reasons for this include the facts that the Dutch earned about 15% more than the OECD average (US$25,740 vs. US$22,387a year)and *72% of its people said they had more positive experiences in an average day* (feelings of rest, pride in accomplishment, enjoyment, etc.) *than negative ones* (pain, worry, sadness, boredom, etc.).Besides, *over 75% of people aged 15 to 64 had a paying job,* above the OECD employment average of 66%. Few employees worked very long hours; the Dutch work 1377 hours a year, less than the OECD average of 1749 hours. Also, *69% of women had jobs* compared to the OECD average of 59%. In addition, young people aged 15-24 in the Netherlands, only faced an unemployment rate of 8.7% compared with the OECD average of 16.7%. The long-term unemployment rate for men and women was the same: 1.2%, lower than the OECD average of 3.0%. The country has a good quality education system, and Dutch students performed better on OECD's Program for International Student Assessment (PISA). The average student scored 519, higher than the OECD average of 497 (OECD, 2012d). *Furthermore, 72% of people said they trust their political institutions,* higher than the OECD average of 56%. In the most recent elections for which data is available, *voter turnout in the Netherlands was 80% of those registered,* higher than the OECD average of 73% *(OECD, 2012d)*. In general, the Dutch are satisfied with their life.

The above stated characteristics with some hard data explain the context that may facilitate the Netherlands in having bright prospects in the future.

Challenges

Although the Netherlands was ranked top ten in its overall NIC, its long-term NIC - human capital and renewal capital lagged behind its counterparts. This finding cast concern in the increasingly knowledge and innovation dependent world economy. In addition, even though the financial soundness of the country has improved, vulnerabilities remain. For the Dutch government, the short-term challenge is that fiscal consolidation should be combined with structural reforms to boost employment and participation rates, whereas the most crucial longer-term challenges are to secure fiscal sustainability and raise potential growth in an aging society (OECD, 2010a). Specifically, the challenges are largely pertaining to aging, reducing debt and deficit, financial sector reform, governance, labor force, transportation, and housing issues.

Aging posits a special challenge for the Dutch government, particularly in restricting growth in aging-related spending, such as healthcare and pensions (OECD, 2010a). According to OECD (2010a), the total costs of aging for the Dutch budget, relative to GDP, are set to increase by over 9 percentage points between 2010 and 2060, the fifth highest in the EU and double the EU average; the costs of long-term care, already the highest in the EU, are expected to rise by 4.6 percentage points – four times the EU average; and the expected 4 percentage point increase in pension spending is also above the EU average. These estimates are likely to increase in response to the upward revision in life expectancy. With respect to pensions, the government should pursue the plans to increase the official retirement age by two years to 67 years and more front-loading of this measure would have stronger effects on fiscal sustainability and reduce early retirement incentives in the transition phase (OECD, 2010a). The main concern is the generosity of the Dutch system and increases in aging-related spending need to be curbed to secure fiscal sustainability (OECD, 2010a), such as controlling health expenses and tightening gate-keeping and medical controls for existing benefit recipients (OECD, 2012a, 2012b).

For reducing debt and deficit, the Dutch government's spending remains high and public finance sustainability has deteriorated following the financial crisis. In a DICE (Database for Institutional Comparisons in Europe) Report, the following measures were proposed to maintain a sustainable economy without raising taxes (Beetsma and Gradus, 2010). First, improvements in the economic structure, such as more research and development and a better educated labor force can increase labor productivity. Second, about one sixth of the sustainability gap can be eliminated by reducing public sector wages and a more efficient public administration will contribute to a deficit reduction of 1.25% of GDP amounting to 25% savings on the expenses of public administration. Third, for the streamlining of administrative processes and administrative bodies, fewer rules and inspections, simplified tax system, and restricted subsidies should be considered. Fourth, government deficit can be reduced by reforming the health care sector, by separating the provision of accommodation from that of long-term care, by transferring curative care to the Health Insurance Law, and by transferring the responsibility for support to the local authorities (Beetsma and Gradus, 2010).

Concerning the financial sector reform, although the Dutch financial institutions have improved after the financial crisis, their short term challenges include high indebtedness of home buyers and active cross-border financial activities. Dutch households remain heavily indebted, amongst the highest in the EU, with the most lending relates to housing encouraged by generous mortgage interest deductibility (Enoch, Moore and Zhou, 2011). As the average loan-to-value ratio is well above 100%, macro-prudential instruments should be developed to lower the system's vulnerability. Another key risk stems from the sizable cross-border activities of Dutch financial institutions and the local activities of foreign-owned financial institutions, which require closer scrutiny and supervisory engagement (Enoch, Moore and Zhou, 2011). Legislative reforms will also be needed to strengthen crisis management and bank resolution capacity, including changes to the deposit guarantee scheme (Enoch, Moore and Zhou, 2011).

To strengthen future financial governance, the following measures should be considered (Enoch, Moore and Zhou, 2011; OECD, 2010a). First, establishing routine reporting requirements to strengthen monitoring and risk supervision of large international financial institutions, especially with greater emphasis on group supervision. Second, developing sound business models and communicating prospective changes are essential. It is also important to strengthen the institutional framework for crisis management by shifting decision-making power from the Judiciary to DNB in the context of bank resolution and by specifying more clearly the respective roles of the Ministry of Finance and DNB in bank resolution. Third, improving macro-prudential regulation and supervision of financial markets in cooperation with international institutions should also be emphasized. Fourth, since regulatory reporting suffers from a lack of timeliness and formalization, consistent and sufficiently comprehensive information should be strengthened to better inform offsite monitoring and to increase capacity for early warning (Enoch, Moore and Zhou, 2011).

Labor utilization remains relatively low in the Netherlands, despite a strengthening of activation policies over the past couple of years (OECD, 2010a). Under-utilized labor resources should be mobilized and resources should be allocated to the most productive use on the increasingly scarce labor resources (OECD, 2012a). Measures could aim at lengthening working careers by offering wage subsidies for hiring older workers and older workers should be encouraged to continue to work through tax incentives. Younger people (less than 27 years) are no longer eligible for passive income support, but are encouraged to work or study. Moreover, there is a need to increase the hours worked by females. Boosting labor mobility by easing rigidities would also improve labor resource utilization (OECD, 2010b). The Dutch government should also prepare the business sector for the ongoing challenges of globalization, and adapt labor market institutions for an older and shrinking labor force (OECD, 2012a). Among key priority areas, the government should initiate reforms in the disability system to increase employment and improve gate-keeping. Above all, the most pressing challenge for the near future is to prevent the cyclical increase in unemployment from becoming structural (OECD, 2010b).

Congestion has also become a burden for the Dutch economy. Commuters and businesses are suffering from the time lost in traffic and the unreliability of travel time. In addition to expanding infrastructure, short to medium-term solutions need to be centered on improvements in the use of existing infrastructure, more efficient public transport and better demand management. Road pricing, fuel taxation, and congestion charges are potential coping measures (OECD, 2010b).

The Dutch housing market is more rigid than in many other OECD countries, as the result of numerous government interventions. The rental sector could be made more attractive and flexible by dismantling strict rent regulation and rigid allocation mechanisms in the social housing sector. Lowering tax incentives to homeowners would improve the allocation of scarce capital and reduce house prices. Easing strict land-use and zoning regulation would increase the supply of all types of housing, reducing prices and allowing the housing stock to adjust better to residents' needs (OECD, 2010b).

Policy Implications

Unexpectedly, what started off as a sub-prime mortgage problem in the U. S. triggered a wide-spread global financial crisis. Even a relatively wealthy and advanced small European country as the Netherlands was not immune from the impact. During the financial crisis, the fiscal policy response of the Netherlands was generally well designed. Nevertheless, the deficit widened significantly and fiscal sustainability deteriorated. As a result, the Dutch government was confronted with the task of consolidating public finances without putting the recovery at risk (OECD, 2010b). In the middle of 2012, economic performance of the Netherlands was still affected by the EU economic slowdown. Globalization and aging of the labor force continuously challenge its world competitiveness and national governance.

Behind the statistics such as percentage GDP growth drop and export volume decrease are the hidden intangibles – the people, systems, governance, market dynamics, overlooked risks, and regulation flaws that resulted in this global financial catastrophe. NIC research reported in this chapter covers human capital, market capital, process capital, and renewal capital that encompassing key intangible elements described above. The data analysis describes national intangible assets to a certain extent and provides valuable information for the policy makers to look back the NIC before the crisis, observe the unfolding of the crisis, and study its progression afterwards. By investigating the GDP per capita (ppp) and NIC co-development spanning 2005-2010, we have been able to see the co-evolution of the tangibles and the intangibles for the Netherlands. Some implications can be drawn from our research findings as follows:

First, the Dutch government's swift and focused intervention of large banks is critical for stabilizing the financial markets thus reduced the negative impact of the financial crisis. One of the key reasons for the relatively good recovery of the Netherlands is the government's swift and focused intervention of large banks in trouble. In the Netherlands, banks are actively expanding their financial activities across national borders, especially in the central and eastern European countries that were seriously impacted by the financial crisis. Shortly after the banking crisis emerged, the government took swift and decisive actions to either nationalize the bank or provide capital support and guarantees. Thus, the financial markets were not disturbed too much to a detrimental level. The effects are manifested by the country's relatively fast recovery. In this regard, process capital such as capital availability and government efficiency are important to weather future similar crisis. The Netherlands has a relatively good degree process capital.

Second, international cooperation to effectively assess cross-border financial information facilitates the supervision of financial activities outside of the country. Due to the small domestic market and the convenience of the Netherlands' geographical location in Europe, the country has to and will continue its financial institution expansion across national borders. The need for intensified international cooperation to ensure effective coordinated supervision, such as pan-European banking supervision mechanisms, was highlighted (IMF, 2009). In this regard, market capital including cross-border ventures and shared information of exports facilitate the so-called pan-European banking supervision. As a nation with a relatively high degree market capital, international cooperation is particularly critical to safeguard this valuable intangible asset.

Third, national intellectual capital development goes together with the economic development and should be regarded as an enhancer of economic growth. From Figure 8, it is very clear that the higher the NIC, the higher the GDP per capita (ppp). This finding provides the rationale for promoting intangible national intellectual capital, especially in the knowledge economy that intangible assets are becoming increasingly important.

Fourth, detecting early warnings and designing country-specific strategy facilitate a more focused NIC development. Even though the Netherlands has relative good performance in terms of overall NIC and GDP per capita (ppp), our research still reveals an early warning – especially a declining renewal capital even after the financial crisis. A related result of this decline is its relatively weak long-term NIC (human capital and renewal capital) compared with three other countries (Israel, Norway, and the U.S.) of similar NIC ranking (Figure 14). For advanced countries, the winning strategy of future national development is innovation. National innovation relies on good human capital and renewal capital. This finding provides a clear direction for the Netherlands to strategize its future national development and well-being.

Fifth, the Netherlands can utilize its strong short-term NIC to boost its weak long-term NIC. The Netherlands has strong short-term NIC (Figure 15), with market capital ranks 4 and process capital ranks 10 among 48 countries. Our other study of the top ten NIC ranking countries reveals that the interplay among the four capitals – human capital, market capital, process capital, and renewal capital – resulted in the best synergic prospect for GDP growth. When their weaker capital interacts with stronger capital, both effects on the GDP are enhanced (Lin, 2011). Since long-term NIC needs time and resources to nurture its improvement, if resources created by the short-term NIC can benefit the development of long-term NIC, the Netherlands has a great potential to become a leading country in Europe.

Conclusion

Over the past few decades, intangible assets, such as knowledge, patents, and innovation, have been identified as fundamental sources of wealth and progress. Peter Drucker predicts the emergence of a society dominated by knowledge-based resources and a competitive landscape in the allocation of intellectual capital (Lin and Edvinsson, 2011: 1). The assessment of national intellectual capital reflects a nation's past efforts in terms of human resource development, national economic relationships, infrastructural investment, renewal capability building, and national financial management. Such capacity also nourishes the social economic development and builds resilience of a nation over time. When crisis hits, oftentimes successful coping measures rely more on the intangibles than the tangibles. This chapter introduces the co-development of these two equally important resources.

In summary, this global financial crisis was triggered in September 2008 by the U.S. sub-prime mortgage problems. As a result, a massive impact on the world economy has occurred, due to the drying-up of the interbank market, the tougher lending terms, higher borrowing costs and tumbling stock markets. GDP has been shrunk world widely as business and consumer confidence has dropped, leading to a marked decline in corporate investment, major destocking and a contraction in world trade, and then followed by a sharp deterioration in labor markets. The high international interdependencies, supervisory and regulatory systems that failed to adequately address the systemic risks, and the insufficient international banks transaction information disclosure all led to the outbreak of 2008 global financial crisis.

Macroeconomic information reported in this chapter showed that the Dutch government has navigated the country through the crisis relatively well. NIC related graphs and statistics also indicate that the Netherlands was able to maintain even to advance its short-term NIC international competitiveness. However, its long-term NIC has room for improvement. Its top ten NIC ranking among 48 countries may have played a role in facilitating its national development and helped withstand the financial turmoil.

Crisis will arise again, national leaders who have the confidence to weather through the crisis need to continuously respond to the social changes and reexamining the adequacy of national strategies, policies, and governance in coping with the increasingly interconnected and rapidly changing global social and economic environment. National development is built upon the well-coordinated tangible and intangible systems, including money, real assets, and human capital, market capital, process capital, and renewal capital systems described in this chapter. As the very origin of the financial crisis – people, systems, governance, market dynamics, and the global interdependence –they are also the keys to the economic recovery in any place and country.

Appendices

Appendix 1

Indicators in each type of capital

Human Capital index	Market capital index
1. Skilled labor[*]	1. Corporate tax[*]
2. Employee training[*]	2. Cross-border venture[*]
3. Literacy rate	3. Openness of culture[*]
4. Higher education enrollment	4. Globalization[*]
5. Pupil-teacher ratio	5. Transparency[*]
6. Internet subscribers	6. Image of country[*]
7. Public expenditure on education	7. Exports of goods
Process capital index	**Renewal capital index**
1. Business competition environment[*]	1. Business R&D spending
2. Government efficiency[*]	2. Basic research[*]
3. Intellectual property rights protection[*]	3. R&D spending/GDP
4. Capital availability[*]	4. R&D researchers
5. Computers in use per capita	5. Cooperation between universities and enterprises[*]
6. Convenience of establishing new firms[*]	6. Scientific articles
7. Mobile phone subscribers	7. Patents per capita (USPTO + EPO)

Remarks:
1. Financial capital is the logarithm of GDP per capita adjusted by purchasing power parity.
2. Indicators marked with an asterisk are rated qualitatively using a scale of 1–10.
3. Indicators with objective numbers are transformed to 1-10 scores, by calculating the ratio to the highest number in that indicator and then multiply 10.
4. Readers can refer to the book *National Intellectual Capital: A Comparison of 40 Countries* for model validation details (www.nic40.org)

Appendix 2

Definition of the indicators

Indicators	Definition
Human Capital	
Skilled labor[*]	Whether skilled labor is readily available
Employee training[*]	Whether employee training is a high propriety in companies
Literacy rate	Adult (over 15 years) literacy rate as a percentage of population
Higher education enrollment	Percentage of population that has attained at least tertiary education
Pupil-teacher ratio	Ratio of teaching staff to students
Internet subscribers	Number of internet users per 1000 people
Public expenditure on education	Total public expenditure on education (percentage of GDP)
Market Capital	
Corporate tax encouragement[*]	Whether corporate taxes encourage entrepreneurial activity
Cross-border venture[*]	Whether international transactions can be freely negotiated with foreign partners
Openness to foreign culture[*]	Whether the national culture is open to foreign culture ideas
Attitudes toward globalization[*]	Whether attitudes toward globalization are generally positive in a given society
Transparency[*]	Whether transparency of government policy is satisfactory
Country image[*]	Whether the image abroad of a given country encourages business development
Exports of goods	Exports of goods (Percentage of GDP)
Process Capital	
Business competition environment[*]	Whether competition legislation is efficient in preventing unfair competition
Government efficiency[*]	Whether government bureaucracy hinders business activity

Definition of the indicators

Indicators	Definition
Process Capital	
Intellectual property rights protection[*]	Whether intellectual property rights are adequately enforced
Capital availability[*]	Whether cost of capital encourages business development
Computers in use per capita	Number of computers per 1000 people
Convenience of establishing new firms[*]	Whether creation of firms is supported by legislation
Mobile phone subscribers	Number of subscribers per 1000 inhabitants
Renewal Capital	
Business R&D spending	Business expenditure on R&D (per capita)
Basic research[*]	Whether basic research enhances long-term economic development
R&D spending/GDP	Total expenditure on R&D (percentage of GDP)
R&D researchers	Total R&D personnel nationwide per capita (Full-time work equivalent per 1000 people)
Cooperation between universities and enterprises[*]	Whether knowledge transfer is highly developed between universities and companies
Scientific articles	Scientific articles published by origin of author (per capita)
Patents per capita (USPTO + EPO)	USPTO and EPO total patents granted (per capita)
Financial Capital	
GDP per capita (PPP) (From IMF)	Gross domestic product based on purchasing-power-parity (PPP) per capita

References

Beetsma, R.& Gradus, R. (2010).Filling the sustainability gap after the crisis: The case of the Netherlands, CESifo DICE Report. Retrieved from http://www.cesifo-group.de/portal/pls/portal/docs/1/1192834.PDF.

Bontis, N. (2004). National intellectual capital index: a United Nations initiative for the Arab region. *Journal of Intellectual Capital*, 5(1), 13-39.

Bounfour, A.& Edvinsson, L. (2004).*IC for communities, nations, regions, cities and other communities*. Boston: Elsevier Butterworth-Heinemann.

Central Intelligence Agency (CIA) (2012). *The world factbook, U. S. A. Central Intelligence Agency.* Retrieved from https://www.cia.gov/library/publications/the-world-factbook/index.html.

CPB Netherlands Bureau for Economic Policy Analysis (December 13, 2011). Dutch economy in recession, prospects for 2012 depend on Eurozone crisis. Retrieved from http://www.cpb.nl/en/pressrelease/3211184/dutch-economy-recession-prospects-2012-depend-eurozone-crisis.

Doerig, H. U. (September 11, 2009) In a better position than before the crisis: The Swiss financial market has 'AAA' opportunities for the future, Credit Suisse Group. Retrieved from https://www.credit-suisse.com/news/doc/speech_doerig_nzz_en.pdf.

Dutch News (December 9, 2011) Dutch economy virtually halted, recession in 2011second-half, Dutch News. Retrieved from http://www. Dutchnews.nl/news/archives/ 2011/12/dutch_economy_virtually_halted.php.

Economist Intelligence Unit (EIU) (October 22, 2010) *Netherlands: Financial services report, Economist Intelligence Unit.* Retrieved from http://www.eiu.com/index.asp?layout=ib3Article&article_id=737549058&pubtypeid=1132462498&category_id=775133077&country_id=1400000140&page_title=Forecast&rf=0.

Edvinsson, L. & Malone, M. S. (1997). *Intellectual Capital: Realizing your company's true value by finding its hidden brainpower.* New York: Harper Business.

Enoch, C., Moore, M., & Zhou, J. (2011). Financial system stability assessment: Netherlands, International Monetary Fund, Monetary and Capital Markets and European Departments. Retrieved from http://www.imf.org/external/pubs/ft/scr/2011/cr11144.pdf.

Heritage Foundation (2012).Economic freedom of the Netherlands, Heritage Foundation. Retrieved from http://www.heritage.org.

International Monetary Fund (IMF) (March 2009). Belgium: 2008 Article IV Consultation: Staff report; staff supplement; and public information notice on the executive board discussion, IMF Country Report No. 09/87. Retrieved from http:// www.imf.org/external/pubs/ft/ scr/2009/cr0987.pdf.

Lin, C. Y. Y. (2011). Leveraging intellectual capital for future competitiveness in Finland, Presentation at Tekes, Helsinki on November 10, 2011.

Lin, C. Y. Y. & Edvinsson, L. (2011).*National Intellectual Capital: A comparison of40 countries.* New York: Springer Publishing Co. ISBN: 978-1-4419-7376-45.

Lin, C.Y.Y., Edvinsson, L., Chen, J. & Beding, T. (2013) National intellectual capital and the financial crisis in Greece, Italy, Portugal, and Spain. New York: Springer Publishing Co. ISBN: 978-1-4614-5989-7.

Masselink, M. & Noord, P. (April 12, 2009). The global financial crisis and its effects on the Netherlands, Economic analysis from the European Commission's Directorate-General for Economic and Financial Affairs. ECFIN Country Focus, 6(10), 1-7. ISSN 1725-8375.Retrieved from http://ec.europa.eu/economy_finance/publications/ publication16339_en.pdf.

OECD (2010a) OECD Economic surveys: Netherlands 2010, OECD. Retrieved from http://www.oecd.org/economy/economicsurveysandcountrysurveyllance/ economic sur veyofthenetherlands2010.htm.

OECD (2010b).Economic surveys and country surveillance, Economic Survey of the Netherlands 2010, OECD. Retrieved from http://www.oecd.org/eco/ economicsurveysandcountrysurveillance/economicsurveyofthenetherlands2010. htm.

OECD (2011). Country notes – Netherlands, Restoring Public Finances, OECD. Retrieved from http://www.oecd.org/dataoecd/36/15/47860186.pdf.

OECD (2012a).Economic Survey of the Netherlands 2012, OECD. Retrieved from http://www.oecd.org/eco/economicsurveyofthenetherlands2012.htm.

OECD (2012b). Economic policy reforms 2012: Going for growth, Netherlands: Country notes, OECD. Retrieved from http://www.oecd.org/netherlands/ 49655268.pdf.

OECD (2012c). Netherlands - Economic forecast summary (May 2012), OECD. Retrieved from http://www.oecd.org/netherlands/netherlands-economicforecastsummarymay2012.htm.

OECD (2012d). Netherlands: OECD better life index, OECD. Retrieved from in September 2012 http://www.oecdbetterlifeindex.org/countries/Netherlands/.

QFinance (n. d.). The Netherlands: Economy, QFinance. Retrieved from http://www. qfi-nance.com/country-profiles/the-netherlands.

Rabobank (2012). Outlook 2012: How resilient is the economy? Rabo-bank, the Netherlands. Retrieved from http://www.rabobank.com/content/images/ Outlook2012EN_tcm43-153694.pdf.

Reavis, C. (2009). The global financial crisis of 2008-2009: The role of greed, fear andoligarchs, *MIT Sloan Management Case #09-093,* published 2009.07.22.

Schwab, K. (Eds.) (2011). *The global competitiveness report 2011-2012.*Geneva: World Economic Forum.

Ståhle, P. and Pöyhönen, A. (2005) 'Intellectual capital and national competitiveness: a critical examination. Case Finland', *Proceedings of the 6th European Conference of Knowledge Management (ECKM)*, University of Limerick, Limerick.

Stewart, T. A. (1997). *Intellectual Capital: The new wealth of organizations*. New York: Nicholas Brealey.

U. S. Department of State (March 22, 2012). Background Note: *The Netherlands, Bureau of European and Eurasian Affairs, U. S.* Department of State: Diplomacy in action. Retrieved from http://www.state.gov/r/pa/ei/bgn/3204.htm.

In: Progress in Economics Research. Volume 27   ISBN: 978-1-62808-201-2
Editor: A. Tavidze   © 2013 Nova Science Publishers, Inc.

Chapter 4

A NEW TWO-STAGE MODEL AND MONEY FLOWS: THE EXPERIENCE OF CHINA'S STOCK MARKET

Chengying He[1,2], Yingqing Gong[2] and Haiping Lan[2]
[1]Zhejiang University of Finance and Economics, Hangzhou, China
[2]Guosen Securities Co. Ltd, Shenzhen, China

Abstract

The direction and calculation of stock markets' money flows is one of the most difficult problems in financial engineering. Based on existing methods of money flows, this paper proposes a new two-stage model, by which we build an index system, and then empirically analyze the money flows of China's stock market. The results show that, the ratio of net money inflow to outflow in the bull market is above 2.3, and the ratio of net money outflow to inflow in the bear market is above 1.3; the ratio of net inflow to outflow is above 1.78 in the high-growth industries, and the ratio of net outflow to inflow is above 1.54 in the low-growth industries; With respect to individual stock, the ratio of net inflow to outflow over 2 is a high-growth stock. This study also find that the net money flows of past 10 days, 20 days and 30 days have a significant role in the prediction of net money flows for the next 10 days, 20 days and 30 days.

Keywords: Two-stage model, Money flow, China's stock market, Index system

1. Introduction

As a common technical index in stock market, money flow has been studied for a long time. Welles Wilder first published money flow index (MFI) in Stock Commodities magazine in 1989, he used the indicators to measure the money and the pulsation of the market. His theory is that, when MFI indicator is higher than 80 the market is in overbought zone, it may reverse and should be selling; when MFI indicator is lower than 20 the market is in oversold zone, it may reverse and should be buying. When MFI close to 50 that means there are no obvious trends in the market. The Wall Street daily first reported the top 30 stocks of net money inflow or net money outflow from daily market in October 1998. Besides, more and more financial web-site began to provide the data of money flow basing on their respective calculation method.

Money flow as a technical index has been widely used in the practical stock market. Although stock analysts focused on statistics of daily or weekly money flow, and published the trend of market and presented their point of view on newspaper and economy media, these researches, however, were much more from the aspect of exchange quantity in the existing literature. Scholars study mostly from four aspects to find the relationship between exchange quantity and other variables: quantity and price of stock(Chen et al,2002; Cai et al., 2006; Huang and Ting, 2008), exchange quantity and gain of shares (Ning and Wirjanto,2009), exchange quantity and running trend (Chordia and Swaminathan, 2000; Glaser and Weber, 2009; Emawtee and Brooks, 2010), and exchange quantity and the fluctuation in price of stock (Wu and Xu, 2002; Tay and Ting, 2006).

Some scholars also directly measure the money flow from aspect of quantity to. Such as, Kim (2000) discovered the uneven stocks order which had negative effect to shares gain forecast used the data of money flow. Bennett and Sias (2001) discovered the money flow positive relate with rate of year return, and the historical data of money flow could predict the money flow in future. But Chan and Lakonishok (1995) also think money flow has positive correlation with historical gain. Frazzini and Lamont (2008) used the flow of Mutual Funds to evaluate the emotion of individual investor and they found high spirits would lead to low gain of shares in future. Campbell and Ramadorai (2009) believed institutions day orders have negative effects to the gain of stock in future, especially the negative effect of institution offering orders to stock gain in future. Li Gao and Weidong Fan (2002) estimate the money flow of China's stock market, analyze the source of money flow in the market, money inflow distribution structure, money use efficiency of the money inflow in the stock market and flow change the macro money structure, which influence the different macroeconomic market behavior. Liuqi Lang (2008) studied the computer auxiliary analysis system in securities trading money flow from the aspect of computing engineering, and he proposed a main method of market trend discovery system from money flow.

However, researches about money flow were mostly focus on the money's effect on stock market's fluctuation. In fact, the result from existing different kinds of calculation methods were big different, which brought doubt to the measurement of money flow in accurate and practical using. Money flow is the result of positive money selection in the stock market, which not only reflects the action model of the investor, but also indicates the change of the stock price in future. Hence, money flow as a direction has been needed in actual operation in stock market. Complying with the above money flow methodology, this article will ameliorate and accomplish existing calculation methods of money flow, separate the money flow as two processes of direction conformation and quantity conformation, primarily promote a theoretical second stage model of money flow, composite the index system and empirically study the relationship of money flow with stocks return rate in the past bull or bear market. In the second stage money flow theory model, we use the Queue Theory and Expected Utility Function to explain the confirmation of the direction and the quantity of money flow. Comparing with existing calculative theory of money flow, our model not only over-all consider the whole process of money flow, but also have a more scientific and practical calculation method.

In this paper, section 2 proposed two-stage money flows model basing on the money flows experienced two stages of amount and direction, and build the index system of calculation of money flows. Section 3 empirically studies the relationship of money flow and the stock returns by using the money flows data calculated by our two-stage model. Section 4 demonstrates the reasonableness of the money flow indicators counted by the two-stage model, and the section is summary and conclusions.

2. Two-Stage Money Flow Model and Its Index System

In the security market, money is the source of the trade chain. Money inflow or money outflow means excess demand or oversupply of the stock market. The change of money flow reflects the transformation of excess demand or over supply.

In general, there are two situations of the money flow: One is the total quantity of money has changed, that means many from outside is flow in or flow out; the other situation is the change of money structure, that means the money of the stock market flow in different industry and stocks.

There are two main money flow calculation method in present, the first method deduce the money inflow or money outflow basing on the price change of the market, that is to say to judge the direction of money flow basing on the market price, that means if the trade price at present time or present interval is rise comparing with the time or the interval before, the money is inflow, otherwise out flow. The second method judge the money inflow or outflow basing on the power between buyer and seller, that is to say judge money inflow or money outflow by calculating the comparative power of initiative buyer with initiative seller, that means if initiative buyers are willing to buy the stock in a higher price the money is inflow; otherwise is outflow. In current, the first method is used by most financial web-sites, such as Wall Street journal, Great wisdom, Sina Financial, Fenghuang Financial etc. Only a few web-sites like Hexun use the second method.

Intuitively speaking, the second calculation method has some defect, because initiative sellers and initiative buyers cannot reflect the strength of the buyers or sellers in the actual transaction. At same time, these two kinds of calculation method only confirm the money flow from one aspect and neglect the necessary of direction confirmation of money flow before quantity confirmation. According to this, the paper advances the two-stage money flow theory and built the money flow index system basing on queue theory.

2.1. Two-Stage Money Flow Model

Money flow of the stock market includes two stages: one is direction confirmation and the other is quantity confirmation. On the first stage, the direction of the money flow is confirmed according to the successfully confirmation of the process of stock trading and the direction of orders basing on the queue theory.

On the second stage, the quantity of the money flow is confirmed according to the statistics results of money flow after the confirmation of the money flow direction basing the efficiency function of the individual investor and institutional investors. The details are as follow:

First Stage: Direction Confirmation of Money Flow

Direction confirmation is based on the successfully trade process of stock, for the market have real money flow only after stock successfully trade, after which it is possible to confirm and judge the direction of the money flow.

According to the practically trade experience in securities market of our country, the principle of order matching and deal reaching are follow the rules of price priority and time priority: committee to buy orders with high prices are prior to that with low price, and committee to sell order with low price orders are prior to that with high price. (2) Committee to sell order with low price orders is prior to the one with high price when the direction and price of the buyer and seller are the same. (3) matching principle of committee to buy order and sell order follow rules of (1)and (2).(4) match processing of buy and sell orders get into the interval after the finish of successfully matching of the order until a new order matching of buy and sell. (5) complete each trade process following the rules of (1), (2), (3) and (4).

Suppose the T in the interval obeys Poisson distribution with parameters λ, the T and its probability density function given by random decomposition results. Hypotheses the time of matching buy orders with sell orders S is a nonnegative random variable with average of $\frac{1}{\mu}$, and it is a generalized distribution function $G(x)$. Hypotheses the T during the interval is a generalized distribution function $G^*(x)$, trading break time V and trading close time C respectively are distribution function of $V(x)$ and $C(x)$, the T during the interval of trading break time V and trading close time C are $V^*(x)\,T$ and $C^*(s)\,T$ respectively. T, S, V and C are independent, and obey the treatment principle of time priority and price priority.

Suppose there are Q_{bt} buying orders in line who want to buy the stocks with price P_t, and it enter into the time of $t+1$ after successfully matching under the current price. In the time of $t+1$, there are $L_{n(t+1)}$ buying orders in line to buy the stocks with the price of P_{t+1} ($P_{t+1} \le P_t$ or $P_{t+1} \ge P_t$), in which the buying order is $L_n\{n \ge 1\}$. So, in the time of $t+n$, there are $L_{n(t+n)}$ buying orders in line to buy the orders with price P_{t+n} ($P_{t+n} \le P_t$, P_{t+1}, ..., P_{t+n-1}; or $P_{t+n} \ge P_t$, P_{t+1}, ..., P_{t+n-1}). Hypotheses trading process in time t completed follow the rules, embed Markov chain when leave, at leaving time, and then prepare to enter the trading process of moment $t+1$.

In the queue of Q_{bt} buying orders, the system deal with j orders by trade rules, the probability of dealing with is b_j, and then b_j is:

$$b_j = P(Q_{bt} = j) = \begin{cases} 1 - c_0 + c_0 \dfrac{v_j}{1 - v_0}, j = 1 \\ c_0 \dfrac{v_j}{1 - v_0}, j \geq 2 \end{cases} \tag{1}$$

Among which c_0 and v_0 are :

$$\begin{cases} v_j = \displaystyle\int_0^\infty \dfrac{(\lambda t)^j}{j!} e^{-\lambda t} dv(t), j \geq 0 \\ c_0 = \displaystyle\int_0^\infty e^{-\lambda t} dC(t) = C^*(\lambda), c_1 = 1 - c_0 \end{cases} \tag{2}$$

According to function (2), when $j = 0$, $v_j = \displaystyle\int_0^\infty e^{-\lambda t} dv(t) = v^*(\lambda)$. Hence, the transition probability matrix of Markov chain $\{L_n, n \geq 1\}$ is:

$$\overset{\bullet}{P} = \begin{vmatrix} k_0 & k_1 & k_2 & K \\ a_0 & a_1 & a_2 & K \\ & a_0 & a_1 & K \\ & & M & M \end{vmatrix} \tag{3}$$

In which, $k_j = P(Q_{bt} - 1 + A = j) = \displaystyle\sum_{i=1}^{j+1} b_i a_{j+1-i}, j \geq 0$, A means the queue that arrived during the match time S, and the probability distribution function is $a_j = \displaystyle\int_0^\infty \dfrac{(\lambda t)^j}{j!} e^{-\lambda t} dG(t)$. According to Foster principle, when and only when $\rho = \lambda \mu^{-1} < 1$, Markov chain $\{L_n, n \geq 1\}$ is positive cycle. When $\rho = \lambda \mu^{-1} < 1$, the probability generating function $Q_{bt}(z)$ and mean function $E(Q_{bt})$ of queue Q_{bt} at t are:

$$Q_{bt}(z) = z \left[1 - C^*(\lambda) + C^*(\lambda) \frac{v_1}{1 - v^*(\lambda)} \right] + \sum_{j=2}^{\infty} C^*(\lambda) v_j z^j$$

$$= z(1 - C^*(\lambda)) + C^*(\lambda) \sum_{j=1}^{\infty} C^*(\lambda) v_j z^j \qquad (4)$$

$$= z(1 - C^*(\lambda)) \frac{C^*(\lambda)}{1 - v^*(\lambda)} \left[v^*(\lambda(1-z)) - v^*(\lambda) \right]$$

$$E(Q_{bt}) = 1 - C^*(\lambda) + \frac{\lambda C^*(\lambda) E(V)}{1 - v^*(\lambda)} \qquad (5)$$

At $t+1$, the length of buying orders queue $L_{v(t+1)}$ in the market is constructed by the queue $L_{(t+1)}$ processed by the trading rules and the addition queue length $L_{d(t+1)}$ entered latterly, that means $L_{v(t+1)} = L_{(t+1)} + L_{d(t+1)}$. Among them, $L_{(t+1)}$, $L_{d(t+1)}$ are independent random variables. According to $M^X/G/1$ queue model and the marginal state change theory (*Xu et al., 2007*), it can be concluded that function (6) is,

$$L_{d(t+1)}(z) = \frac{1 - z(1 - C^*(\lambda)) - \dfrac{C^*(\lambda)}{1 - v^*(\lambda)} \left[v^*(\lambda(1-z)) - v^*(\lambda) \right]}{\beta(1-z)} \qquad (6)$$

In (6), $\beta = 1 - C^*(\lambda) + \dfrac{\lambda C^*(\lambda) E(V)}{1 - v^*(\lambda)}$

According to stochastic decomposition results, Equation(5), Equation(6) and $L_{(t+1)}(z) = \dfrac{(1-\rho)(1-z)\beta^*(\lambda(1-z))}{\beta^*(\lambda(1-z)) - z}$, probability generating function variable of additional queue length $L_{d(t+1)}$ is:

$$L_{d(t+1)}(z) = \frac{1-C^*(\lambda)}{\beta} + \frac{\lambda C^*(\lambda)E(V)}{\beta(1-v^*(\lambda))} \frac{1-v^*(\lambda(1-z))}{\lambda E(V)(1-z)} \qquad (7)$$

From the Equation (7), the length of additional queue $L_{d(t+1)}$ is zero when the probability is $\dfrac{1-C^*(\lambda)}{\beta}$, and it is the length of additional queue arrived in the rest relax time V_r when the probability is $\dfrac{\dfrac{1}{1-v^*(\lambda)}\lambda C^*(\lambda)E(V)}{\beta}$.

According to the L'Hospital rules, the average length of buying order queue $L_{v(t+1)}$ and additional queue $L_{d(t+1)}$ at $t+1$ are:

$$E(L_{d(t+1)}) = L'_{d(t+1)}$$

$$= \lim_{z \to 1} \frac{1}{\beta(1-z)^2} \left[\begin{array}{l} \dfrac{\lambda C^*(\lambda)}{1-v^*(\lambda)}v^*(\lambda(1-z)) - (1-C^*(\lambda)) + \\[2mm] 1 - z(1-C^*(\lambda)) - \dfrac{C^*(\lambda)}{1-v^*(\lambda)}v^*(\lambda(1-z)) - v^*(\lambda) \end{array} \right] \qquad (8)$$

$$= \lim_{z \to 1} \frac{\lambda^2 C^*(\lambda)}{2\beta(1-v^*(\lambda))}v^*(\lambda(1-z))$$

$$= \frac{\lambda^2 C^*(\lambda)E[(V-1)]}{2\beta(1-v^*(\lambda))}$$

$$E[L_{v(t+1)}] = \frac{\lambda^2 C^*(\lambda)E[V(V-1)]}{2\beta(1-v^*(\lambda))} + \frac{\lambda b^{(2)}}{2(1-\rho)} \qquad (9)$$

Analyzing the stock trade process and the direction of money flow at successful time t, $t+1$ and $t+n$ according to the queue theory of price priority and time priority, the direction of the money flow is relate to the stock trading price P_t, P_{t+1}, ..., P_{t+n}. The direction of the money flow includes three ways: inflow, outflow or neither. When compare trading price P_{t+1} in $t+1$ with price

P_t in t, if $P_{t+1} > P_t$, that means money inflow; If $P_{t+1} < P_t$, that means money outflow. If $P_{t+1} = P_t$, it means neither money flows in nor out.

The Second Stage: Quantity Confirms

There are two kinds of investors in the stock market, individual investors and institutional investors, and the latter one include administration department, financial institutions, enterprises and all kinds of fund. Therefore, the investors participating in stock trading include both individual and institutional investors in this paper.

Individual investors and institutional investors have the same possibility to buy or sell stocks in t, that means the buy and sell orders may be committed by either individual or institutional investor.

Thus, there are four trade situations in this matching process of "buy-sell sheet": "individual investors buying orders-individual investors selling orders, individual investors buying orders-institutional investors selling orders, institutional investors buying orders- institutional investors selling orders and institutional investors buying orders-individual selling orders". Hypothesis the probability of individual investors buy the shares is ε, and the probability of institutional investors buy the shares is η, then they probability of selling the shares are $1-\varepsilon$ and $1-\eta$ respectively. From Table1, the probabilities of four trading situation in t are $\varepsilon(1-\varepsilon)$, $\varepsilon(1-\eta)$, $\eta(1-\eta)$ and $\eta(1-\varepsilon)$ respectively, where $\varepsilon(1-\varepsilon)+\varepsilon(1-\eta)+\eta(1-\eta)+\eta(1-\varepsilon)=1$.

Hypothesis individual investors have the same risk preference, information and transaction mode. According to the hypothesizing, individual investors' expected utility function in the moment $t+1$ are $E_{t+1}^{S}\left[-e^{-M_{T+1}^{S}}\right]$, in which $E[\cdot]$ is the conditional variances in the moment t. $T+1$ is the deadline of the target, M is the individual investors' money invest in the market, and S are individual investors. Suppose the individual investors' money invest in the market are $k \times M_t^{S}$ in which $0 \le k \le 1$, k is the rate of money invest in the stock market. If the individual investor's increased (decreased) money from the stock trading in $t+1$ are ΔM_{t+1}^{S}, compare his money ΔM_t^{S} in t his expect incomes in $T+1$ is $\left[\Delta M_{t+1}^{S} + k \times M_t^{S} - \Delta M_t^{S}\right] - k \times M_t^{S}$, simplify as $\Delta M_{t+1}^{S} - \Delta M_t^{S}$. Therefore, individual investors' expect utility function of incomes in moment $T+1$ are $E_{t+1}^{S}[e^{-(\Delta M_{t+1}^{S}-\Delta M_{t}^{S})}]$.

Individual investor need to maximize his expected utility by transaction process, the first order condition of his expected utility function is $M_{t+1}^{S}=\dfrac{\mu_{t+1}^{S}-\Delta M_{t+1}^{S}}{\sigma^{2}}$, from which, the individual investor's money M_{t}^{S} of having stocks depends on the acquirement of money volume μ_{t+1}^{S} form expected trade and acquirement of money volume ΔM_{t+1}^{S} form actual trade. The higher the expected returns on investment, the more money hold by individual investors, and the less of the probability of trading desire, the higher returns from trade, and the more probability of trading for individual investors.

Table 1. Four Stock Trade Situations

	Individual investor's probability of buying the shares ε	Institutional investor's probability of buying the shares η
Individual investor's probability of selling the shares $1-\varepsilon$	$\varepsilon(1-\varepsilon)$	$\eta(1-\varepsilon)$
Institutional investor's probability of selling the shares $1-\eta$	$\varepsilon(1-\eta)$	$\eta(1-\eta)$

Institutional investors have two trading purposes: one is to control the price to confuse the public and make the price rise to the expected level, the other is to earn their expect profit (Bing Wang and Fengming Song, 2006).

In the opinion of individual investors, if a deal is following the intuitional investor's purpose of confusing the public, then the deal itself does not contain the information of affecting the trend of stock price.

If a deal is following the purpose of making profit, the institutional investors will achieve the maximum expected returns from the trade, then the trade will become the signal of to the trend of the stock price. In the view of individual investors, the maximum expected profit of institutional investors is

$\max\limits_{M_t^Z} E[\mu_t^Z - M_t^Z]$, in which μ_t^Z is expected trade money volume, M_t^Z is actual

trade money volume, and M_t^Z is algebraic quantity with positive and negative sign, in which positive sign means money inflow, i.e. the institutional investors buying behavior, and negative sign means money outflow, i.e. the institutional investors selling behavior. When $\mu_t^Z > M_t^Z$, institutional investors choose money inflow. When $\mu_t^Z < M_t^Z$, institutional investors choose money outflow instead.

Suppose individual and institutional investors incline to maximize their profit., when there are π traders (included individual investors and institutional investors) consider $\sum\limits_{\pi}{}' \mu_{t+1} > \sum\limits_{\pi}{}' M_{t+1}$ in $t+1$, and the actual trade price

$P_{t+1} > P_t$, it will be calculated as the money outflow. When there are θ traders consider $\sum\limits_{\theta}{}' \mu_{t+1} > \sum\limits_{\theta}{}' M_{t+1}$ and the actual trade price $P_{t+1} < P_t$, it will be calculated as the money inflow.

When there are τ traders consider $\sum\limits_{\tau}{}' \mu_{t+1} > \sum\limits_{\tau}{}' M_{t+1}$ and the actual trade

price $P_{t+1} = P_t$, it will be calculated as money neither inflow nor outflow, and will not be included in the calculation of money flows, basing on that, calculate the quantity of money inflows and money outflows according to the statistics of money inflows or outflows in every moment.

2.2. Building of Money Flows Index System

Among three directions of money flow, only money inflow and money outflow have significant effect to the direction of the securities market. Therefore, we could divide money flows into the directions of money inflows and money outflows according to the two-stage theoretical model, and build the index system. The money flows index system includes absolute indexes and relative indexes. Absolute indexes includes the amount of money inflow/outflow, the net amount and the accumulate amount of money inflow/outflow. The relative index includes relative money inflows/outflows and the rate of money net inflow to outflow. (See table 2)

Table 2. Index system of money flow

Money Flow Index		Method of Calculation
Absolute index	Amount of money inflow	money inflow $\sum_{1}^{t} M_t^I$ calculated according to $\sum_{\pi}^{'} \mu_t > \sum_{\pi}^{'} M_t$ and transaction price $P_t > P_{t-1}$,
	Amount of money outflow	money outflow $\sum_{1}^{t} M_t^E$ calculated according to $\sum_{\pi}^{'} \mu_t < \sum_{\pi}^{'} M_t$ and transaction price $P_t < P_{t-1}$
	Net money inflow	When $\sum_{1}^{t} M_t^I > \sum_{1}^{t} M_t^E$, net money inflow is $\sum_{1}^{t} M_t^I - \sum_{1}^{t} M_t^E$
	Net money outflow	When $\sum_{1}^{t} M_t^I < \sum_{1}^{t} M_t^E$, net money inflow is $\sum_{1}^{t} M_t^E - \sum_{1}^{t} M_t^I$
	Accumulate net money inflow	The sum of money inflow in N days is $\sum_{N} \left(\sum_{1}^{t} M_t^I - \sum_{1}^{t} M_t^E \right)$
	Accumulate net money outflow	The sum of money inflow in N days is $\sum_{N} \left(\sum_{1}^{t} M_t^E - \sum_{1}^{t} M_t^I \right)$

Table 2. (Continued)

Money Flow Index		Method of Calculation
Relative index	Relative money inflow	The rate of net money inflow to market moneyization $\dfrac{\sum\limits_{1}^{t} M_t^I - \sum\limits_{1}^{t} M_t^E}{MV}$, MV represent marke0t moneyization
	Relative money outflow	The rate of net money outflow to market moneyization $\dfrac{\sum\limits_{1}^{t} M_t^E - \sum\limits_{1}^{t} M_t^I}{MV}$
	Rate of money inflow	The rate of net money inflow to money inflow $\dfrac{\sum\limits_{1}^{t} M_t^I - \sum\limits_{1}^{t} M_t^E}{\sum\limits_{1}^{t} M_t^I}$
	Rate of money outflow	The rate of net money outflow to money outflow $\dfrac{\sum\limits_{1}^{t} M_t^E - \sum\limits_{1}^{t} M_t^I}{\sum\limits_{1}^{t} M_t^E}$

3. Empirical Analysis of China Stock Market

For the second-stage money flow model, different transaction data sets indeed will lead to different results. In general, we can use the mostly common market data, i.e., Level-1, and Level-2 data sets for model estimations. Level-1 access presents real time bid/ask data with the lowest ask and highest bid every 6 seconds. Level-2 data provide 10 bid-ask quotes one by one separately every 3 seconds. The results we present here use Level-1 data sets for the second-stage money flow model estimation. The overall money flow index ranges from December 19th, 1990 to April 15th, 2010. We then carry out statistical analysis on the money flow index for different market situations, i.e, bull or bear markets, various industry sectors and individual stocks. In the end, we further study empirically the prediction power of the money flow index and its relation with stock return rate.

3.1. Statistical Characteristics of Markets' Money Flows

China stock market has been operated for over twenty years since December 19th 1990. We then classify the different market states according to its performance as five bull markets and five bear markets for our further analysis as shown in Table 3.

Table 3. Bull and Bear Markets of China Stock Market

Bull Markets	Bear Markets
1st （1990.12.19~1992.5.25）	1st （1992.5.26~1996.01.17）
2nd （1996.01.18~1997.05.12）	2nd （1997.05.13~1999.05.18）
3rd （1999.05.19~2001.06.13）	3rd （2001.06.14~2005.6.3）
4th （2005.06.06~2007.10.16）	4th （2007.10.17~2008.10.27）
5th （2008.10.28~2009.8.4）	5th (2009.08.05~2010.4.15)

Table 4. Money flows for bull markets

	Inflow/Outflow	Sampling Days	Min	Max	Average
1st Bull Market	Inflow （100 M）	358	0.00065	1.133	0.052
	Outflow （100 M）	358	0.00001	1.09	0.049
	Net Inflow （100 M）	275	0.0000	0.088	0.005
	Net Outflow （100 M）	83	0.041	0.062	0.006
2nd Bull Market	Inflow （100 M）	315	0.608	114.721	27.373
	Outflow （100 M）	315	0.603	107.992	23.666
	Net Inflow (100 M)	211	0.010	41.253	6.962
	Net Outflow (100 M)	104	0.026	2.987	2.987
3rd Bull Market	Inflow (100 M)	497	8.541	248.366	65.015
	Outflow (100 M)	497	10.616	250.722	57.824
	Net Inflow (100 M)	300	0.306	90.728	17.582
	Net Outflow (100 M)	197	0.061	39.276	8.633
4th Bull Market	Inflow (100 M)	575	4.873	1489.512	309.786
	Outflow (100 M)	575	15.257	1223.429	258.386
	Net Inflow (100 M)	434	0.140	346.669	79.127
	Net Outflow (100 M)	141	0.149	174.787	33.942
5th Bull Market	Inflow (100 M)	190	102.630	1567.533	652.961
	Outflow (100 M)	190	109.052	1401.724	542.638
	Net Inflow (100 M)	140	7.772	613.348	180.087
	Net Outflow (100 M)	50	5.981	201.630	85.013

At the early stage, there were only several stocks for trading in the secondary market. Which leads to serious out-of-balance between supply and demand? As a result, the stock prices rose up sharply in the first two years.

At the first bull market stage, there were net money inflow and net money outflow per day in the market with both small absolute values. With the market gradually expanded, the corporations listed increased. Thus, more and more money flew into the market and the trading volume gradually increased.

Especially after 2000, the entire money flow increased obviously, and the trading days of net money flow more than 10 billion Yuan appeared and increased. At the fifth bull market and fifth bear market, the net money inflow and outflow reach the historical maximum. We then summarize results in Table 4 and Table 5.

Table 5. Money flows for bear markets

	Inflow/Outflow	Sampling Days	Min	Max	Average
1st Bear Market	Inflow (100 M)	916	0.215	97.209	6.094
	Outflow (100 M)	916	0.201	63.213	6.149
	Net Inflow (100 M)	367	0.000	36.882	1.596
	Net Outflow (100 M)	549	0.000	25.104	1.159
2nd Bear Market	Inflow (100 M)	491	4.910	69.689	24.386
	Outflow (100 M)	491	6.075	66.779	23.273
	Net Inflow (100 M)	225	0.017	13.415	4.305
	Net Outflow (100 M)	266	0.000	21.756	5.695
3rd Bear Market	Inflow (100 M)	952	3.744	259.499	42.453
	Outflow (100 M)	952	13.185	235.299	42.579
	Net Inflow (100 M)	381	0.010	107.992	14.532
	Net Outflow (100 M)	571	0.004	44.812	9.906
4th Bear Market	Inflow (100 M)	252	78.828	988.560	390.946
	Outflow (100 M)	252	135.050	964.909	403.368
	Net Inflow (100 M)	91	0.166	219.521	62.217
	Net Outflow (100 M)	162	0.029	194.608	54.272
5th Bear Market	Inflow (100 M)	169	309.254	1417.634	696.426
	Outflow (100 M)	169	281.483	1491.415	671.851
	Net Inflow (100 M)	98	0.389	298.625	124.819
	Net Outflow (100 M)	71	4.899	338.803	113.790

3.2. Money Flow of Industry Sectors

As shown in Figure 1 the industry distribution chart for the money flow of past bull markets, the average net money inflow index of all sectors are lower than 0.2.

The net money inflow index of the mechanical equipment sector, petrochemical industry and real estate industry are relatively higher while the extractive industry, building industry and agriculture animal husbandry are under 0.05. Under the bull market there is a net money inflow for all industries but the net money inflow indexes are different among sectors. The difference among the sectors' net money inflow leads to the different interval growth rate of each sector. The change of money inflow index of each sector for past bull markets show the overall performance and the characteristics of the hotspot change of each industry.

From the money flow of past bear markets of different industries' distribution chart, the average net money outflow index of all industries are lower than 0.18. The money flows out from the mechanical equipment sector; petrochemical industry and real estate industry are relatively lower while the net money outflow rate of the extractive industry, building industry and agriculture animal husbandry are under 0.025. Under the bear markets there is a net money outflow for all industries but the net money outflow indexes are different among sectors.

This difference of net money outflow leads to the different interval collapse rate of each sector. The change of money outflow index of each industry for past bear markets shows the evaluation of the market to the industry.

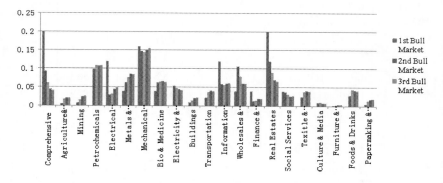

Figure 1. Distribution of net inflow across sectors for bull markets.

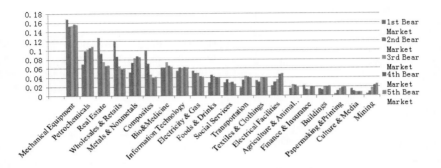

Figure 2. Distribution of net outflow across sectors for bear markets.

As the total market values of each industry are different, it is improper to compare absolute value for the money flow between sectors. In order to analyze the industry's distribution of money flow, we use relative net money inflow index to evaluate the situation of money flow of the industries and statistic the industries which has the highest net money inflow/outflow in the past bull/bear markets. For the past bull markets, the average relative net money inflow is 0.0242 and the rate of net money inflow, is 1.78 and the cumulative net money inflow is 97.555 billion RMB, and the relative net money inflow is 0.045 for the real estate sector during the 5th bull market (see Table 6). For the past bear markets, the average relative net money outflow is 0.0246,while the cumulative net money outflow of the real estate sector is 98.035 billion RMB, and the relative net money inflow is 0.055 for the 4th bear market (see Table 7).

Table 6. Net money flow in past bull markets and sectors

Stages	Industry	The rate of net money inflow and money outflow	Cumulative net money inflow (00,000,000)	Average relative net money inflow
The 1st bull market	Comprehensive	1.83	0.43	0.004
The 2nd bull market	Metal and non-metal	1.73	100.73	0.009
The 3rd bull market	Fossil fuel, chemical, plastic	2.18	320.81	0.028
The 4th bull market	Machine, equipment, instrument	1.65	780.85	0.035
The 5th bull market	Real estate	1.78	975.55	0.045

Table 7. Net money flow in past bear markets and sectors

Stages	Industry	The rate of net money inflow and money outflow	Cumulative net money inflow (00,000,000)	Average relative net money inflow
The 1st bear market	Machine, equipment, instrument	1.54	0.67	0.003
The 2nd bear market	Pharmaceutical biology	1.67	113.27	0.007
The 3rd bear market	Metal and non-metal	2.18	390.81	0.023
The 4th bear market	Real estate	2.78	980.35	0.055
The 5th bear market	Fossil fuel, chemical, plastic	1.76	578.46	0.035

3.3. Individual Stocks' Money Flow and Return Rate

Based on above analysis of money flows for past bull and bear markets, it clearly shows that net money inflows and cumulative net money inflows push up the markets and industry indexes, and net money outflows and cumulative net money outflows cause the market and industry index down. Intuitively, there is a certain relation between money flows and the stock market performance. Whether this relation holds in the future? What is the relation between money flows and stocks' return rate? Based on the model of Bennett and Sias (2001) for money flows and stocks return rate, we then have regression functions for a large sample analysis:

$$NMF_{t+f,i} = \beta_0 + \beta_1 NMF_{t-b,i} + \beta_2 R_{t-b,i} + \varepsilon_i \qquad (10)$$

$$R_{t+f,i} = \beta_0 + \beta_3 NMF_{t-b,i} + \beta_4 R_{t-b,i} + \varepsilon_i \qquad (11)$$

where $NMF_{t+f,i}$ is the relative accumulation of net money inflows/outflows of the stocks i in the future $(t+f)$ days., $R_{t-b,i}$ is the relative accumulation of net money inflows/outflows of the stocks i in the past $(t-b)$ days. $R_{t+f,i}$ is the relative accumulation of return rate of the stocks i in the future $(t+f)$ days.

Table 8. Past and future net money flows/Stock returns

	Full samples				Bull market samples				Bear market samples			
	Equation (10)		Equation (11)		Equation(10)		Equation (11)		Equation(10)		Equation(11)	
Average index	0.080	-0.305	0.002	-0.021	0.087	-0.236	0.003	-0.031	0.078	-0.327	0.004	-0.043
Positive index%	75	20	28	55	90	27	35	51	87	23	25	45
Significance level%	61	7	12	52	69	11	15	49	64	13	12	41
Adjusted mean	0.67%		0.58%		0.97%		0.47%		0.82%		0.49%	
Average index	0.173	-0.015	0.022	-0.018	0.236	-0.010	0.027	-0.002	0.210	-0.018	0.026	-0.019
Positive index%	97	27	39	45	100	29	44	48	99	25	38	43
Significance level%	95	15	21	47	99	17	28	55	99	21	23	47
Adjusted mean	2.58%		0.51%		4.15%		0.59%		3.23%		0.43%	
Average index	0.214	-0.009	0.039	-0.006	0.264	-0.008	0.031	-0.008	0.234	-0.010	0.026	-0.008
Positive index%	98	31	47	56	100	36	37	43	99	32	41	41
Significance level%	99	33	17	45	100	41	26	38	100	34	18	39
Adjusted mean	5.75%		0.45%		6.42%		0.51%		6.26%		0.41%	
Average index	0.377	-0.006	0.031	-0.004	0.416	-0.006	0.038	-0.004	0.413	-0.008	0.032	-0.003
Positive index%	100	37	56	43	100	41	61	52	100	39	57	43
Significance level%	100	42	19	51	100	45	25	45	100	43	21	39
Adjusted mean	10.56%		0.67%		12.16%		0.83%		11.35%		0.72%	
Average index	0.407	-0.004	0.032	-0.003	0.451	-0.004	0.037	-0.003	0.457	-0.005	0.038	-0.003
Positive index%	100	45	63	47	100	48	61	56	100	41	57	51
Significance level%	100	51	25	54	100	53	23	49	100	46	21	47
Adjusted mean	15.13%		1.14%		16.25%		1.29%		15.76%		1.05%	

$R_{t-b,i}$ is the relative accumulation of return rate of the stocks i in the past $(t-b)$ days. The residual is ε_i, where f and b were taken 1 day, 5days, 10days, 20days and 30day. Therefore, our results are shown in Table 3, where f and b are (1,1), (5,5), (10,10), (20, 20) and (30, 30) respectively.

The regression results clearly show that the past net money flows have a predictive power for the future net money flows. Past net money flows of 10days, 20days and 30days have positive relations with future net money flows in 10 days, 20days and 30days (Of 99% significant level). It means that a stock with higher past net money flows should keep higher net money flows in future, while a stock with lower past net money flows should keep low net money flows in future.

The average autocorrelation coefficient of money flows gradually increases and becomes more and more significant. In the meantime, adjustment R^2 also gradually increases if it increases in past days. From the future stock return rate and the net money flow of regression result (Equation(11)), it can be found that the future stock return rate and past money flows has a positive relation (coefficient β_3). The stock return rate in future 5 days, 10 days 20 days positively depends on the money flow past 5days, 10days and 20 days. It means that the continuous net money outflows in the past will engender negative stock return rate although this positive relation is not significant as shown in Table 3. The results show that the more days of past money flows in, the more highly autocorrelation relation and significant level of money flows are. But the relation of future money flow and past stock return rate (coefficient β_2), future stock return rate and past stock return rate (coefficient β_4) are not significant.

Conclusion

Money flow is an important momentum index that people cares very much in stock market, which not only shows the investors' track but also largely indicates the change of the stock price in the future, because it could reflects the excess demand and supply in current and future stock as well. The estimation of money flow plays a critical role in both the trend of stock market analysis and individual stocks operation. In the three directions of money flow, only money inflow and outflow plays a key role in the direction choice of stock market. Money inflow indicates the excess demand of market for stocks, while money outflow means the excess supply of market for stocks. If there is consistent excess money demand or supply, then it will be excess net money inflow or outflow which will lead to the increase or decrease of stock price, in another word, the money flow is related to the return of stocks.

This paper firstly builds a two-stage money flow theoretical model, which principle is that the direction confirmation of the money flow on the first stage is basing on the confirmation of the stock trading process successfully completed by using the queuing theory and the orders direction judgment in the process of trading; and the quantity confirmation of the money flow on the second stage is basing on the statistics of the result of money flow direction after the confirmation of direction of money flow on the first stage by using the utility function of private investor and institutional private investor.

Use the money flow data calculated by the two-stage model as sample, mathematical process them in accordance with the absolute and relative money flow index built in this article, and then empirically analyze the money flows of China's stock market, the results show that, firstly, the direction of net money flows and the stock index of the entire market are basically the same, the accumulated money net inflow in the bull market promote the rise of the stock index, and the accumulated money net out flow in the bear market form stock index fell, the ratio of net money inflow to outflow in the bull market is above 2.3,and the ratio of net money outflow to inflow in the bear market is above 1.3; the average net inflows during the top of a bull market account 14.84% to the overall net inflows, and the average net outflows during the bottom of a bear market account 50.80% to the overall net outflows; Secondly, the ratio of net inflow to outflow is above 1.78 in the high-growth industries, and the ratio of net outflow to inflow is above 1.54 in the low-growth industries. With respect to an individual stock, the ratio of net inflow to outflow over 2 is a high-growth stock. The rate of net outflow of money and net money inflow in bull and bear markets are Significantly different from each industry sector, which Industry average net inflows in the bull market rate below 0.2 while the rate of net outflow of money in the bear market is below 0.18; This study also found that the net money flows of past 10 days, 20 days and 30 days have a significant role in the prediction of net money flows for the next 10 days, 20 days and 30 days. The historical net money flows are positively correlated to the future stock return, in another words, the past continued net money flows has positive impact on stock returns in the future, but the positive relationship is not significant.

From the empirical results, net money flow is sustainable, that is to say that those stock with the money flow direction of net inflow or outflow in history will keep net inflow or outflow in the future for some time . The money flows change of net inflow to net outflow can be seen as leading indicators of the stock trading.

For example, continuously 5 days' net money inflow followed by another 5 days, could be seen as the signal for stock exchange. Also, net money flow could predict the stock return to some degree, if history net money flow of the stocks is in/out; their future stock yield will be positive/negative. Though the prediction is not significant tested by large sample, it still has some reference value for investors. Let us say, when the net money inflow of stocks last for 10 days, it could be seen as the stock price will rise then investors could buy the stocks at the right time; it is the same in reverse. So investors can buy or sell the stocks according to the position of net money flow and the days it lasts.

References

Bennett, J.A., and Sias, R.W (2001). Can money flows predict stock returns? *Financial Analysts Journal,* 57, 64-77.

Cai, B.M., Cai, C.X., and Keasey, K(2006). Which trades move prices in emerging markets? Evidence from China's stock market. *Pacific-Basin Finance Journal,* 14,453-466.

Campbell, J.Y., Ramadorai, T., and Schwartz, A (2009). Caught on tape: Institutional trading, stock returns, and earnings announcements. *Journal of Financial Economics,* 92, 66-91.

Chan, K., and Lakonishok, J (1995). The Behavior of Stock Prices around Institutional Trades. *Journal of Finance,* 50, 1147-1174.

Chen J, Hong H, and Stein J (2002). Breadth of Ownership and Stock Returns. *Journal of Financial Economics,* 66, 71-205.

Chordia, T., and Swaminathan (2000). Trade volume and cross-autocorrelations in stock returns. *Journal of Finance,* 55,913-935.

Emawtee, B.B., and Brooks, R.D (2010). Does volume help in predicting stock returns? an analysis of the Australian market. *Research in International Business and Finance,* 24,146-157.

Frazzini, A., and Lamont, O.A (2008). Dumb money: Mutual fund flows and the cross-section of stock Returns. *Journal of Financial Economics,* 88,299-322.

Glaser, M., and Weber, M (2009). Which past returns affect trading volume? *Journal of Financial Markets,* 12, 1-31.

Huang, R.D., and Ting (2008), C. A functional approach to the price impact of stock trades and the implied true price. *Journal of Empirical Finance,* 15, 1-16.

Kim, Jung-Wook (2000). An analysis of the impact of trades on stock returns using money flow data. Harvard University paper.

Ning, C., and Wirjanto, T. S(2009). Extreme return–volume dependence in East-Asian stock markets: A copula approach. *Finance Research Letters,* 6(4), 202-209.

Qingzhen, Xu, and Xiaonan, Luo (2007). Continuous time M/G/1 queue with multiple vacations and server close-down time. *Journal of Computational Information Systems,*3(2), 753-757.

Tay, A.S., and Ting, C (2006). Intraday stock price, volume, and duration: a nonparametric conditional density analysis. *Empirical Economics*, 30, 827-842.

Wu, C.C., and Xu, X.Q(2002). Return volatility, trading imbalance and the information content of volume. *Reviews of Quantitative Finance and Accounting*, 14, 53-131.

In: Progress in Economics Research. Volume 27   ISBN: 978-1-62808-201-2
Editor: A. Tavidze   © 2013 Nova Science Publishers, Inc.

Chapter 5

DO THE RICH SAVE MORE? A REVISIT TO THE THEORIES OF THE CONSUMPTION FUNCTION

C. Simon Fan[*]
Department of Economics, Lingnan University,
Tuen Mun, Hong Kong

1. Introduction

Modern macroeconomic research on consumption/saving starts with Keynes (1936), who puts forward his well-known consumption function. The Keynesian consumption function can be written as follows,

$$C = a + bY$$

where C denotes consumption, Y denotes disposable income, a and b are both positive coefficient, and $0 < b < 1$. An important implication of the Keynesian consumption function is that saving rate increases with income. However, while this predication is consistent with cross-section evidence, it is not consistent with time-series evidence. For example, in a seminal contribution, Kuznets (1946) discovered that the saving rate in the United States was remarkably stable from 1869 to 1938, although people's income increased significantly over this

[*]E-mail address: fansimon@ln.edu.hk, Tel: 852-2616-7206, Fax: 852-2891-7940

period. Thus, the long-run consumption function implies that saving rate is constant with economic development. Indeed, a key assumption of the Solow growth model that the saving rate of an economy is constant with economic development (Solow, 1956).

More recently, an empirical contribution by Dynan, Skinner and Zeldes (2004) find a strong positive relationship between saving rates and lifetime income. This important empirical finding makes the old "consumption puzzle" more intriguing, because it shows that the average propensity to consume decreases not only with current income but also with lifetime income. This puzzle can be illustrated by the familiar international comparison of saving rates: If richer people have higher saving rates, why hasn't the United States, which has been the most wealthy nation in the world, had a higher saving rate than many much poorer countries?

The current paper attempts to provides a rigorous framework that helps resolve this puzzle. This model extends the related literature by examining individuals' intertemporal choices with the consideration of intergenerational interactions. This extension is empirically important because intergenerational transfers account for an important part of aggregate saving.[1] This chapter is based on the same essential idea as Fan (2006), but it develops a different model. Our model implies that an individual is more concerned about her offspring's well-being when the offspring's future mean income is lower. In a Markovian game framework, the model shows that the bequests from parents to children decrease with the mean income of future generations. Meanwhile, *ceteris paribus*, an individual's bequests to her children increase with her own wealth. Thus, the model has the following implications. First, at a given point in time, richer people have higher saving rates, because they are concerned that their children are likely to receive lower incomes than theirs. In other words, a household with higher lifetime income saves more in order to leave more bequests to its offspring, who are likely to be worse off. Second, over time, when an economy experiences economic growth and the mean income of the economy rises, individuals will reduce their bequests because their offspring are expected to be equally well off due to the economic growth. Consequently, the saving rate can be approximately constant over time if the impacts of the increase in one's lifetime income and the increase in her offspring's future mean income on her consumption cancel out each other. Thus, this model helps explain the consumption

---

[1] For example, see the surveys by Kotlikoff (1988) and Gale and Scholz (1994).

puzzle and reconcile the short-run and long-run consumption functions.

This paper is closely related to Fan (2006), who studied a model that aims to achieve the same purpose as the current paper. However, this paper builds on a model that is very different from Fan (2006). In Fan (2006), it is assumed that parents get utility from their children's future wealth. In contrast, the current paper is in line with Fan (2001), who assumes that parents get utility from the quality of their grandchildren as well as their children. Consequently, the current paper studies a framework in which intergenerational conflicts and intergenerational commonality co-exist. Thus, while it is based on the same essential idea of Fan (2006), this paper examines this important issue from a different angle from Fan (2006).

In what follows, Section 2 summarizes a framework on which the current model is based; Section 3 is the core of the paper, which examines the consumption functions both in the long run and in the short run and provides an explanation for the consumption puzzle; Section 4 further illustrates the intuition of the paper with an example; Section 5 offers the concluding remarks.

1.1. Models of Intergenerational Transfers

The most commonly used model of bequests is Barro (1974), who assumes that parents obtain utility from their children's utility. In fact, this altruism model is theoretically identical to the infinitely-lived "representative agent" model. However, despite its theoretical elegance, detailed empirical studies have consistently shown that the assumption that parents' utility depends on children's utility is not consistent with the observed evidence on intergenerational transfers.[2] In fact, it has been recognized that a problem of the "representative agent" model in explaining intergenerational interactions is that it implies that there is no intergenerational conflict.

The statistical rejections of the predominant model of altruism stimulated the development of other theories of bequests. For example, Pollak (1988) and Chu (1991) argue that altruism can be better understood from *paternalistic* and evolutionary perspectives. Pollak (1988) suggests an interesting idea that parents' utility depends on the pattern of their children's consumption. For example, he observes that most parents in the U.S. are willing to spend money on children's college education and are willing to provide some of the down pay-

---

[2]For example, see Altonji, Hayashi and Kotlikoff (1992, 1997); Hayashi (1995); Cox and Rank (1992); Wilhelm (1996).

ments for children's home purchases, but will not give the children the same amount of money to buy sports cars or other forms of entertainment. On the basis of anthropologists' extensive research, Chu (1991) proposes that the "altruism" from parents to children arises from parents' concern about the survival of their genes. Based on this assumption, he explains that primogeniture emerged as family heads' optimal policy to minimize the probability of their lineal extinction. Chu (1991) also demonstrates that a model based on this assumption can provide a satisfactory explanation for primogeniture, while the commonly used altruism model of Barro (1974) that assume parents' utility depends on children's utility cannot. However, because of the mathematical difficulty, Chu (1991) focuses on the division of bequests by assuming that the total amount of the bequest is given by habit or custom and is not a choice variable.

Along the line of Pollak (1988) and Chu (1991), Fan (2001) provides a rigorous model of intergenerational transfers. In a Markovian game framework, Fan (2001) formalizes the idea that transfers from parents to children are to improve certain characteristics of the offspring, that is, the quantity and the quality of the offspring in terms of Becker (1991). Because Fan (2001) posits that parents care about children's characteristics rather than utility, it implies the coexistence of intergenerational conflicts and intergenerational commonality and hence is more consistent with the observed patterns of intergenerational transfers.[3] Meanwhile, as will be described in the next section, the reduced form of Fan (2001) is similar to the "joy of giving" model of bequests (e.g., Blinder, 1973; Yarri, 1965). So, Fan (2001) provides a much simpler and more tractable than the commonly used altruism model of Barro (1974), particularly when there is uncertainty for the earnings of every generation.[4] Therefore, the current paper will be based on Fan (2001) to set up its basic analytical framework.

---

[3]Due to the technical difficulty of the Markovian game, Fan (2001) uses some restrictive assumptions. However, it has the advantage over most other bequest models in accounting for intergenerational strategic interactions.

[4]If we instead adopt the commonly used altruism model of Barro (1974), we will have to deal with a complicated problem of stochastic dynamic programming since the income distribution is non-degenerate for the purpose of our study.

2. The Basic Analytical Framework

The basic analytic framework is based on Fan (2001), which can be briefly described as follows. Consider a small open economy that operates in a perfectly competitive world in which economic activity extends over an infinite discrete time. Every individual in this economy makes economic decisions only for one period. An individual obtains utility from her material consumption, C_t and (2) the quantity and quality, or certain "desired characteristics", of her children and grandchildren. Fan (2001) assumes that every individual has a child, and the child can be either a "high quality" (or type H) child or "low quality" (or type L) child. If an individual chooses to have a type H child, she first needs to spend a fixed cost, d. Then, an individual's utility function is defined as

$$u(C_t) + \chi(\text{child is of type } H)X + \chi(\text{grandchild is of type } H)\gamma X \quad (1)$$

where χ is an indicator function; C_t is the material consumption of an individual who is "born" at time t; $u()$ is the utility function from material consumption, and $u'() > 0$, $u''() < 0$, and $u()$ satisfies the Inada conditions; X ($X > 0$) and γX ($\gamma > 0$) denote the utility that an individual gets from having a type H child and a type H grandchild respectively. (Note that in a poor country, the utility function, (1), can be reinterpreted as that an individual obtains utility from having (survived) children and grandchildren as well as her own consumption. In this case, the assumption here is essentially the same as the key assumption in Chu (1991).)

The total wealth of an individual of generation t, Y_t, consists of her own endowment, w_t, and non-negative bequests from her parents, B_{t-1}. Then $Y_t = w_t + (1+r)B_{t-1}$, where r is the interest rate. If an individual has a type L child, she gets utility from her own consumption only and her utility is $u(Y_t)$. If an individual has a type H child, she will divide her wealth into her consumption and bequest, B_t. Suppose the probability that the child will have a grandchild is denoted by p, then the parent's expected utility function is

$$u(C_t) + X + p\gamma X \quad (2)$$

"p" is endogenously determined by the strategic interactions of different generations. An individual's future own endowment, $\tilde{w}$, is a random variable (before she is "born") and $\tilde{w} \sim (0, \infty)$. $\tilde{w}$ is time-invariant, and the cumulative distribution function of $\tilde{w}$, $F()$, is twice differentiable. A main result of Fan (2001) is as follows.

Theorem 1. (1) *There exists a stationary Markov perfect equilibrium in which an individual will choose to have a type H child if and only if her total wealth is greater than or equal to a threshold level of wealth $\bar{Y}$.*

(2) *Given a Markov Perfect equilibrium characterized by a threshold $\bar{Y}$, there exists a unique Y^c, such that an individual will leave a positive amount of transfer if and only if the amount of her wealth is greater than Y^c.*

From Theorem 1, it is easy to derive that

$$p = 1 - F[\bar{Y} - (1+r)B_t, \mu] \tag{3}$$

where μ is the mean of the distribution function "$F(,)$". Hence, (2) can be rewritten as,

$$u(Y_t - d - B_t) + (1+\gamma)X - F[\bar{Y} - (1+r)B_t, \mu]\gamma X \tag{4}$$

It is easy to see that the reduced form, (4), is just like the "joy of giving" model of bequests. However, from (4) and the above descriptions of the model, we know that $F()$ and $\bar{Y}$ depend on μ. Thus, (4) implies that B_t depends on μ as well as Y_t.

3. Consumption Functions

This section is the core of the current paper. It aims to examine the consumption functions both in the short run and in the long run and provide an explanation for the consumption puzzle described in Sections 1 and 2. We do so by exploring the impacts of the changes of individual income and mean income on consumption and saving. (Note that in this model, saving is equal to bequests.) This paper focuses on the case in which bequests are positive. Then, taking the derivation of (4) with respect to B_t, we get the first order condition as

$$-u'(Y_t - d - B_t) + \gamma(1+r)Xf[\bar{Y} - (1+r)B_t, \mu] = 0 \tag{5}$$

where "$f(,)$" is the density function of "$F(,)$".

From (5), we first have the following proposition.

Proposition 1. (1) *An individual's bequests increase with her wealth, that is,* $\frac{dB_t}{dY_t} > 0$.

(2) $\frac{dB_t}{dY_t} < 1$ *if and only if* $f_1 < 0$.

Proof. Totally differentiating (5) with respect to B_t, Y_t and rearranging, we get

$$\frac{dB_t}{dY_t} = \frac{u''}{u'' - \gamma(1+r)Xf_1} \tag{6}$$

Note that the denominator of (6) is just the second order condition, which must be negative when B_t is optimally chosen. Thus, we always have $\frac{dB_t}{dY_t} > 0$.

Meanwhile, when $f_1 < 0$, both the numerator and the denominator of (6) are negative and the absolute value of the denominator is greater. Thus, we have $\frac{dB_t}{dY_t} < 1$. $\qquad\square$

A comment for Proposition 1 is that the condition, $f_1 < 0$, guarantees that the objective function, (4), is convex with respect to B_t.

Next, we will examine the relationship between B_t and μ, which can be derived by the total differentiation of (5). In the derivation, it should be noted that $\bar{Y}$ is a function of μ. From the analysis in the last section, we know that at wealth $\bar{Y}$, if an individual chooses to have a type L child, her utility is $u(\bar{Y})$; if she chooses to have a type H child, her utility is

$$u(\bar{Y} - d - (1+r)B) + (1+\gamma)X - \gamma XF[\bar{Y} - (1+r)B, \mu]$$

For technical simplicity, we assume,

$$\bar{Y} \leq Y^c \tag{7}$$

This assumption means that at wealth $\bar{Y}$, $B = 0$. Namely, if an individual's wealth just reaches the threshold level of having a type H child, she will not leave any bequests to her child. It is clearly consistent with empirical observations. So, we have[5]

$$u(\bar{Y} - d) + (1+\gamma)X - \gamma XF[\bar{Y}, \mu] = u(\bar{Y}) \tag{8}$$

The relationship between $\bar{Y}$ and μ is determined by the above equation.

Then, we have the following proposition.

---

[5]From the proof in Fan (2001), it is easy to see that at wealth $\bar{Y}$, an individual is indifferent to whether to have a a type H child or not.

Proposition 2. *An individual's bequests decrease with the mean income of her offspring (i.e. $\frac{dB_t}{d\mu} < 0$) if and only if*

$$f_2 + \frac{\gamma X f_1 F_2(\bar{Y})}{u'(\bar{Y} - d) - u'(\bar{Y}) - \gamma X f(\bar{Y})} < 0 \tag{9}$$

Proof. Totally differentiating (5) with respect to B_t, μ, and $\bar{Y}$, we have,

$$u''(Y_t - d - B_t)dB_t + \gamma(1+r)X[f_1 d\bar{Y} - (1+r)f_1 dB_t + f_2 d\mu] = 0 \tag{10}$$

Meanwhile, totally differentiating (8) with respect to μ and $\bar{Y}$ and rearranging, we have,

$$d\bar{Y} = [\frac{\gamma X F_2(\bar{Y})}{u'(\bar{Y} - d) - u'(\bar{Y}) - \gamma X f(\bar{Y})}]d\mu \tag{11}$$

Plugging (11) into (10) and rearranging, we have

$$\frac{dB_t}{d\mu} = -\frac{\gamma(1+r)X[f_2 + \frac{\gamma X f_1 F_2(\bar{Y})}{u'(\bar{Y}-d)-u'(\bar{Y})-\gamma X f(\bar{Y})}]}{u''(Y_t - d - B_t) - \gamma(1+r)^2 X f_1} \tag{12}$$

Note that the denominator of (12) is just the second order condition, which must be negative when B_t is optimally chosen. Thus, when (9) is satisfied, we have

$$\frac{dB_t}{d\mu} < 0$$

□

Under some reasonable conditions, Proposition 2 indicates that when future generations get richer (i.e. mean income increases), parents will leave fewer bequests, holding parents' wealth constant. An interesting testable implication of this proposition is that for the same income groups in two different countries, the one in the poorer country has a higher saving rate. Meanwhile, we can see from (9) that the less f_2 (i.e. $\frac{\partial f}{\partial \mu}$) is, the more likely the bequests will decrease with the mean of her offspring's future earnings. The intuition is as follows: From (3), we have

$$\frac{dp}{dB_t} = (1+r)f$$

So, the marginal benefit of bequests is an increasing function of f. Meanwhile, $f_2 < 0$ means that f will decrease as the mean of children's future incomes increases. So, the less f_2 is, the less benefit parents will get from leaving bequests to their children.

Noting $C_t = Y_t - d - B_t$, from Propositions 1 and 2, obviously, we have the following corollary.

Corollary 1. Under the above stated assumptions, we have

$$0 < \frac{\partial C_t}{\partial Y_t} < 1, \ \frac{\partial C_t}{\partial \mu} > 0$$

Corollary 1 implies that as a first order approximation, we can write an individual's "consumption function" as follows:

$$C_t = \lambda Y_t + \pi \mu \tag{13}$$

where $\lambda = \frac{\partial C_t}{\partial Y_t}$, $\pi = \frac{\partial C_t}{\partial \mu}$. By Corollary 1, $\pi > 0$, and the "marginal propensity to consume," λ, is between 0 and 1. In the following, we can show that the consumption function (13) provides an explanation for the empirical observation about the "average propensity to consume" (i.e. $\frac{C_t}{Y_t}$) in the short run and in the long run.

An important component of Keynes' *general theory* (1936) is the Keynesian consumption function, which implies the average propensity to consume decreases with income. Empirical evidence shows that at a given point in time, households with higher income save a larger fraction of their income, which confirms Keynes' conjecture. However, over time, when an economy experiences economic growth and every household in the economy gets richer, the time-series evidence indicates that the saving rates are often approximately constant. For example, Kuznets (1946) shows that the ratio of consumption (saving) to income in the United States had been remarkably stable since the middle of the nineteenth century, despite large increases in per capita income over time.

This paper helps explain these seemingly contradictory findings. From (13), the "average propensity to consume" is

$$\frac{C_t}{Y_t} = \lambda + \pi \frac{\mu}{Y_t} \tag{14}$$

In the short run, μ is constant, so the "average propensity to consume", $\frac{C_t}{Y_t}$, decreases with income, Y_t. This implication is consistent with the empirical finding by Dynan, Skinner and Zeldes (2004) that there is a strong negative relationship between consumption rates and lifetime income. In the long run, μ and Y_t increase in the same proportion in aggregate, so the "average propensity to consume" remains approximately constant as Y_t (and μ) rises. Thus, from an intergenerational perspective, Corollary 1 provides a new explanation for the consumption puzzle and a reconciliation for the short-run and long-run consumption functions.[6]

Meanwhile, this model extends the permanent-income hypothesis, by examining offspring's mean income as a permanent income for a dynasty. Since there is intergenerational altruism, the mean income of the offspring is clearly a permanent income for a dynasty. In fact, as the economy lasts infinitely, we can regard the mean income of (infinite) future generations, μ, as the permanent income of a dynasty, and regard the income of the current generation, Y_t, as the "transitory income" of a dynasty.[7] Meanwhile, this extension is particularly in the spirit of the permanent-income hypothesis, which emphasizes that people experience random and temporary changes in their incomes, because the randomness of children's and grandchildren's future incomes is usually much greater than the randomness of one's own income. Thus, this paper complements the existing literature.

4. An Example

In this section, to further explore the intuition of the results in Section 4, we will consider an example, in which the distribution of earnings is *log-normal*, that is,

$$\ln(\tilde{w}) \sim N(\mu, \delta^2)$$

This assumption, which roughly means individuals' own endowment (e.g. labor income) follows a *log-normal* distribution, is largely consistent with empirical evidence and is commonly used in the existing literature.

---

[6]However, it should be noted that our analysis focuses on the situation in which bequests are positive. So, the model has less applicability in the situation in which few people transfer wealth to their children. In fact, Fan (2001) shows that as people's incomes continue to rise beyond a certain level (i.e. $\mu \to \infty$), the relative importance of bequests in aggregate saving will tend to be small, and he argues that this result provides an explanation for the recent decline of the saving rates in the U.S. and other developed countries.

[7]Note that for simplicity, we abstract from the consideration of the income fluctuations across different subperiods within a single generation.

As p is a function of B_t only, we can define "$p \equiv Q(B_t)$". Then, we have

$$
\begin{aligned}
Q(B_t) &= P\{\tilde{w} : \tilde{w} \geq \bar{Y} - (1+r)B_t\} \\
&= 1 - P\{\tilde{w} : \tilde{w} < \bar{Y} - (1+r)B_t\} \\
&= 1 - P\{\tilde{w} : \ln \tilde{w} \leq \ln(\bar{Y} - (1+r)B_t)\} \\
&= 1 - \Phi(\frac{\ln(\bar{Y} - (1+r)B_t) - \mu}{\delta})
\end{aligned}
$$

where Φ denotes the cumulative function of the standard normal distribution. So,

$$
\frac{dQ}{dB_t} = \frac{1+r}{\bar{Y} - (1+r)B_t} \frac{1}{\sqrt{2\pi}\delta} e^{-\frac{[\ln(\bar{Y}-(1+r)B_t)-\mu]^2}{2\delta^2}} \tag{15}
$$

Then we can write the first order condition (5) as

$$
u'(Y_t - d - B_t) = \frac{(1+r)\gamma X}{\sqrt{2\pi}\delta(\bar{Y} - (1+r)B_t)} e^{-\frac{[\ln(\bar{Y}-(1+r)B_t)-\mu]^2}{2\delta^2}} \tag{16}
$$

We make the following technical assumptions in this section.

$$
\mu > \delta^2 + \ln \bar{Y} \tag{17}
$$

$$
u'(\bar{Y} - d) - u'(\bar{Y}) > \frac{\gamma X}{\bar{Y}} \frac{1}{\sqrt{2\pi}\delta} e^{-\frac{\delta^2}{2}} \tag{18}
$$

From the proof below, we can see that (17) serves as a sufficient condition for the convexity of the probability density function. (18) relates the utility function ($u()$) to the probability density function. Simply speaking, the left hand side of (18) is the difference of the marginal utility from material consumption between having a type H child and having a type L child for an individual whose wealth is $\bar{Y}$. Clearly, (18) will be satisfied if and only if the cost of having a type H child, "d", is sufficiently high. From the proof below, , we can see that (18) serves as a sufficient but not necessary condition for the result that we are going to obtain.

We now state the following proposition.

Proposition 3. If the distribution of earnings is *log-normal* and the conditions (17) and (18) are satisfied, then we have

$$
0 < \frac{\partial C_t}{\partial Y_t} < 1, \quad \frac{\partial C_t}{\partial \mu} > 0
$$

Proof. First, we try to prove (1) $\frac{\partial^2 Q}{\partial B_t^2} < 0$. (2) $\frac{\partial^2 Q}{\partial B_t \partial \mu} < 0$.

Note that because $Q'(B_t) > 0$ and

$$\frac{dQ'(B_t)}{dx} = Q'(B_t)\frac{d\ln[Q'(B_t)]}{dx}$$

it is equivalent to prove above results with $\ln[Q'(B_t)]$ instead of $Q'(B_t)$.

From (15), we have

$$\ln Q'(B_t) = \ln\frac{1+r}{\sqrt{2\pi}} - \ln\delta - \ln(\bar{Y} - (1+r)B_t) - \frac{(\ln(\bar{Y} - (1+r)B_t) - \mu)^2}{2\delta^2}$$
(19)

Then, taking the derivative of $\ln Q'$, and rearranging, we get

$$\frac{d(\ln Q'(B_t))}{dB_t} = \frac{1+r}{\bar{Y} - (1+r)B_t}\left[\frac{\delta^2 + \ln(\bar{Y} - (1+r)B_t) - \mu}{\delta^2}\right]$$

When (17) is satisfied,

$$\delta^2 + \ln(\bar{Y} - (1+r)B_t) - \mu \leq \delta^2 + \ln\bar{Y} - \mu < 0$$

Meanwhile, we can show that

$$\bar{Y} - (1+r)B_t > 0$$
(20)

Because when B_t is large enough so that $(1+r)B_t > \bar{Y}$ or $\bar{Y} - (1+r)B_t > 0$, the parent will be certain that the child will have a type H grandchild regardless of the child's future income. So, an individual will never transfer more than $\frac{\bar{Y}}{1+r}$ since her marginal utility from material consumption is assumed to be strictly positive. Also, we claim that $B^* \neq \frac{\bar{Y}}{1+r}$. Suppose not, Plugging $B_t = \frac{\bar{Y}}{1+r}$ into the first order condition (16), then we can see that the right hand side of (16) will be equal to positive infinity and its left-hand side is finite, which results in contradiction. In other words, $B_t = \frac{\bar{Y}}{1+r}$ can never satisfy the first order condition, and hence is not the optimal solution. So, (20) is always satisfied. Thus, $\frac{d(\ln Q'(B_t))}{dB_t} > 0$, which implies

$$\frac{\partial^2 Q}{\partial B_t^2} < 0$$
(21)

Next, taking the derivative of $\ln Q'(B_t)$ (i.e. Equation (19)) and rearranging, we get

$$\frac{\partial(\ln Q'(B_t))}{\partial \bar{Y}} = -\frac{1}{\bar{Y} - (1+r)B_t} \cdot \frac{\delta^2 + \ln(\bar{Y} - (1+r)B_t) - \mu}{\delta^2}$$

Similar to the proof in the above, we can show that when (17) is satisfied, we have $\frac{\partial(\ln Q'(B_t))}{\partial \bar{Y}} > 0$, which implies

$$\frac{\partial Q'(B_t)}{\partial \bar{Y}} > 0 \tag{22}$$

Next, by (7), we know that when $Y_t = \bar{Y}$, we have $B_t = 0$. In this case, the probability that the child has a type H grandchild is

$$p = P\{\tilde{w} : \tilde{w} \geq \bar{Y}\} = 1 - P\{\tilde{w} : \ln \tilde{w} < \ln \bar{Y}\} = 1 - \Phi(\frac{\ln \bar{Y} - \mu}{\delta})$$

which implies that the utility from having a Type H child is

$$v(\bar{Y}) \equiv u(\bar{Y} - d) + (1+\gamma)X - \Phi(\frac{\ln \bar{Y} - \mu}{\delta})\gamma X$$

From the analysis in the previous section, we know

$$v(\bar{Y}) = u(\bar{Y})$$

we define,

$$K \equiv v(\bar{Y}) - u(\bar{Y})$$
$$= u(\bar{Y} - d) + (1+\gamma)X - \Phi(\frac{\ln \bar{Y} - \mu}{\delta})\gamma X - u(\bar{Y}) = 0$$

So,

$$\frac{\partial K}{\partial \bar{Y}} = u'(\bar{Y} - d) - u'(\bar{Y}) - \frac{\gamma X}{\bar{Y}} \frac{1}{\sqrt{2\pi}\delta} e^{-\frac{(\ln \bar{Y} - \mu)^2}{2\delta^2}} \tag{23}$$

Noticing (17), we have

$$\frac{(\mu - \ln \bar{Y})^2}{2\delta^2} \geq \frac{\delta^4}{2\delta^2} = \frac{\delta^2}{2}$$

Therefore, we have

$$e^{-\frac{(\mu - \ln \bar{Y})^2}{2\delta^2}} \leq e^{-\frac{\delta^2}{2}}$$

Noticing (18), from (23), we have

$$\frac{\partial K}{\partial \bar{Y}} \geq u'(\bar{Y} - d) - u'(\bar{Y}) - \frac{\gamma X}{\bar{Y}} \frac{1}{\sqrt{2\pi}\delta} e^{-\frac{\delta^2}{2}} > 0 \qquad (24)$$

Also, it is easy to see that

$$\frac{\partial K}{\partial \mu} = \frac{1}{\delta} \Phi' \gamma X > 0$$

Therefore, noting (24), we have

$$\frac{\partial \bar{Y}}{\partial \mu} = -\frac{\partial K}{\partial \mu} \Big/ \frac{\partial K}{\partial \bar{Y}} < 0 \qquad (25)$$

Now, holding $\bar{Y}$ constant, we have

$$\frac{\partial Q'(B_t)}{\partial \mu}\Big|_{\bar{Y}} = \frac{2(\ln(\bar{Y} - (1+r)B_t) - \mu)}{\delta^2} < \frac{2(\ln \bar{Y} - \mu)}{\delta^2} < 0 \qquad (26)$$

Thus, from (22), (25), and (26), we have

$$\frac{\partial^2 Q}{\partial B_t \partial \mu} \equiv \frac{\partial Q'(B_t)}{\partial \mu} = \frac{\partial Q'(B_t)}{\partial \mu}\Big|_{\bar{Y}} + \frac{\partial Q'(B_t)}{\partial \bar{Y}}\Big|_{\mu} \frac{\partial \bar{Y}}{\partial \mu} < 0 \qquad (27)$$

Next, we note that the first order condition, (16), can be written as

$$u'(Y_t - d - B_t) = \gamma X Q'(B_t) \qquad (28)$$

Totally differentiating it with respect to B_t, μ and rearranging, then yields,

$$\frac{dB_t}{d\mu} = -\frac{\gamma X \frac{\partial^2 Q}{\partial B_t \partial \mu}}{u'' + \gamma X \frac{\partial^2 Q}{\partial B_t^2}}$$

So, we have

$$\frac{dC_t}{d\mu} = -\frac{dB_t}{d\mu} = \frac{\gamma X \frac{\partial^2 Q}{\partial B_t \partial \mu}}{u'' + \gamma X \frac{\partial^2 Q}{\partial B_t^2}} \qquad (29)$$

Noting (27), we can see that the numerator and the denominator of the right hand side of (29) are both negative. Thus,

$$\frac{dC_t}{d\mu} > 0$$

Totally differentiating (28) with respect to Y_t and B_t and rearranging, it yields,

$$\frac{dB_t}{dY_t} = \frac{u''}{u'' + \gamma X \frac{\partial^2 Q}{\partial B_t^2}}$$

So, we have

$$\frac{dC_t}{dY_t} = 1 - \frac{dB_t}{dY_t} = \frac{\gamma X \frac{\partial^2 Q}{\partial B_t^2}}{u'' + \gamma X \frac{\partial^2 Q}{\partial B_t^2}} \tag{30}$$

From (21), we know that $\frac{\partial^2 Q}{\partial B_t^2} < 0$. Meanwhile, noting $u'' < 0$, we have

$$0 < \frac{dC_t}{dY_t} < 1$$

$\square$

The model investigates the effects of the changes of offspring's mean income and an individual's own income on her consumption/saving behaviors. This proposition illustrates that under some plausible conditions, the marginal propensity to consume is between zero and one and the average propensity to consume decreases with one's income in the short run. In the long run, an increase in mean income will reduce saving (bequests) and increase consumption. The intuition is that as the child's expected future income increases, the child is more likely to have a high-quality grandchild without receiving more bequests. Hence, in the long run, the average propensity to consume can be stable over time. Meanwhile, the proofs of the proposition clearly indicate that the impacts of offspring's mean income on an individual's consumption are qualitatively different from those of her own earnings.[8]

5.   Conclusion

Based on the essential idea of Fan (2006), this chapter investigates the consumption puzzle from an intergenerational perspective. Our model implies that

---

[8]In the existing literature, intergenerational altruism is usually formalized by the assumption that an individual obtains utility from her children's utility. In this case, as shown by Barro (1974), the decision making of a dynasty is equivalent to that of an infinitely lived "representative agent." Consequently, in the existing literature, there is no essential difference between the impacts of offsprings' mean income on an individual's consumption and those of her own earnings.

an individual is more concerned about her offspring's well-being when the offspring's future mean income is lower. In a Markovian game framework, the model shows that the bequests from parents to children decrease with the mean income of future generations. Meanwhile, *ceteris paribus*, an individual's bequests to her children increase with her own wealth. Thus, the model has the following implications. First, at a given point in time, richer people have higher saving rates, because they are concerned that their children are likely to receive lower incomes than theirs. In other words, a household with higher lifetime income saves more in order to leave more bequests to its offspring, who are likely to be worse off. Second, over time, when an economy experiences economic growth and the mean income of the economy rises, individuals will reduce their bequests because their offspring are expected to be equally well off due to the economic growth. Consequently, the saving rate can be approximately constant over time if the impacts of the increase in one's lifetime income and the increase in her offspring's future mean income on her consumption cancel out each other. Thus, this model helps explain the consumption puzzle and reconcile the short-run and long-run consumption functions. This paper is closely related to Fan (2006), who studied a model that aims to achieve the same purpose as the current paper. However, this paper builds on a model that is very different from Fan (2006), and hence this paper examines this important issue from a different angle from Fan (2006).

Further, this model extends the permanent-income hypothesis of Friedman (1957) by noting that the mean income of the offspring is a permanent income for a dynasty. Since the randomness of children's and grandchildren's future incomes is usually much greater than the randomness of one's own income, the study of the permanent-income hypothesis in intergenerational context is particularly important. Meanwhile, as there are both intergenerational conflicts and intergenerational commonality, the model shows that the impacts of offspring's mean income on an individual's consumption are qualitatively different from those of the permanent income of her own earnings.

References

[1] Altonji, J., F. Hayashi, and L. Kotlikoff (1992) "Is the Extended Family Altruistically Linked? Direct Tests Using Micro Data," *American Economic Review* 82(5): 1177-1198.

[2] Altonji, J., F. Hayashi, and L. Kotlikoff (1997) "Parental Altruism and Inter Vivos Transfer: Theory and Evidence," *Journal of Political Economy,* 105(6): 1121-1166.

[3] Barro, R. J. (1974) "Are Government Bonds Net Wealth?" *Journal of Political Economy* 48(6): 1095-1118.

[4] Becker, G. S. (1991) *A Treatise of the Family*, Cambridge, M.A.: Harvard University Press.

[5] Blinder, A. S. (1973) "A Model of Inherited Wealth," *Quarterly Journal of Economics* 87(4): 608-626.

[6] Chu, C.Y.C. (1991) "Primogeniture," *Journal of Political Economy* 99, 78-99.

[7] Cox, D. and M. Rank (1992) "Inter-Vivos Transfers and Intergenerational Exchange," *Review of Economics and Statistics* 74(2): 305-314.

[8] Dynan, K. E., J. Skinner and S. P. Zeldes (2004) "Do the Rich Save More?" *Journal of Political Economy,* 112(2): 397-444.

[9] Fan, C. S. (2001) "A Model of Intergenerational Transfers," *Economic Theory*, 17(2): 399-418.

[10] Fan, C. S. (2006) "Do the Rich Save More? A New View Based on Intergenerational Transfers," *Southern Economic Journal*, 73(2): 362-373.

[11] Friedman, M. (1957) *A Theory of the Consumption Function*, Princeton: Princeton University Press.

[12] Gale, W. G. and J. K. Scholz (1994) "Intergenerational Transfers and the Accumulation of Wealth," *Journal of Economic Perspectives* 8(4): 145-60.

[13] Hayashi, F. (1995) "Is the Japanese Extended Family Altruistically Linked? A Test Based on Engle Curves," *Journal of Political Economy*, 103(3): 661-674.

[14] Keynes, J. M. (1936), *General Theory of Employment, Interest and Money*, New York: Harcourt, Brace.

[15] Kotlikoff, L. J. (1988) "Intergenerational Transfers and Saving," *Journal of Economic Perspectives* 2: 41-58.

[16] Kuznets, S. S. (1946) *National Income: A Summary of Findings*, NBER, New York: Arno Press.

[17] Pollak, R. (1988) "Tied Transfers and Paternalistic Preferences," *American Economic Review* (*Papers and Proceedings*) 78: 240-4.

[18] Solow, R. M. (1956), "A Contribution to the Theory of Economic Growth," *Quarterly Journal of Economics*, 70(1): 65-94.

[19] Wilhelm, M. O. (1996) "Bequest Behavior and the Effect of Heirs' Earnings: Testing the Altruistic Model of Bequests," *American Economic Review* 86(4): 874-892.

[20] Yarri, Menahem E. (1965) "Uncertain Lifetime, Life Insurance and the Theory of the Consumer," *Review of Economic Studies* 32: 137-50.

In: Progress in Economics Research. Volume 27   ISBN: 978-1-62808-201-2
Editor: A. Tavidze   © 2013 Nova Science Publishers, Inc.

Chapter 6

PSYCHOLOGY OF PUBLIC SPENDING

Monica Auteri[*]
Dipartimento di Scienze Politiche
Università Roma Tre and CREI, Italy

Abstract

The size and role of the government is one of the most fundamental
and enduring debates that has attracted the attention of researchers for
decades. Politicians, social scientists, and citizens disagree sharply about
the appropriate public spending, as well as the size of government. Many
see government as an agent striving to correct the inadequacies and excesses of the unrestrained markets. Others view politicians, public sector
employees, and special interest groups as seeking to use the power of the
government for their own purposes. The purpose of this paper is to investigate the reasons that determine the preferred size of government, and
the role of government.

1. Introduction

Politicians, social scientists, and citizens disagree sharply about the appropriate public spending, as well as the size of government. Many see government
as an agent striving to correct the inadequacies and excesses of the unrestrained
markets. The government provides the public goods the market is incapable of

[*]E-mail address: monica.auteri@uniroma3.it

providing and removes the distortions in the allocation of resources due to externalities. Others view politicians, public sector employees, and special interest groups as seeking to use the power of the government for their own purposes. Distortions arising from political decision making can outweigh the benefits from government activities, thus reducing social welfare. When this occurs, government is no longer a solution but is a problem. The purpose of this paper is to investigate the psychological reasons that determine the preferred size of government, e.g. the share of government spending that maximizes economic growth.

2.   Government Size and Economic Growth

The size and role of the government is one of the most fundamental and enduring debates that has attracted the attention of researchers for decades.

The most basic function of Government is the protection of people and property which is the foundation for the efficient operation of a market economy. In addition, a provision of limited set goods and services, called public goods, such as roads and national defense, may also enhance economic growth.

Most economists believe a larger government size than a certain optimal level has detrimental impact on economic growth due to the inefficiencies inherent in government.

Gwartney et al. (2008) states, "as governments move beyond the core functions, they will adversely affect economic growth because of (a) the disincentive effects of higher taxes and crowding-out effect of public investment in relation to private investment, (b) diminishing returns as governments undertake some activities for which they are not well-suited, and (c) an interference with the wealth creation process, because governments are not as good as markets in adjusting to changing circumstances and finding innovative new ways of increasing the value of resources". Daniel Mitchell concludes "government spending undermines economic growth by displacing private-sector activity. Whether financed by taxes or borrowing, government spending imposes heavy extraction and displacement costs on the productive sector."

There are some economists who argue that a larger government is likely to speed economic growth by providing public goods and correcting for market failures.

According to this school, government consumption is also likely to increase investment and employment via multiplier effects on aggregate demand.

In addition, Wagner's Law suggests a more-than-proportionate increase in government expenditure when economic growth accelerates because there will be a need for more administrative and protective functions of the state, a need for increased provision of social and cultural goods and services, and an increased need for provision of proper administrative and bureaucratic controls to ensure the smooth operation of market forces (Bird, 2011).

3.   Efficiency

Even if it is clear that some government policies raise economic efficiency and some lower efficiency, all spending decisions made by the government today are justified on efficiency grounds.

As opposed to its popular usage, economic efficiency does not involve economic growth, wealth, or productivity.

An outcome is economically efficient if the marginal cost of producing one more unit of a good is equivalent to the marginal benefit of consuming one more unit of the good. When market is characterized by many buyers and sellers, no barriers to entry, perfect information, and the costs and benefits of the transaction are completely borne by the buyer and seller, then the markets function perfectly and an economically efficient outcome will occur. In this case government intervention can only reduce efficiency, but when there are market failures, government intervention has the potential to improve efficiency by moving away from the economically inefficient outcome produced by the market.

Therefore the need for government intervention in market affairs should be limited.

According to Adam Smith in the normal state of affairs, markets work better when government leaves them alone and focuses instead on maintaining order and administering justice.

The idea that the market work well provided that the state does little more than ensure peace, easy taxes, and a tolerable administration of justice, might be susceptible to revision on empirical grounds has many roots, including the work of Barro.

Barro (1997), in a cross-country analysis, finds that smaller government consumption and the rule of law help economic growth; Sala-i Martin (1997) finds that the rule of law and openness of the economy contribute to growth; and Djankov et al. (2002) show that complex business regulation restrains growth. However as Von Mises and Greaves (1949) pointed out, there is no need for extensive empirical research to determine how humans respond to incentives. When left alone to pursue their own goals and plans, individuals do well and create prosperity that spreads to everyone else in the society. Institutional structures that enable individuals to follow their personal goals are most likely to result in widespread economic prosperity.

However government intervention in market affairs has grown in the twentieth century to unprecedented levels and remains persistent.

4. Public Choice Perspective

Public-choice theorists have developed a number of useful concepts to explain the motives for government intervention in the economy. The core assumption is that public officials, like other people, respond to incentives and pursue their own interests, which naturally leads governments to shape legislation and policies in ways that maximize politicians' power. Public-choice analysts also assume an uninformed and poorly motivated voter, as described by Downs (1957). As the individual cost of voting is greater than the possible benefit of any individual vote, voters do not acquire information as it is costly and because gathering it does not serve their interest. The resulting ignorance allows politicians to constantly cheat on voters not only by shirking on responsibilities, but also by adopting legislation that voters might not want or would oppose if they knew about it.

In addition the median voter prefers high spending. He desires high spending currently more then low (or no) deficits. This is Buchanan and Wagner (1977)'s argument in *Democracy in Deficit: The Political Legacy of Lord Keynes*.

A neglected dimension of Buchanan and Wagner's book is its in-depth treatment of voters being fooled by their own cognitive biases. From 1977 Buchanan and Wagner are already incorporating what are now called "behavioral" arguments into the macroeconomic consequences of fiscal and monetary policy. This, alongside their more traditional interest group argument, runs through almost every chapter of their book and forms the backbone of their analysis.

Three decades after, Caplan (2011) in *The Myth of the Rational Voter: Why Democracies Choose Bad Policies*, argues that voters may be "rationally irrational" — holding beliefs that are simply not true, but which cost them little to maintain. Failure to grasp certain economic realities, such as the benefits of free trade, likely will have no direct cost to a single voter. While the consumer who fails to do a little research before buying a car may end up with a lemon, the voter with economically incorrect ideas is not likely to change the course of an election. But the effects of cognitive biases can add up. When many voters think high tariffs will make them richer, they're likely to get what they want (tariffs, not riches).

Caplan points out that most people overestimate the percentage of the federal budget that goes to foreign aid. No surprise, then, that "cutting foreign aid" would be seen as a meaningful attempt to address the budget crisis. In reality, a much broader conversation about entitlements will be required.

It emerges then that public-choice theory – as for log rolling, rent seeking, budget-maximizing bureaucracy, and powerful interest groups (Buchanan and Tullock, 1962; Olson, 1965; Tullock, 1967; Niskanen, 1971) – assume that individuals are rational and selfish and that voters are deeply ignorant about political issues.

The public-choice explanation is widely accepted among economists today. There is a wide consensus on the believes that special interests play a major role in policy formulation as stated in a survey by Davis and Figgins (2012).

5.   General Public and Intellectual Elites

Public choice usually focuses on the supply side of government growth, but somehow neglects the demand side, that it is at least equally important. It actually seems that voters seek government involvement in many different areas. Higgs (1987) explains how once a change has been introduced, the public more readily perceives the change's visible benefits than its invisible opportunity costs. Therefore, many expansions of government power that politicians introduce as temporary measures in times of crisis become irreversible. However once we recognize the general preference for government activity, it is not clear why people prefer government action over the spontaneous market order in the first place?

The reason may be found in what Buchanan (2005) calls "parentalism".

Buchanan's term is not to be confused with "paternalism", the familiar idea that sometimes people—other people—need to be restrained for their own protection from making poor choices. (In some cases, as with children, this may be right.) Parentalism is in a sense more insidious: it emerges when we begin to suspect that we ourselves are not competent to make our own choices, to yearn for someone to relieve us of the burden of choice. As Buchanan puts it:

> [Economists and political theorists] have assumed that, other things
> being equal, persons want to be at liberty to make their own
> choices, to be free from coercion by others, including indirect
> coercion through means of persuasion. They have failed to em-
> phasize sufficiently, and to examine the implications of the fact
> that liberty carries with it responsibility, and it seems evident
> that many persons do not want to shoulder the final responsibil-
> ity for their own actions..[They] want to be told what to do and
> when to do it; they seek order rather than uncertainty, and order
> comes at an opportunity cost they seem willing to bear.

Even if the general public is the ultimate source of the demand for government intervention in the market, intellectual elites usually reinforce this public
attitude, given their ability to influence public opinion (Zaller, 1992).

Klein and Stern (2005) surveyed six national social science associations in
the United States and found that the ratio of Democratic voters to Republican
voters among their members was fifteen to one. Horowitz and Lehrer (2002)
report that the same ratio for U.S. University departments was approximately
ten to one. It seems then that intellectuals tend to belong to left-wing political
parties and therefore for the most part, they favor big government.

Market does not reward intellectual work, so in Von Mises ((1956)'s view,
intellectuals are prone to socialism because they tend to overestimate their own
value, and they often believe that they deserve greater rewards than business
people. Before Mises, Hayek (1949) offered a partial explanation in his essay
The Intellectuals and Socialism. Hayek asked why the more active, intelligent
and original men among [American] intellectuals ... most frequently incline
toward socialism. His answer is based on the opportunities available to people
of varying talents.

Intelligent people hold a variety of views. Some are lovers of liberty, defenders of property, and supporters of the *natural order* — i.e., defenders of the
market. Others are reformers, wanting to remake the world according to their
own visions of the ideal society.

Hayek argues that exceptionally intelligent people, who favor the market
tend to find opportunities for professional and financial success in the business
or professional world. Those who are highly intelligent but ill-disposed toward
the market are more likely to choose an academic career and form the so-called
cultural elite. For this reason, the universities come to be filled with those intellectuals who were favorably disposed toward socialism from the beginning.

This *sample selection bias* erroneously suggest that more intelligent people tend to favor socialism.

6.   The Psychology of Budget Choice

It seems clear now that people disagree sharply about the appropriate size of government. A reason can be found in the fact that citizens will fail to integrate their beliefs and actions over time. Anti-government partisans fear that citizens will want programs now, neglecting their long-term costs, and then will be reluctant to cut these programs later. Pro-government partisans fear that citizens will support tax cuts now, ignoring the long-term effects of any resulting deficit (or diminished surplus) on the ability of the government to continue to provide public goods and services in the future. These two sets of attitudes stand in contrast to the "rational choice" or "rational expectations" model of politics, where citizens properly integrate their actions over time. Thus, Barro (1974) has argued that government deficits may not even matter, because forward-looking citizens in an overlapping generations framework will rationally save today in anticipation of increased taxes tomorrow; conversely, surpluses today can lead to greater private debt in anticipation of lower taxes tomorrow. Standard findings in cognitive psychology, most notably prospect theory and the endowment effect (Kahneman and Tversky, 1979; Kahneman et al., 1991), support the popular understanding that timing matters. Once a government program is in place, it will become part of the status quo, and can be hard to cut. This implies a continuous government growth. On the other hand, citizens are averse to taxes, a phenomenon that itself has cognitive psychological dimensions. People react disproportionately to taxes and fail to consider the off-setting benefits of government programs (McCaffery and Baron, 2006); people are also likely to code a tax increase as a loss, making it hard to ever raise taxes.

A psychologically political strategy used by those who favor smaller government has come to be called "starve the beast". The idea is to cut taxes in order to deprive the government of revenue in a deliberate effort to force the federal government to reduce spending. Politicians may want to cut taxes before cutting spending, then use the resulting deficit as a political argument to reduce spending, or to reject new spending, therefore they prefer large deficits that result from fiscal policies. Then it seems that if citizens are fully rational and consistent in the manner of Barro, such budgetary and political manipulations would not matter: private actions would perfectly counterbalance the public ones. Or citizens might be fully rational, anticipating the ultimate tax increases or spending cuts that deficits imply, but distrust their own discipline. In such a case, citizens would rationally want balanced budgets today as a self-commitment mechanism (Schelling, 1980) (Schelling, 1984), and politicians who cut taxes without reducing spending would lose public support. In these rational choice settings, either deficits do not matter or they cannot get started, and there is no room for the "starve the beast" technique to have real effects. We now have abundant evidence that ordinary people are not always rational, in the simple sense of having stable consistent preferences over choices and outcomes as they might accept tax cuts in the absence of spending cuts. One, people might think excessively or even exclusively about the short term and they neglect the fact that deficits must be covered in the future. More generally, they have an optimism bias (Kahneman and Lovallo, 1993; Camerer and Lovallo, 1999), so they favor budget deficits in the short term and respond differently when asked about the future than when asked about the present. Two, people might think differently about tax cuts and spending cuts today because of their different ability to consider future consequences. Specifically, people are averse to taxes (Fennell and Fennell, 2003), and so support specific tax cuts. They actually favor fiscal discipline, that is, balanced budgets, but are thinking about spending cuts. Later, the same people generally oppose cuts in particular government programs. It seems that people anchor on current levels of taxation and government spending, so their preferred levels of each do not go far enough to remove the deficit, once a deficit exists.

References

Auteri, M. (2003). The entrepreneurial establishment of a nonprofit organization, *Public Organization Review* 3(2): 171–189.

Auteri, M. and Wagner, R. E. (2007). The organizational architecture of nonprofit governance: Economic calculation within an ecology of enterprises, *Public Organization Review* 7(1): 57–68.

Barro, R. (1997). *Determinants of Economic Growth*, Cambridge, Mass.: MIT Press.

Barro, R. J. (1974). Are government bonds net wealth?, *The Journal of Political Economy* 82(6): 1095–1117.

Bird, R. M. (2011). Wagner's o law' of expanding state activity, *Public Finance=Finances publiques* 26(1): 1–26.

Buchanan, J. M. (2005). Afraid to be free: Dependency as desideratum, *Public Choice* 124(1-2): 19–31.

Buchanan, J. M. and Tullock, G. (1962). The calculus of consent, *Ann Arbor: University of Michigan Press*.

Buchanan, J. M. and Wagner, R. E. (1977). *Democracy in deficit: The political legacy of Lord Keynes*, Vol. 16, Academic Press New York.

Camerer, C. and Lovallo, D. (1999). Overconfidence and excess entry: An experimental approach, *The American Economic Review* 89(1): 306–318.

Caplan, B. (2011). *The Myth of the Rational Voter: Why Democracies Choose Bad Policies (New Edition)*, Princeton University Press.

Davis, W. L. and Figgins, B. (2012). Do economists believe american democracy is working?, *Econ Journal Watch* 6(2): 195–202.

Djankov, S., La Porta, R., Lopez-de Silanes, F. and Shleifer, A. (2002). The regulation of entry, *The Quarterly Journal of Economics* 117(1): 1–37.

Downs, A. (1957). An economic theory of bureaucracy.

Fennell, C. and Fennell, L. (2003). Fear and greed in tax policy: A qualitative research agenda, *Washington University Journal of Law and Policy* 13: 75.

Gwartney, J. D., Stroup, R. L., Sobel, R. S. and Macpherson, D. A. (2008). *Economics: Private and public choice*, South-Western Pub.

Hayek, F. A. (1949). The intellectuals and socialism, *The University of Chicago Law Review* pp. 417–433.

Higgs, R. (1987). *Crisis and Leviathan: Critical episodes in the growth of American government*, Oxford University Press New York.

Horowitz, D. and Lehrer, E. (2002). Political bias in the administrations and faculties of 32 elite colleges and universities, *A Report of the Center for the Study of Popular Culture. Online http://www. frontpagemag. com/Content/read. asp.*

Kahneman, D., Knetsch, J. L. and Thaler, R. H. (1991). Anomalies: The endowment effect, loss aversion, and status quo bias, *The journal of economic perspectives* 5(1): 193–206.

Kahneman, D. and Lovallo, D. (1993). Timid choices and bold forecasts: A cognitive perspective on risk taking, *Management science* 39(1): 17–31.

Kahneman, D. and Tversky, A. (1979). Prospect theory: An analysis of decision under risk, *Econometrica: Journal of the Econometric Society* pp. 263–291.

Klein, D. B. and Stern, C. (2005). Professors and their politics: The policy views of social scientists, *Critical Review* 17(3-4): 257–303.

McCaffery, E. J. and Baron, J. (2006). Thinking about tax, *Psychology, Public Policy, and Law* 12: 106–419.

Niskanen, W. A. (1971). *Bureaucracy and representative government*, Vol. 18, E. Elgar Aldersho.

Olson, M. (1965). *The logic of collective action: public goods and the theory of groups.*, Vol. 124, Harvard University Press.

Sala-i Martin, X. X. (1997). I just ran two million regressions, *The American Economic Review* pp. 178–183.

Schelling, T. (1980). The intimate contest for self-command, *The Public Interest*, 60: 94-118.

Tullock, G. (1967). The welfare costs of tariffs, monopolies, and theft, *Economic Inquiry* 5(3): 224–232.

Von Mises, L. ((1956)1972). *The anti-capitalistic mentality*, South Holland, Ill.: Libertarian Press.

Von Mises, L. and Greaves, B. B. (1949). *Human action*, Liberty Fund.

Zaller, J. (1992). *The nature and origins of mass opinion*, Cambridge university press.

INDEX

H

I

T